IMAGES
of Rail

Middletown and Unionville Railroad

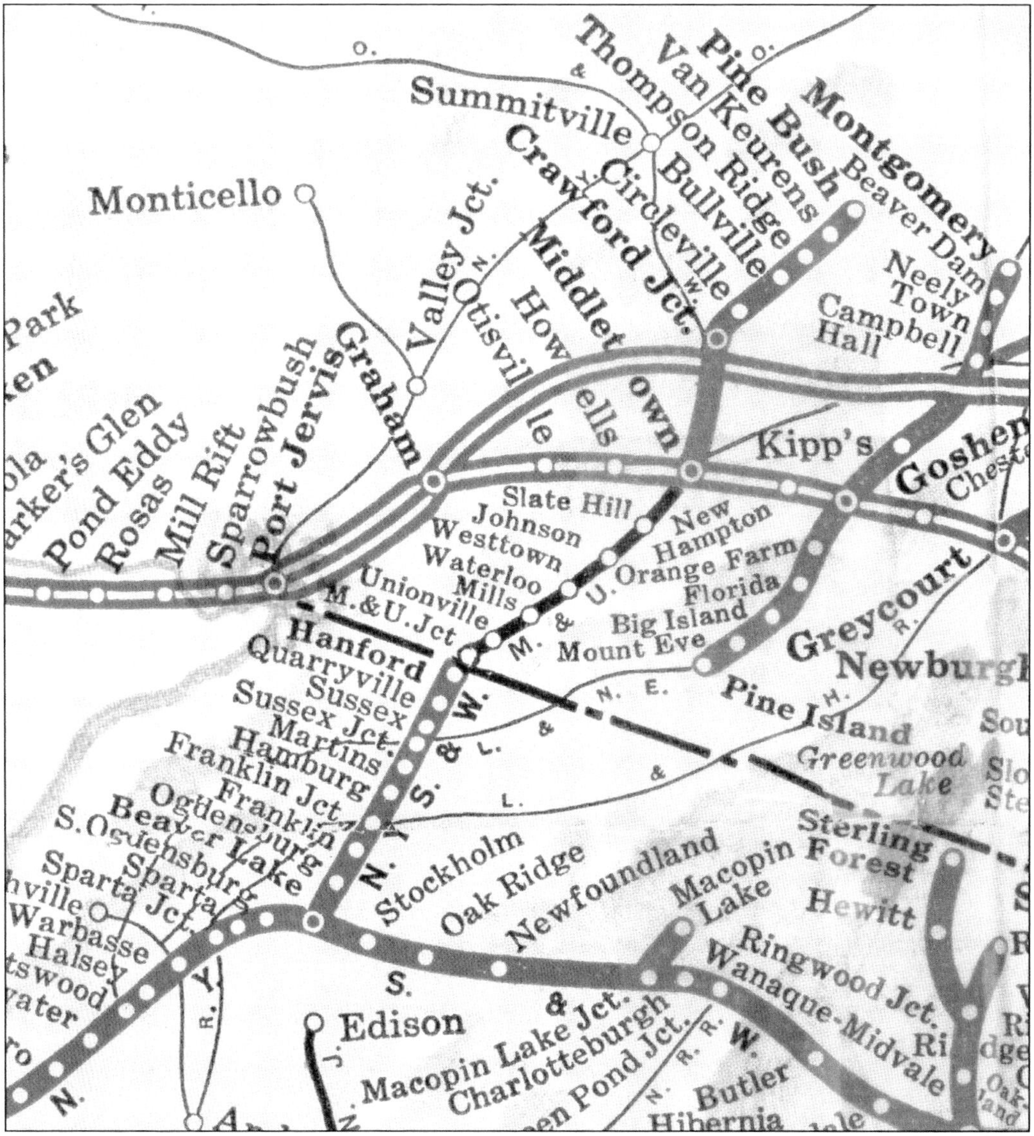

The Middletown and Unionville Railroad (M&U) is centrally located running from Middletown to Hanford. Note M&U Junction is actually in New Jersey and was the same location as Hanford. The NYS&W Hanford branch and main line are visible below. The NYO&W is the thin line over the word "Kipp's" but is bold from Middletown to Crawford Junction showing the Erie's trackage rights to the Pine Bush Branch. The Erie main line runs from Port Jervis through Graham, Middletown, and Goshen. (Erie System map 1930, author's collection.)

On the Cover: Heading for the NYS&W interchange at Hanford Junction Middletown and Unionville, No. 7 is hustling an eastbound freight near Westtown, New York. (Ray Brown Collection, M&NJRHS Archives.)

IMAGES
of Rail

MIDDLETOWN AND UNIONVILLE RAILROAD

Douglas Barberio

ARCADIA
PUBLISHING

ISBN 978-0-7385-7317-5

Published by Arcadia Publishing
Charleston, South Carolina

Printed in the United States of America

Library of Congress Control Number: 2009943001

For all general information contact Arcadia Publishing at:
Telephone 843-853-2070
Fax 843-853-0044
E-mail sales@arcadiapublishing.com
For customer service and orders:
Toll-Free 1-888-313-2665

Visit us on the Internet at www.arcadiapublishing.com

To the M&NJ employees who I called my friends: Peter Brill, Harold Rasmussen, and those departed—Raymond Brown, Carl Detwyler, Jerry Dilger, and Pierre Rasmussen

Contents

ACKNOWLEDGMENTS

Peter Brill was a conductor on the Middletown and New Jersey Railway from 1987 until 2002. We became friends and with the help of M&NJ president Pierre Rasmussen and his son, Harold, who was the engineer, we started the Middletown and New Jersey Railway Historical Society in 1994. As the editor of our newsletter, the *Unionville Flyer*, Peter Brill has been a very valuable source of historical information and has identified and discussed areas of M&U history that have had to be reexamined as a result of this project. Peter provided much of the inspiration for this book, and it could not have been completed without him.

The M&NJ Railway during the period 1994 to 2003 allowed the historical society access to historical documents for research. Pierre Rasmussen donated many Middletown and Unionville Railroad documents to the M&NJRHS including the general manager and vice president files of J. A. Smith, dated from 1913 to 1940. This formed the foundation that allowed this book project to be considered and ultimately become reality. The M&NJRHS photograph collections of the M&U/M&NJ from three deceased photographers, Ray Brown, Carl Detwyler, and John Stellwagen, made this book possible.

Special thanks go to Ruth Stellwagen for allowing the use of her late husband's Erie photograph collection. Also to Carol Van Buren, town historian for Minisink and the Town of Minisink Museum, for allowing the use of their extensive photograph collection. The New Jersey Midland Railroad Historical Society and archivist Curtis Carlough graciously allowed me to use their 1910 station images that were taken just three years before the M&U would begin independent operation. The Ontario and Western Railway Historical Society was critically important for the use of their extensive photograph and negative collection that allowed the close relationship between the M&U and the NYO&W to be depicted. Author and railroad historian Robert Mohowski graciously allowed me to use images from former NYS&W conductor John Treen making the last chapter on the NYS&W Hanford branch possible. Lastly to my loving wife, Catherine, who is indispensable with her computer expertise and toleration of my many hours delving into the history of local railroads.

Introduction

On June 1, 1843, the New York and Erie became the first railroad to reach the hamlet of Middletown, New York, propelling the growth of its population and industry toward a city while also stimulating the growth of the dairy industry in Orange County. At a meeting in Middletown on March 3, 1866, a board of directors was elected for the newly organized Middletown, Unionville, and Water Gap Railroad. The railroad was built to the Erie's 6-foot broad gauge as the Erie was contracted to run the railroad. The first train of the Middletown, Unionville, and Water Gap ran on January 14, 1868, from Middletown to Unionville. Stations were built at Slate Hill, Johnson, Westtown, and Unionville. The railroad connected directly with the Erie as it entered Middletown from Goshen resulting in the MU&WG using the Erie's Middletown depot. The distance from the Erie's Middletown depot to Unionville was 13.89 miles.

The New York and Oswego Midland's first train reached Middletown during January 1872, but they had already leased the MU&WG on May 1, 1871, for 99 years beginning with the New Jersey Midland's completion to the New York and New Jersey border and connection to the MU&WG at Unionville. The NY&OM converted the MU&WG to standard gauge and built a 1.1-mile extension from just west of Dolson Avenue, which required a bridge over the Erie to reach the East Main Street connection with their main line. The NY&OM built the depot at East Main Street in 1872. The NY&OM operations of the MU&WG began on April 1, 1872. During the panic of 1873, the NY&OM entered bankruptcy and reorganized as the New York, Ontario, and Western Railway in 1879. The MU&WG lease was passed to the NJM but it also entered receivership emerging on March 31, 1881 as the New York, Susquehanna, and Western Railroad Company holding the MU&WG lease. The NYO&W rerouted most of its traffic off the MU&WG when it opened its Middletown branch on June 4, 1883, from Middletown to the West Shore Railroad at Cornwall, New York. The NYS&W extended its main line from Two Bridges, New Jersey, to East Stroudsburg, Pennsylvania, connecting with a new subsidiary, the Wilkes Barre and Eastern that reached the northern anthracite coalfields. Overhead traffic dropped on the former 34-mile main line to Middletown as it became the NYS&W's Middletown branch. Ever-increasing milk traffic to New York City markets from the MU&WG's numerous milk stations earned the little railroad the unofficial distinction that mile for mile it had the greatest milk traffic in the country. The Erie Railroad emerged in 1895 after several reorganizations to gain control over the NYS&W along with the MU&WG on July 1, 1898. When the Erie failed to pay interest due on the MU&WG mortgage bonds on September 8, 1913, it allowed the mortgage holders to take control and organize the independent Middletown and Unionville Railroad that began operations on December 1, 1913. Throughout the corporate existence of the M&U and first decade of its successor, the Middletown and New Jersey Railway, the connections to the Erie, NYO&W, and the NYS&W would remain the same.

The Middletown and Unionville Railroad leased for 999 years the 1.1-mile extension from East Main Street to Dolson Avenue from the NYO&W giving the M&U a main line of 14.12 miles and an additional 1.46 miles of yard tracks and sidings along with stations from Middletown to Unionville. The M&U's main offices and yard were in Middletown. The former MU&WG Unionville turntable and one stall engine house were replaced by a cost effective wye track for turning larger locomotives. The M&U and the NYS&W interchanged freight at Unionville until January 30, 1914. During 1914, the NYS&W and the M&U each built 900-foot interchange tracks, along the New York and New Jersey border, with each railroad granting the other 1,300 feet of trackage rights to interchange freight. In 1917, the NYS&W built a turntable and water tank on the eastern end of their interchange track. On the NYS&W and the M&U, this location was known as M&U or Hanford Junction respectively. The NYS&W's 21-mile branch from Beaver Lake, formerly Two Bridges, to M&U Junction was referred to as the Hanford branch.

The M&U hired veteran railroader John A. Smith as vice president and general manager from December 1, 1913, until his retirement in 1940 when he was replaced by W. R. Durland. Smith maintained detailed notes and files throughout his tenure. In a statement he wrote to the ICC during 1920, he listed the companies along the railroad as one file manufacturing facility, six coal dealers with yards, five feed dealers, three wholesale oil dealers, one cheese factory, five cattle dealers, five automobile dealers, one fur factory, one silk mill, eight creameries, two gravel banks, and twenty merchants.

During 1914, the M&U ran two westbound milk trains and one eastbound, but by 1919, only one milk train ran in each direction. During 1922, only a mixed train in each direction provided service to the various creameries. From 1921 through 1938, milk revenue constituted 51 percent to 76 percent of the railroad's earnings with the peak year being 1927. Diversion of milk traffic to truck competition began a decline from 1927 until the end of milk traffic in 1941. To support the dairy industry, feed mills developed in every village and generated heavy inbound feed traffic during the M&U era. With its passenger service in direct competition with automobiles, the M&U purchased a series of rail buses and gas electric motor cars. Only the contract to transport students to Middletown High School kept passenger service in operation until June 1940. Overhead coal traffic from the NYO&W via the M&U to the NYS&W at Hanford Junction during the early 1940s helped the struggling short line compensate for some of the lost milk revenue.

The Erie would use the M&U Middletown yard, known as "DG Yard," for storing commuter coaches for trains terminating in Middletown along with servicing their local freight and commuter engines including use of the M&U's 75-foot turntable until May 10, 1949, when diesels became the local Erie freight power. The Erie also would run trains from its Middletown yard via trackage rights over the M&U and NYO&W to reach their disconnected Pine Bush branch. Once independent from the Erie on January 1, 1940, the NYS&W sent via the M&U steam locomotives and equipment requiring major repairs to the NYO&W Middletown shops until 1943.

The M&U filed for bankruptcy in 1943 with M&U official Louis F. Zieres becoming the trustee. The M&U's financial situation was irreversible as feed and overhead traffic between the NYO&W and the NYS&W continued to decline. Manning, Simmons, and Clark were feed dealers along the railroad and members of the M&U's board of directors who purchased a General Electric diesel leasing it back to the railroad on April 19, 1946. The diesel's arrival could not stop an embargo of the railroad during the last week of May 1946. The M&U's last train operated on May 31, 1946. Manning, Simmons and Clark secured control of the M&U stocks and bonds, forcing the foreclosure of the M&U and its reorganization as the Middletown and New Jersey Railway.

One

Locomotives, Equipment, and Leased Power

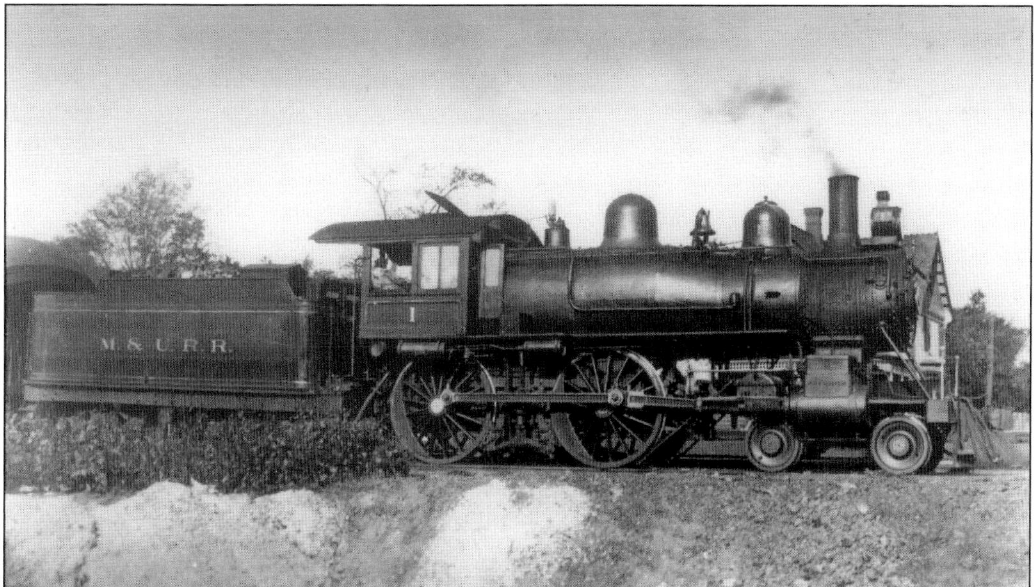

M&U No. 1, a 4-4-0 American locomotive, is seen here in the M&U's Middletown yard on August 10, 1915, pulling a passenger train eastbound to Unionville. (John Stellwagen Collection, M&NJRHS Archives.)

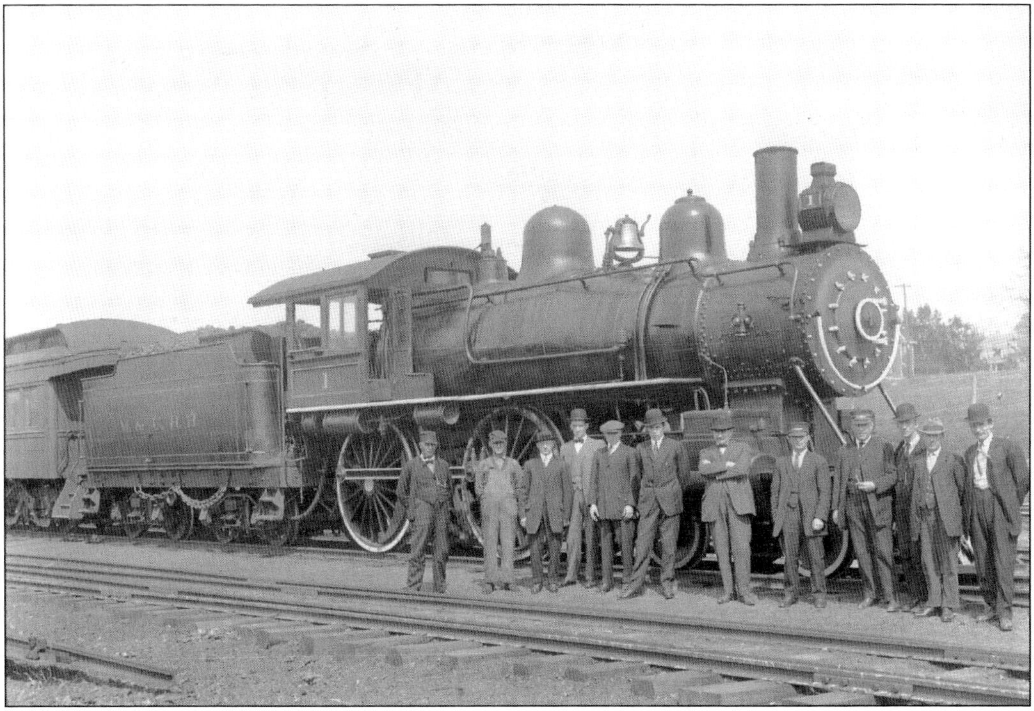

M&U No. 1 poses with the train crew and railroad officials. No. 1 was purchased from the Pittsburgh and Lake Erie Railroad prior to the M&U becoming operational. The M&U sold this locomotive during November 1924. The gentleman in the center with his arms crossed was J. A. Smith, general manager and vice president of the railroad from 1913 until 1940. His meticulous files document the history of the M&U. (Ray Brown Collection, M&NJRHS Archives.)

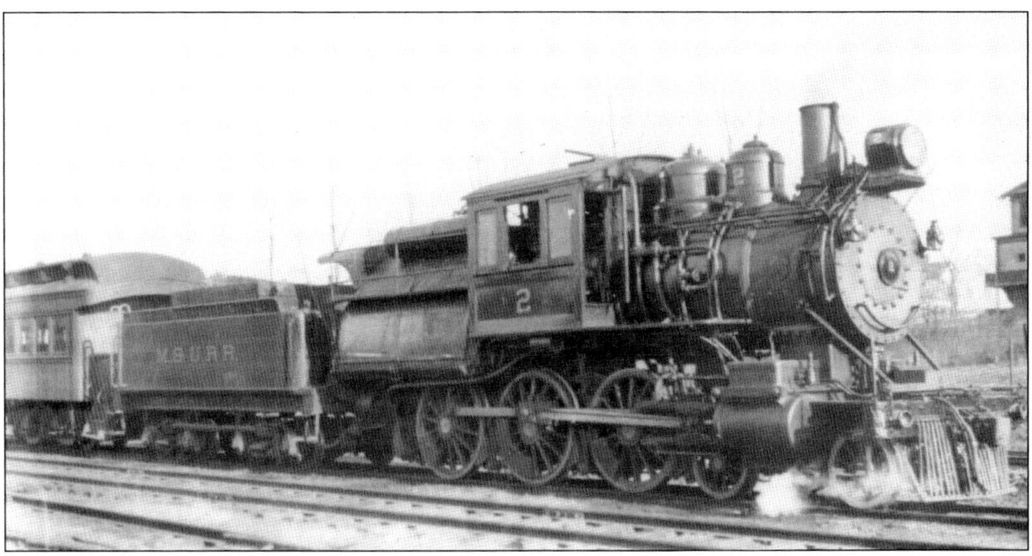

The No. 2 in this photograph was actually the second locomotive of that number. The first was former NYO&W engine No. 109, which was only operated from July 30, 1917, until September 26, 1917. Second No. 2 was purchased from the Lehigh and Hudson River Railway on October 1, 1922, and was sold on December 31, 1930. (Ray Brown Collection, M&NJRHS Archives.)

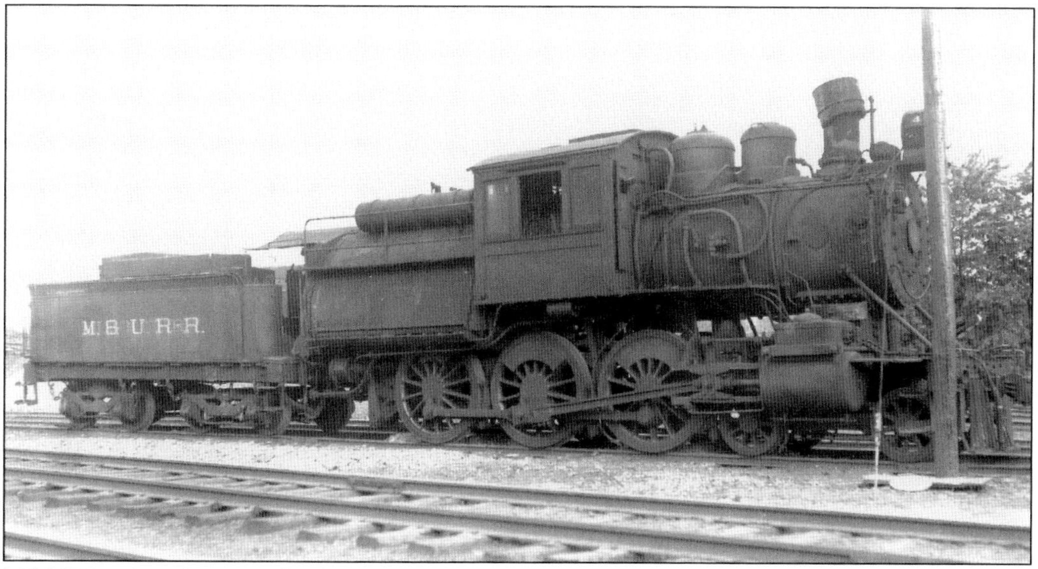

M&U Nos. 3 and 4 were also former Lehigh and Hudson River locomotives and along with No.2 were the only camelbacks owned by the M&U as well as the only 4-6-0 locomotives. No. 4, shown here with its stack capped as it awaits scrapping, was purchased on September 1, 1924, and sold on December 1, 1927. (Ray Brown Collection, M&NJRHS Archives.)

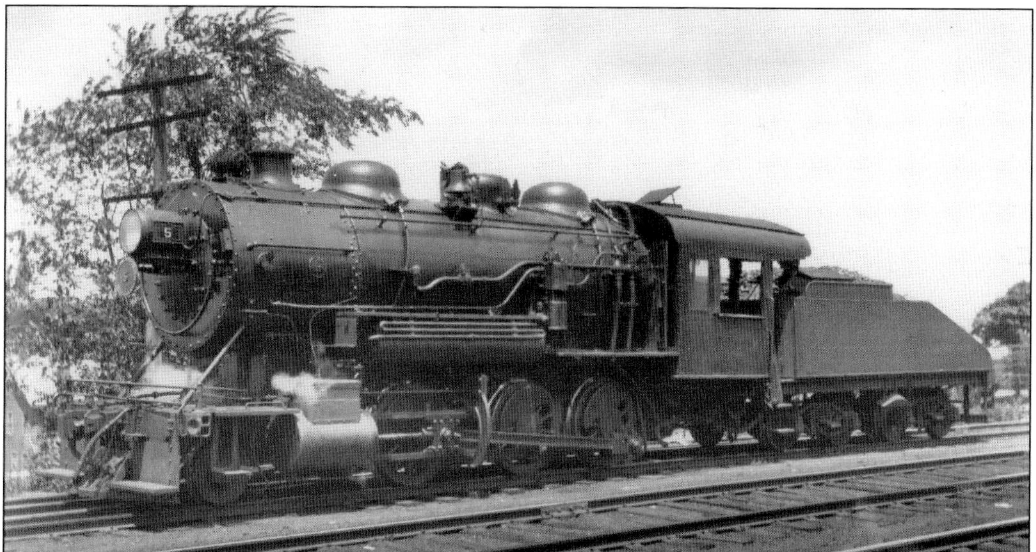

M&U No. 5 shown here in DG yard during May 1931 ran as rough as it was esthetically unappealing. It was purchased on December 12, 1930, from the Mount Hope Mineral Railroad in New Jersey and sold during November 1935 to the West Pittston and Exeter in Pennsylvania. (Ray Brown Collection, M&NJRHS Archives.)

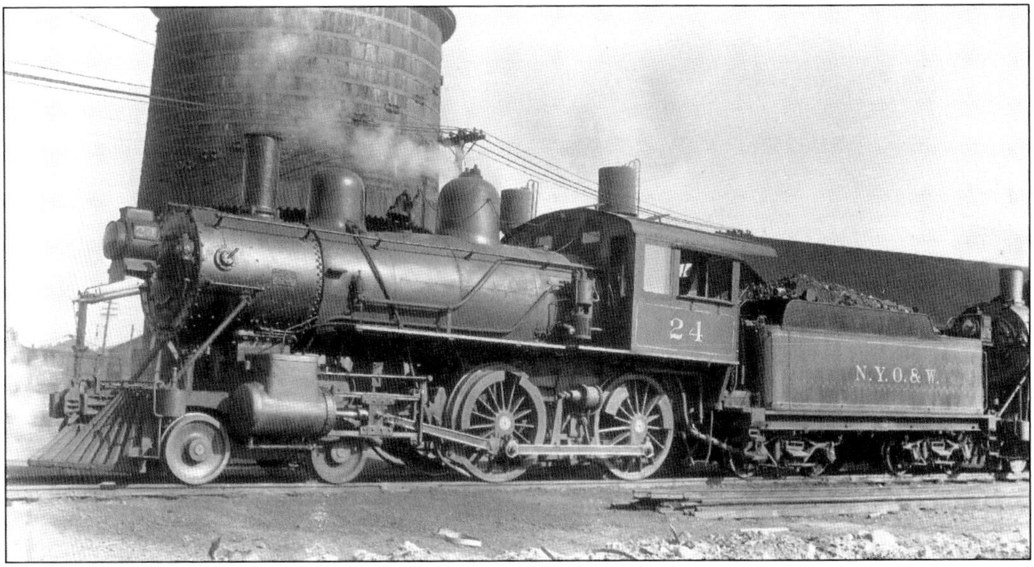

NYO&W No. 24 would later be bought by the M&U and become No. 6. Shown here at the Middletown shops, No. 24 was built in 1908 by Cooke locomotive works in Paterson, New Jersey. The M&U leased her on occasions to power their passenger and freight trains when No. 2 or No. 3 was in the NYO&W shop. (Ray Brown Collection, M&NJRHS Archives.)

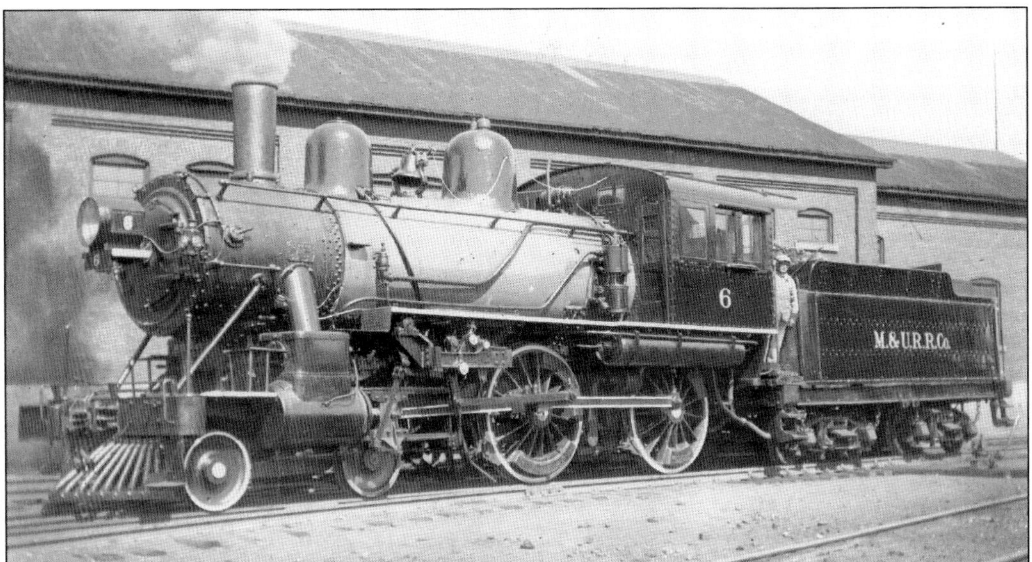

The M&U purchased No. 24 from the NYO&W for $2,500 on June 24, 1935, and the engine was serviced and painted at the NYO&W's Norwich, New York, shops. No. 6 made its inaugural run on the M&U on July 19, 1935. (Ray Brown Collection, M&NJRHS Archives.)

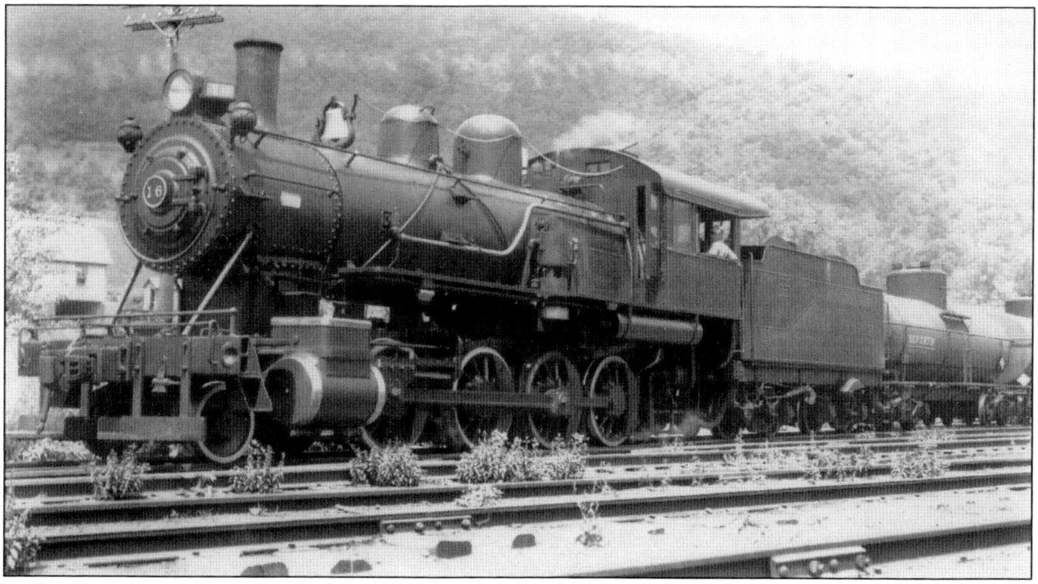

Bellefonte Central No. 16, a 2-8-0, was former Detroit, Toledo, and Ironton No. 76. It was sold to the A. A. Morrison Company of Buffalo, New York, who in turn sold it to the M&U on June 1, 1940. Unfortunately for the M&U coping with heavy coal traffic, the actual tractive effort of 26,868 pounds fell short of the stated 31,000 pounds. (Ray Brown Collection, M&NJRHS Archives.)

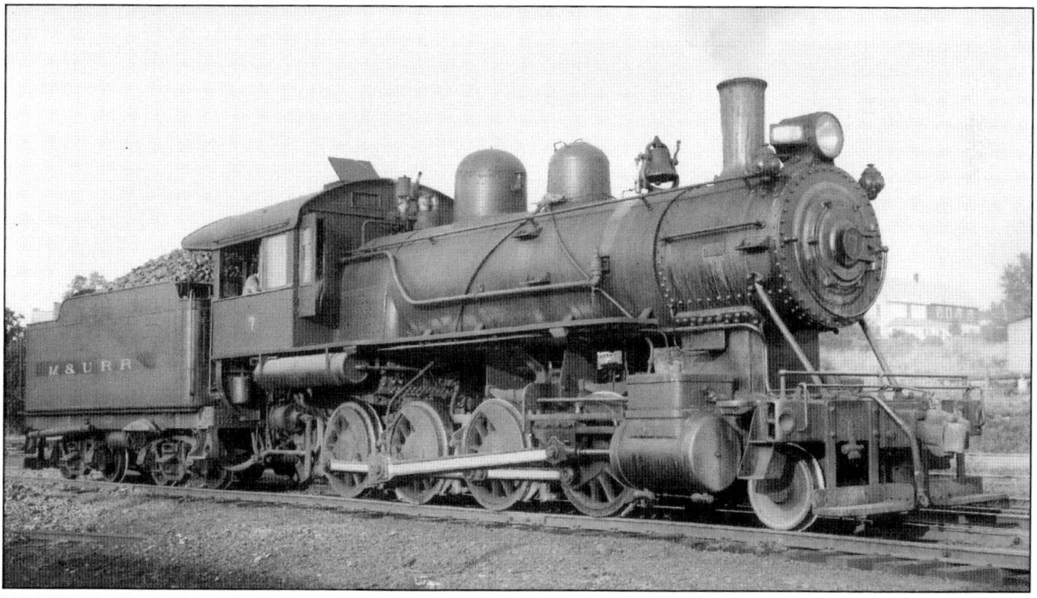

No. 7, the last steam locomotive purchased by the M&U, was bought on June 1, 1940, at a cost of $4,150 that included $1,000 for scrapping the No. 6. As a saturated locomotive built in 1902 No. 7 was actually older than the No. 6. She made her first run on June 9, 1940, and was retired on April 23, 1944. (Robert Collins Photograph, M&NJRHS Archives.)

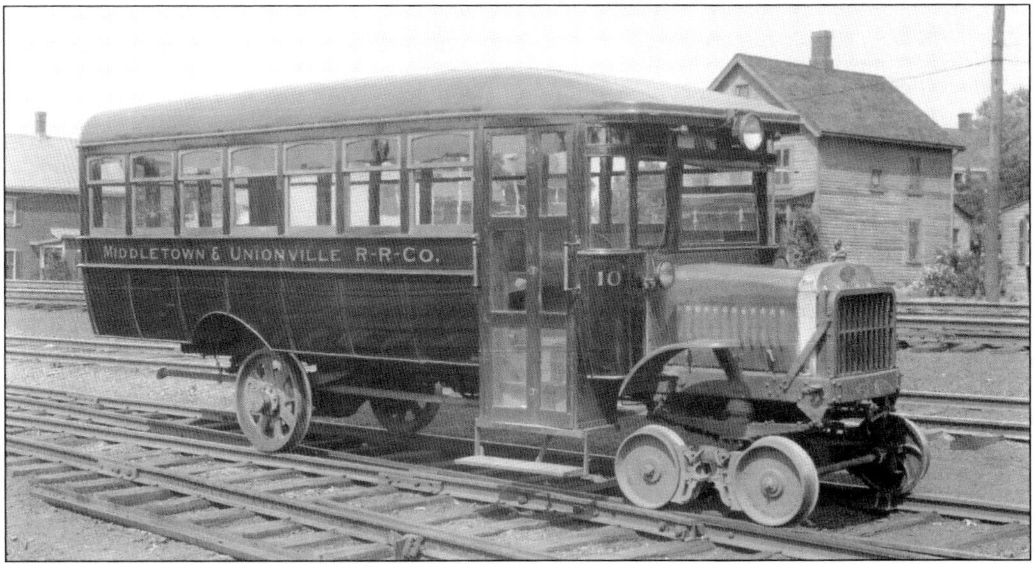

The M&U had five different types of the Reo rail bus. The No. 10 shown above was the larger of two that the M&U had during 1922 and carried as many as 30 people. This unit was wrecked when it was struck by a drunk driver at Dolson Avenue on June 28, 1922. It was traded in on a Gramm-Bernstein model that was numbered 10. (M&NJRHS Archives.)

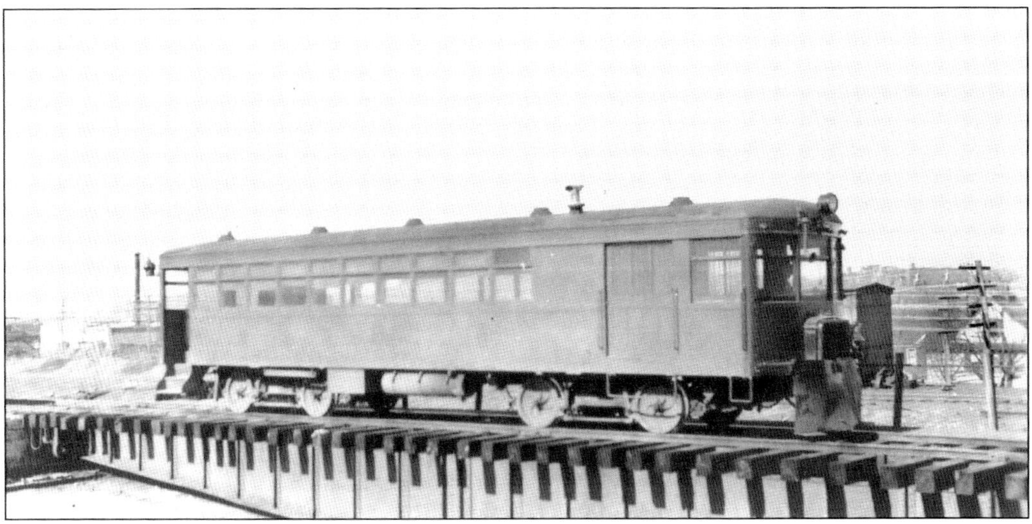

The Middletown and Unionville M-55 Brill Car was a gas electric motor car used to cut passenger service costs by replacing a steam locomotive passenger train. The M-55 Brill Car was purchased in 1926 and remained in service until the end of passenger service in the spring of 1940 when the M&U lost the contract to transport students to Middletown High School. (Ray Brown Collection, M&NJRHS Archives.)

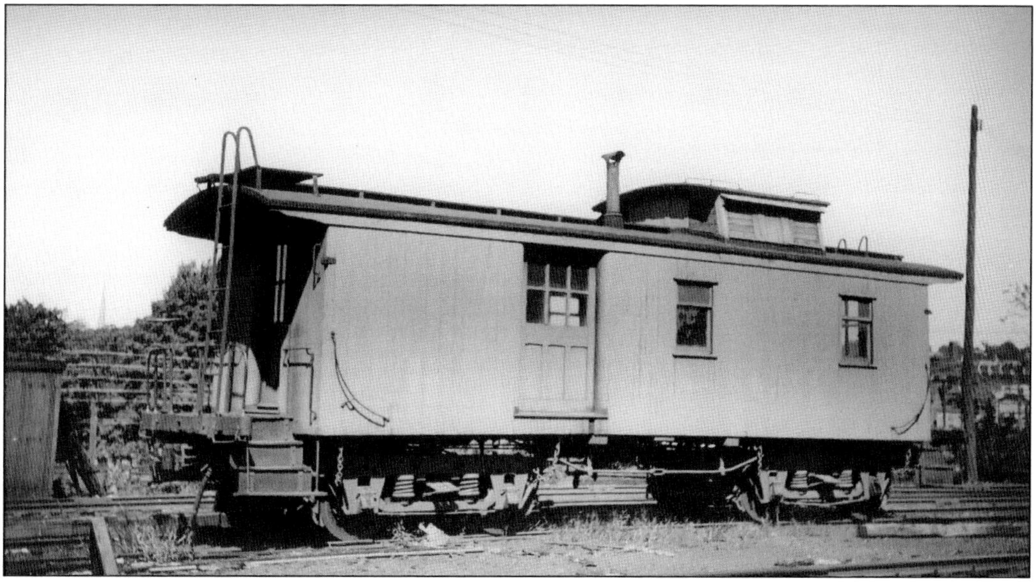

The M&U's first caboose, No. 50, is shown here in DG yard on August 25, 1935. It was purchased from the Ulster and Delaware Railroad during November 1925 and was retired in 1937. (Ray Brown Collection, M&NJRHS Archives.)

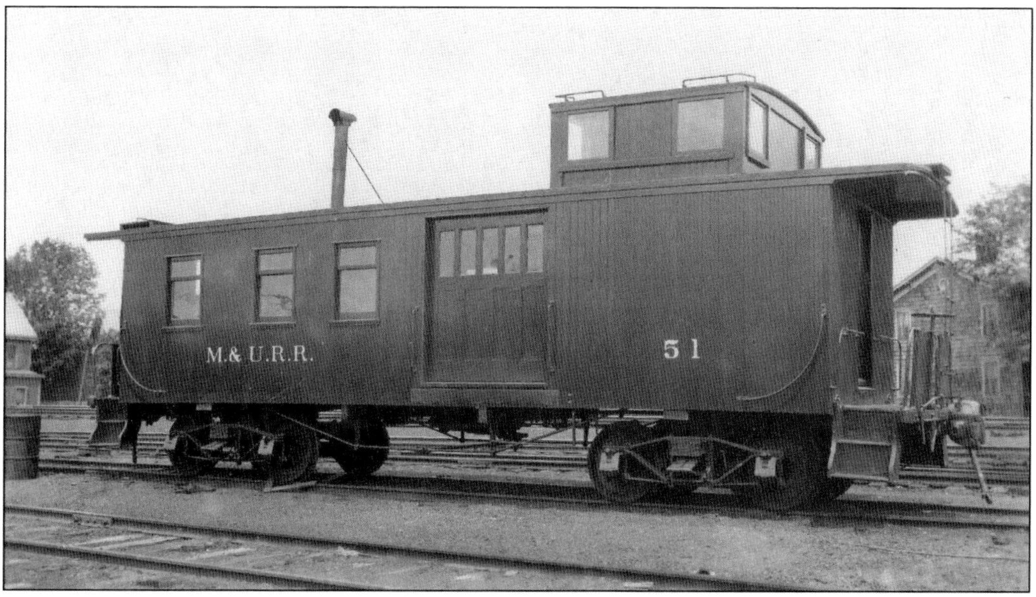

The second caboose was No. 51 shown here in the M&U's Middletown yard during May 1935. It was a former Delray Connecting Railroad caboose purchased on May 22, 1928, from the General Equipment Company. (George Votava Photograph, M&NJRHS Archives.)

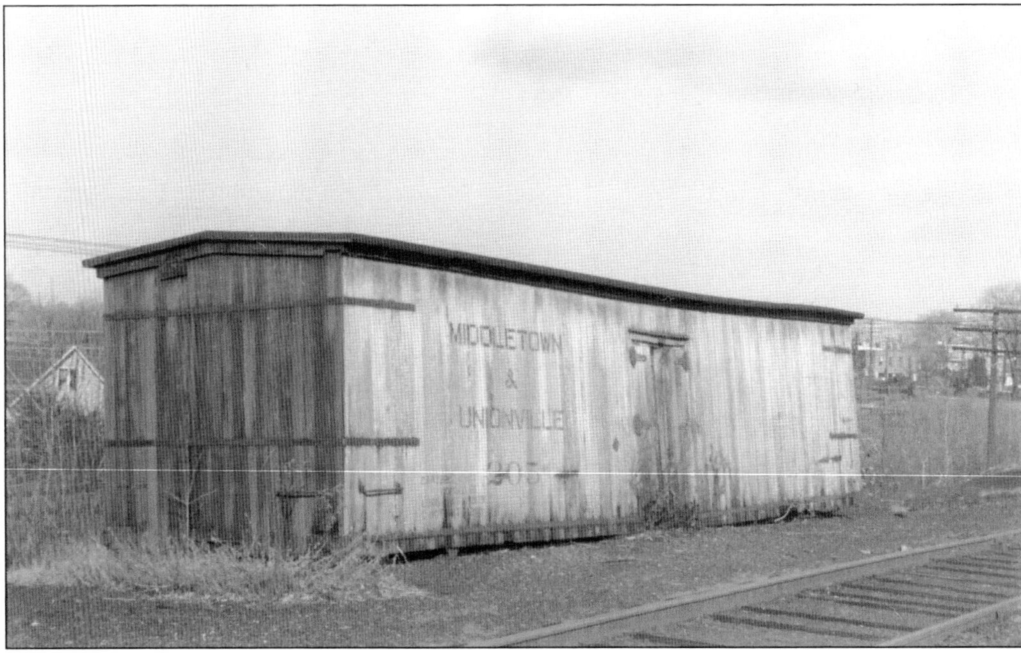

The frugal M&U salvaged the bodies of retired freight cars, such as refrigerator car No. 205 seen here, and used them in DG yard as storehouses. In its first life, No. 205 carried tens of thousands of gallons of milk from creameries along the M&U to the New York metropolitan market. (John Stellwagen Collection, M&NJRHS Archives.)

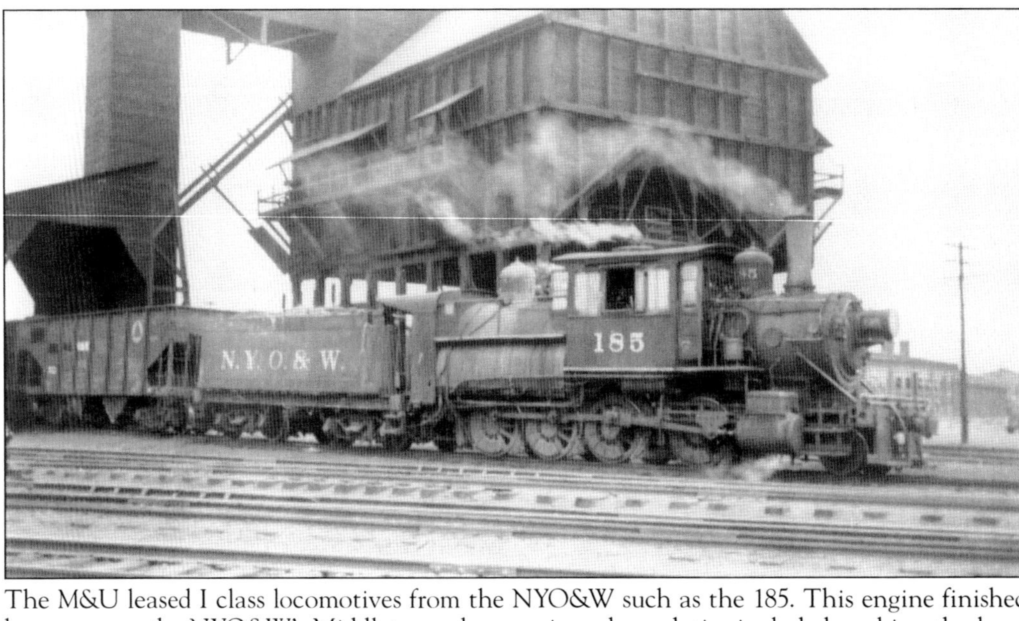

The M&U leased I class locomotives from the NYO&W such as the 185. This engine finished her career as the NYO&W's Middletown shop engine whose duties included working the large Fairbanks Morse coal tipple on Wisner Avenue. (Peter Brill Collection.)

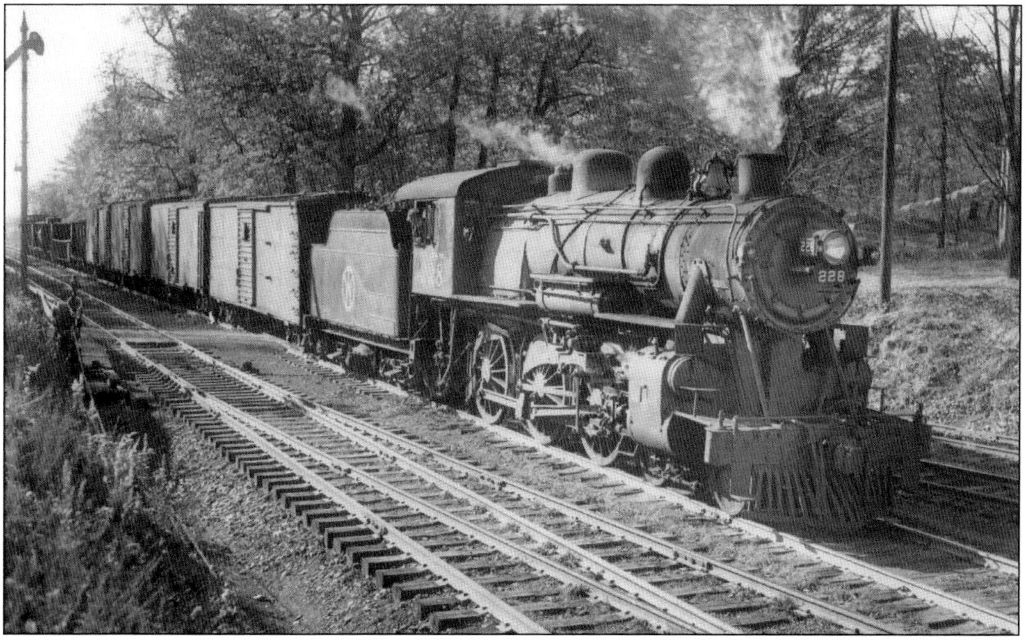

The M&U also leased NYO&W E class 4-6-0 ten wheelers. Although built for speed and passenger service, these locomotives did see freight duty. The 228 is at Campbell Hall headed southbound on the NYO&W with the Cornwall turn. The nine-car consist is similar in size and makeup to an M&U freight train. (Author's collection.)

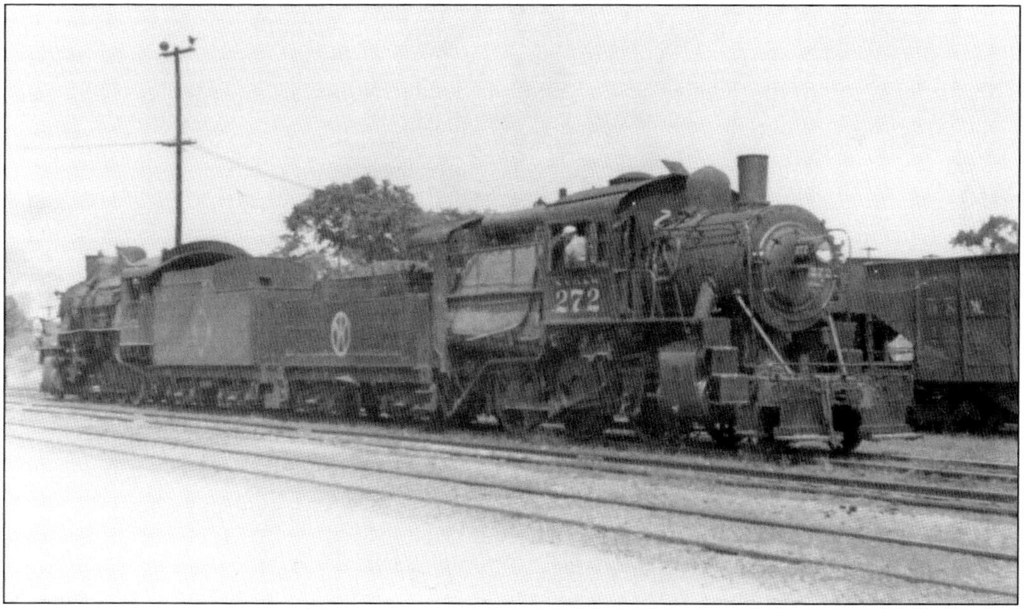

The M&U on occasion leased from the NYO&W V class 2-6-0's such as the 272 shown here in Middletown, New York. The 272 is pushing Erie J2 class 2-10-0 No. 2452 to the NYO&W shops for repairs during the period of 1940 to 1943 when large numbers of the NYS&W locomotive fleet were repaired by the NYO&W. The 2452 arrived at Middletown via the M&U from Hanford Junction. (Steven Maguire Photograph, M&NJRHS Archives.)

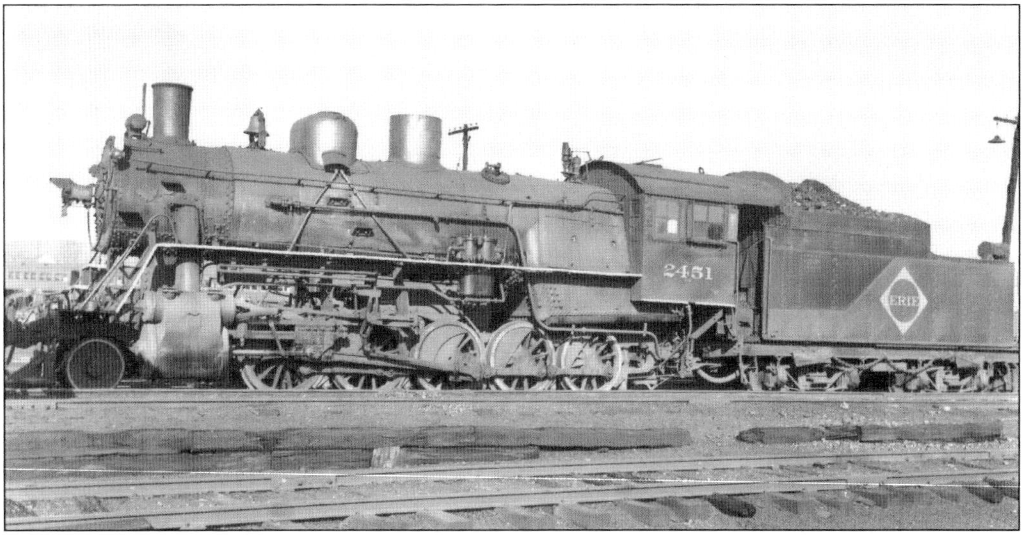

Some Erie J2 class 2-10-0 Decapods such as the 2451 were eventually sold to the NYS&W. Four of these NYS&W locomotives were leased by the M&U from July 22, 1945, to April 19, 1946. The M&U leased the 2435, 2451, 2461, and 2492. (Ray Brown Collection, M&NJRHS Archives.)

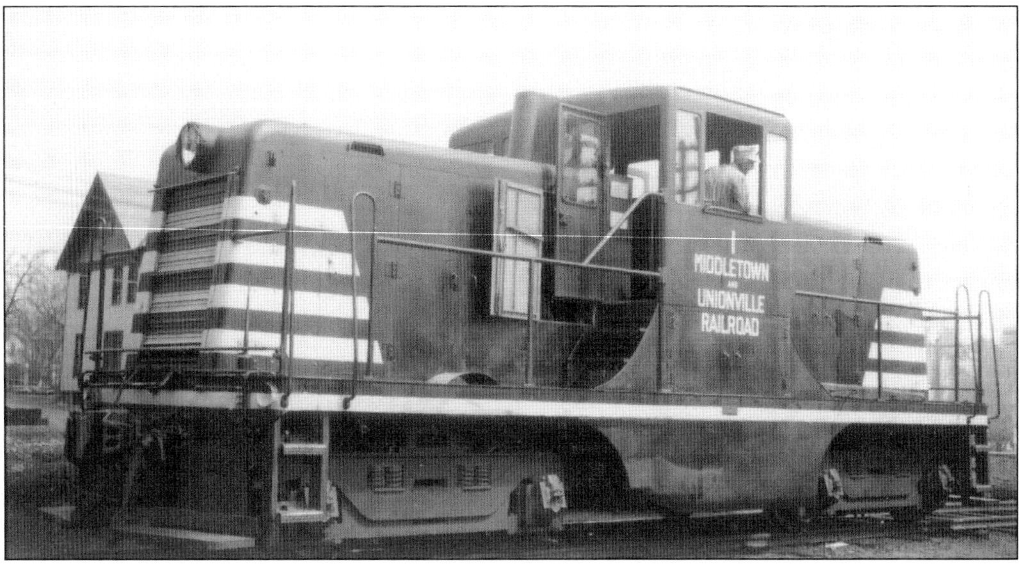

The Middletown and Unionville operated only one new locomotive. Diesel electric No. 1 was a 44-ton center-cab switcher manufactured by General Electric. It was built in April 1946 and had a starting tractive effort of 26,400 pounds. It was delivered on April 19, 1946, at Hanford Junction and made its first run that afternoon westward to Middletown. (Rasmussen Family Collection.)

Two

MIDDLETOWN AND WESTERN CONNECTIONS

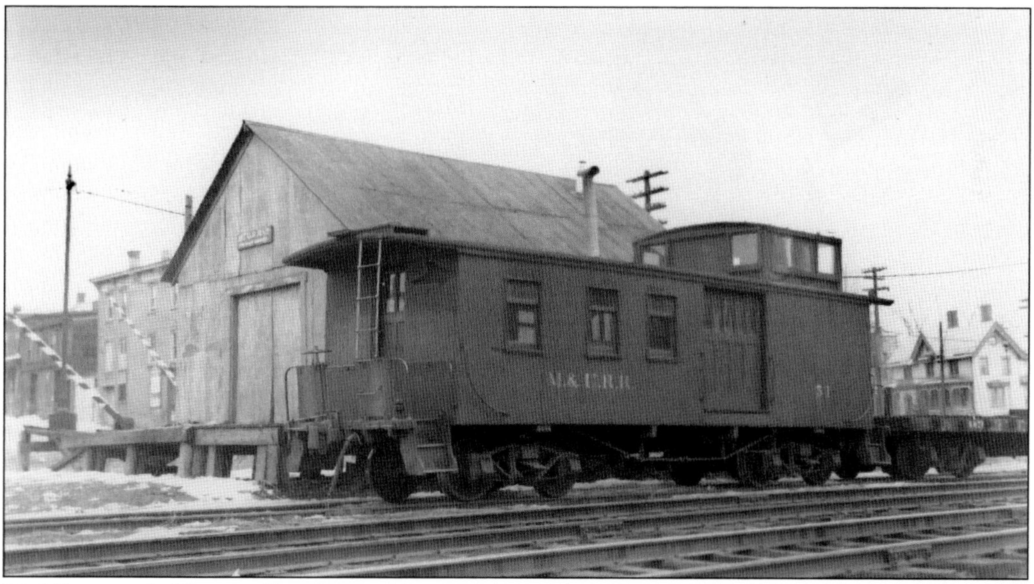

Middletown & Unionville caboose 51 sits next to the M&U freight house on March 16, 1941. The structure was located off Railroad Avenue in Middletown, north of East Main Street and the M&U's passenger station. The M&U leased the freight depot's site from the O&W. The crossing gates in the background are on Railroad Avenue protecting motorists and pedestrians from traffic on the O&W. (John Stellwagen Collection, M&NJRHS Archives.)

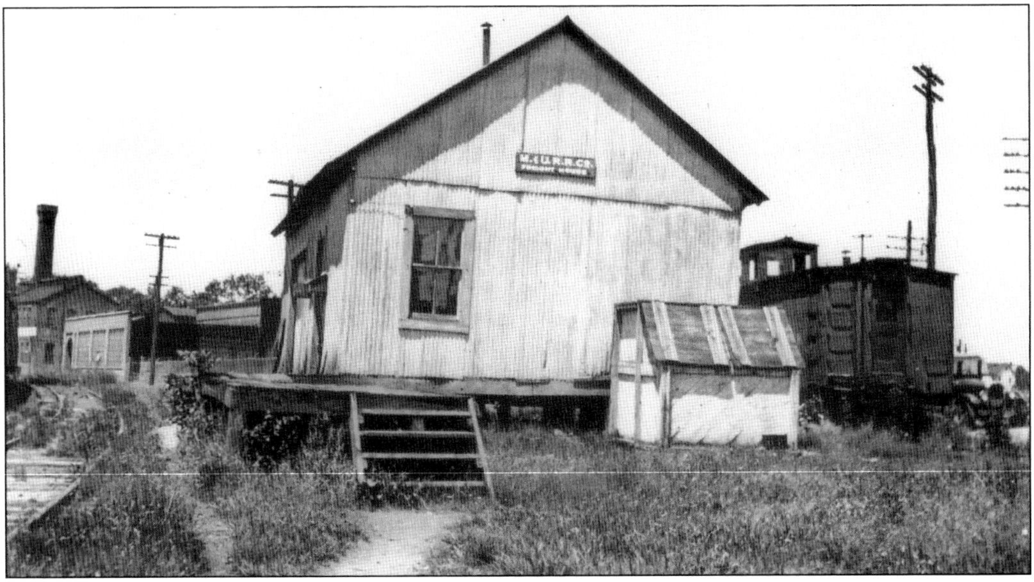

This view of the M&U freight house was taken from East Main Street looking west. The M&U flanger is on the right side of the building. Note the platform that runs along the left side. To the extreme left are a number of cars on the interchange track. Clemson Hack Saw works are in the background along Railroad Avenue. (Ray Brown Collection, M&NJRHS Archives.)

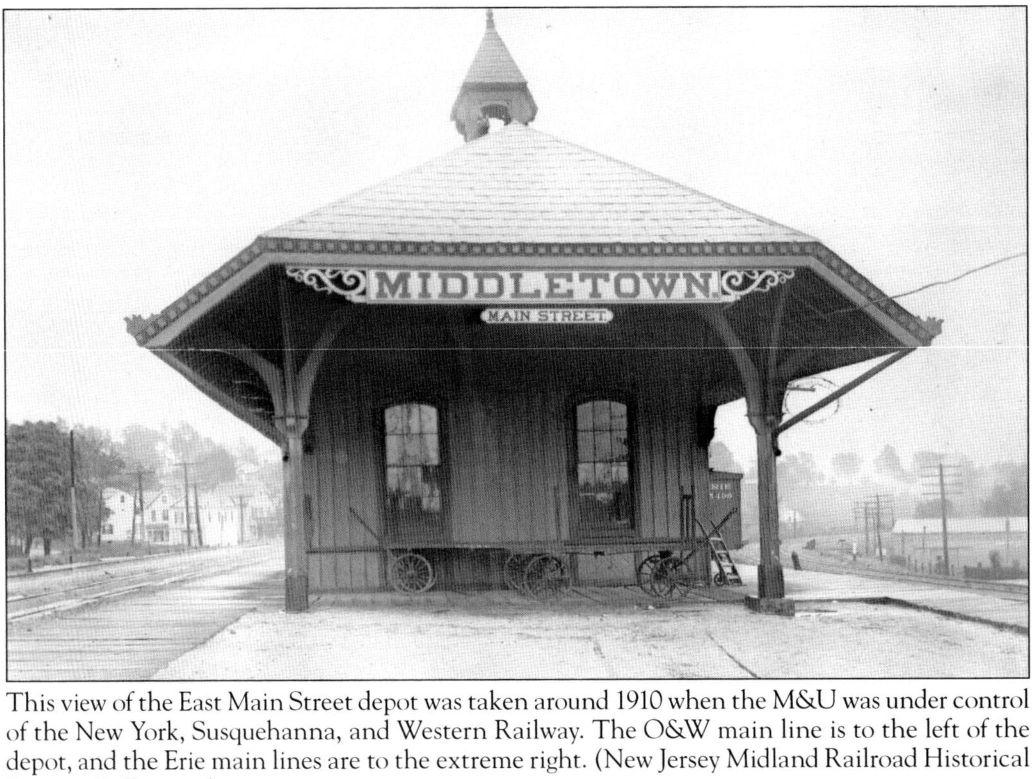

This view of the East Main Street depot was taken around 1910 when the M&U was under control of the New York, Susquehanna, and Western Railway. The O&W main line is to the left of the depot, and the Erie main lines are to the extreme right. (New Jersey Midland Railroad Historical Society Collection.)

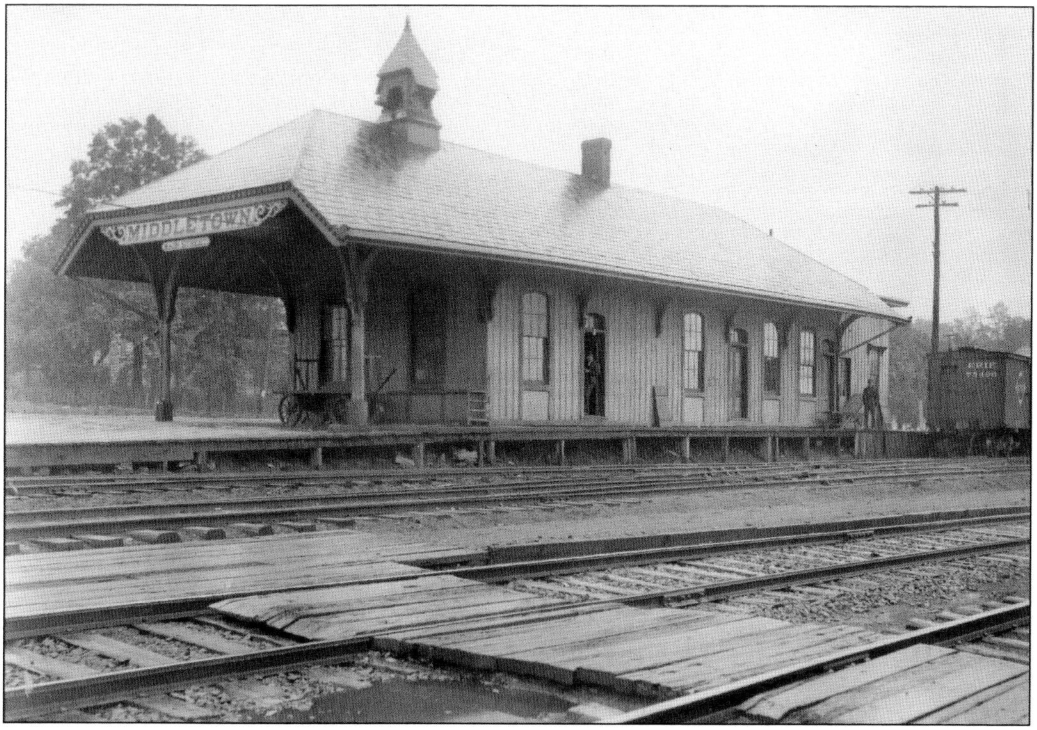

This view of the East Main Street depot around 1910 shows the Erie side of the depot. Note the wooden platform used during this time period for less-than-carload traffic. The station's telegraph call letter was "DG." The Erie double-track main line is at the bottom of the photograph. (New Jersey Midland Railroad Historical Society Collection.)

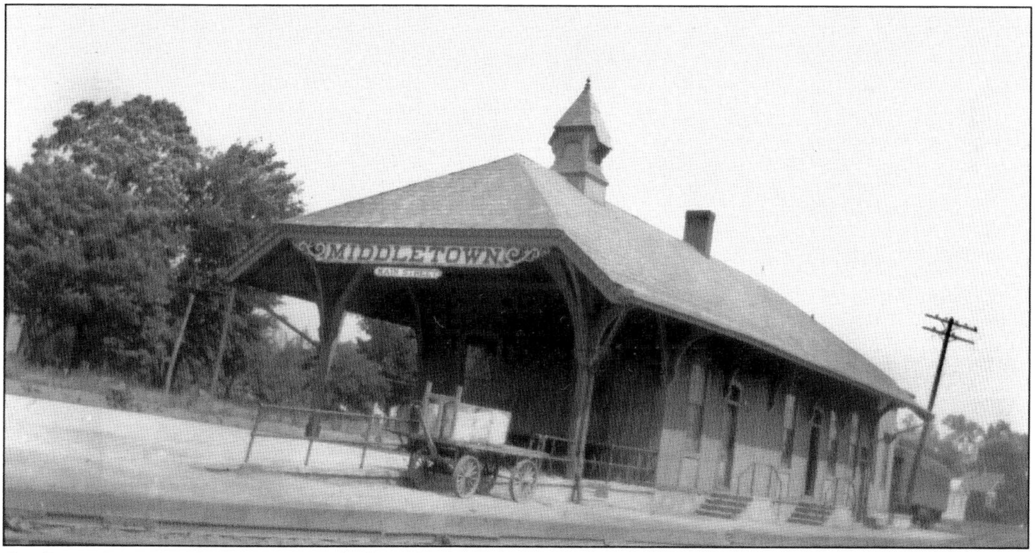

On June 21, 1921, Jim Speer took this photograph showing the M&U's Middletown depot at East Main Street. The M&U main track runs alongside the depot. During the M&U era, the wooden platform was removed and concrete steps installed at each door. Less-than-carload freight could now be handled at the M&U's freight house across East Main Street. (Ray Brown Collection, M&NJRHS Archives.)

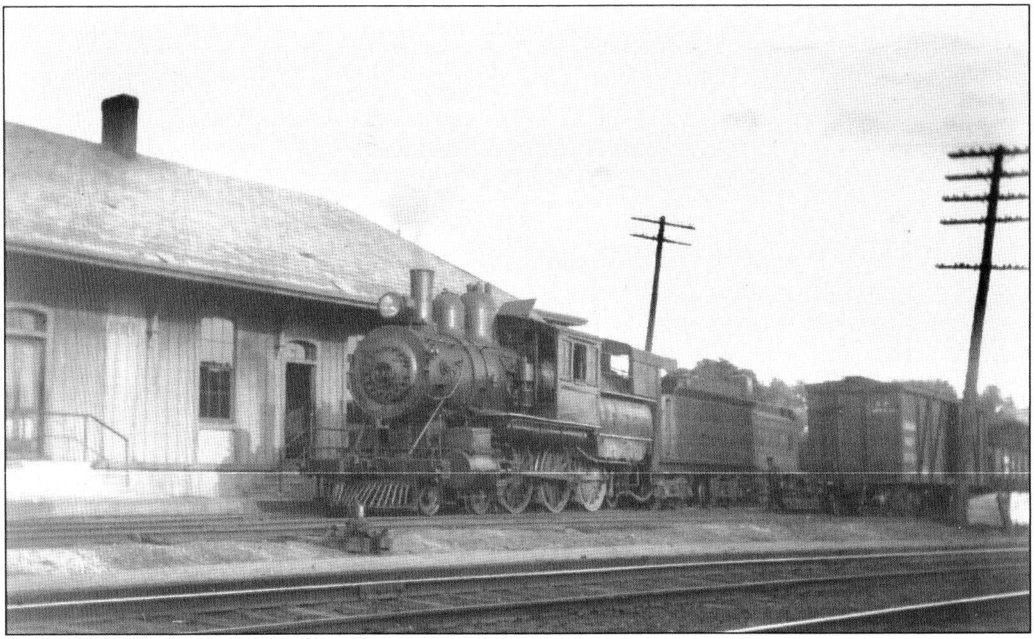

Erie class G8 4-6-0 camelback pushes her train into the M&U's DG yard. The Erie 893 will park her train and use the turntable to prepare for the next eastbound trip to Jersey City. The name "camelback" was applied to steam locomotives with an engineer's cab astride the boiler and a rear cab used by the fireman to fire the locomotive. (John Stellwagen Collection.)

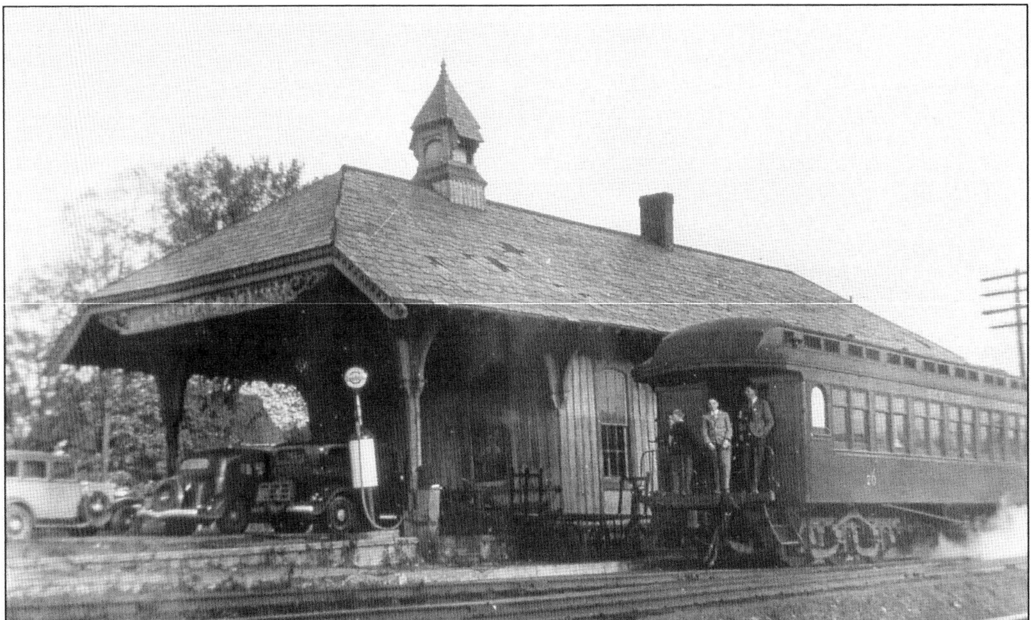

An eastbound Erie passenger train slowly backs out of the M&U's DG yard past the East Main Street depot. From here, the train will return to Erie rails on the opposite side of East Main Street on the third track leading to the Erie's Middletown passenger depot a half mile away. (Carl Detwyler Collection, M&NJRHS Archives.)

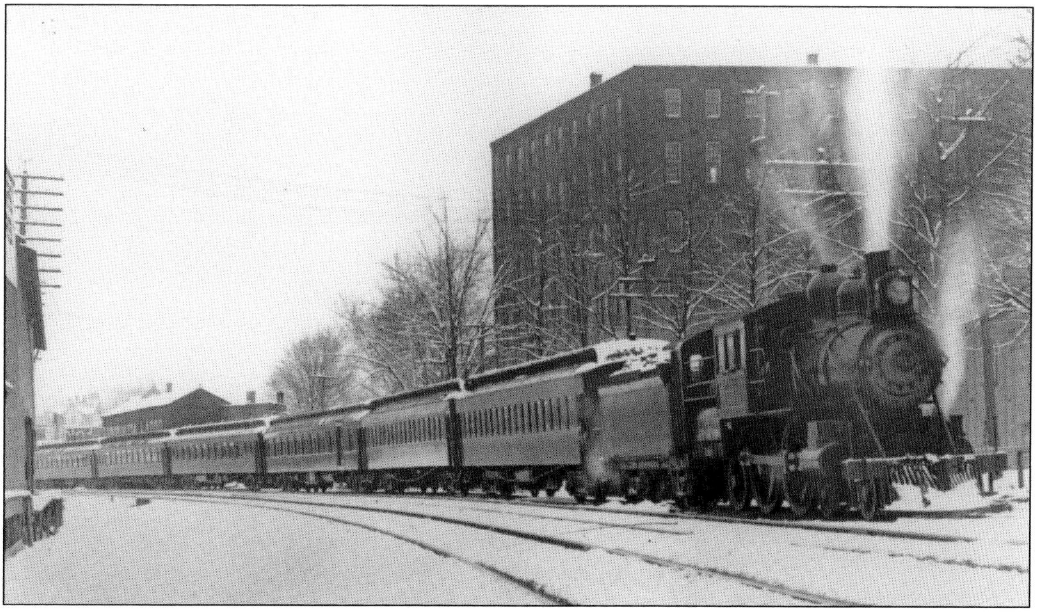

Erie G8 camelback 519 is backing its train from the Middletown, Unionville, and Water Gap's yard on the Erie's third track to the Erie's Middletown yard. The Susquehanna is currently running the MU&WG. The train will cross over to the eastbound main and head to Jersey City. The large building in the background is the former New York Piano Key Manufacturing Company that burned to the ground on April 26, 1911. (Ray Brown Collection, M&NJRHS Archives.)

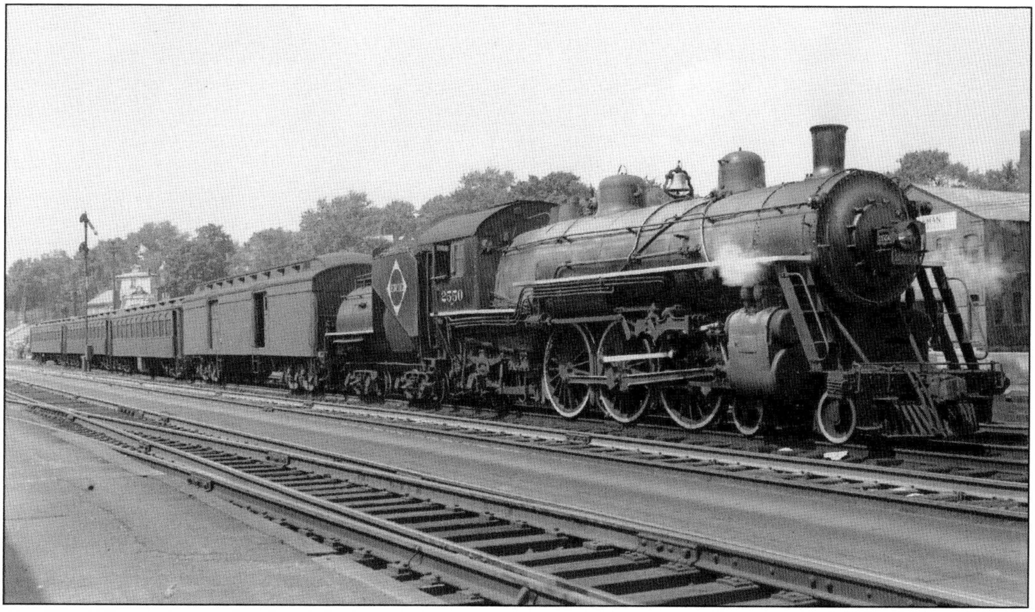

On September 3, 1938, Erie K-1 Pacific 2550 has backed her train out of the M&U's DG yard to the Erie's DW Middletown yard. When the 2550 is given clearance by the Middletown operator, the engineer will back his train through two pairs of crossover switches to enter the eastbound main to the left. The 2550 will then pick up any passengers at the Erie's Middletown depot for the trip to Jersey City. (George Votava Photograph, author's collection.)

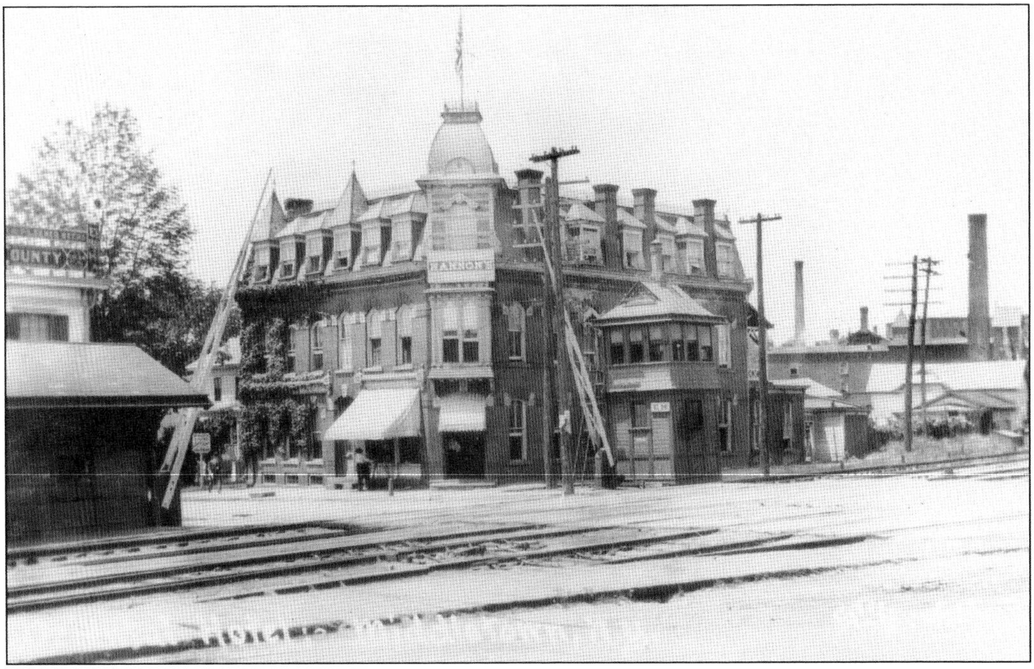

Across East Main Street was Hannon's Hotel behind the Erie's EM tower. To the left is the Erie's East Main Street depot, which stood until the 1930s. All three railroads stopped at this location, thus making this the closest facility to a union station that the City of Middletown would ever have. (Ray Brown Collection, M&NJRHS Archives.)

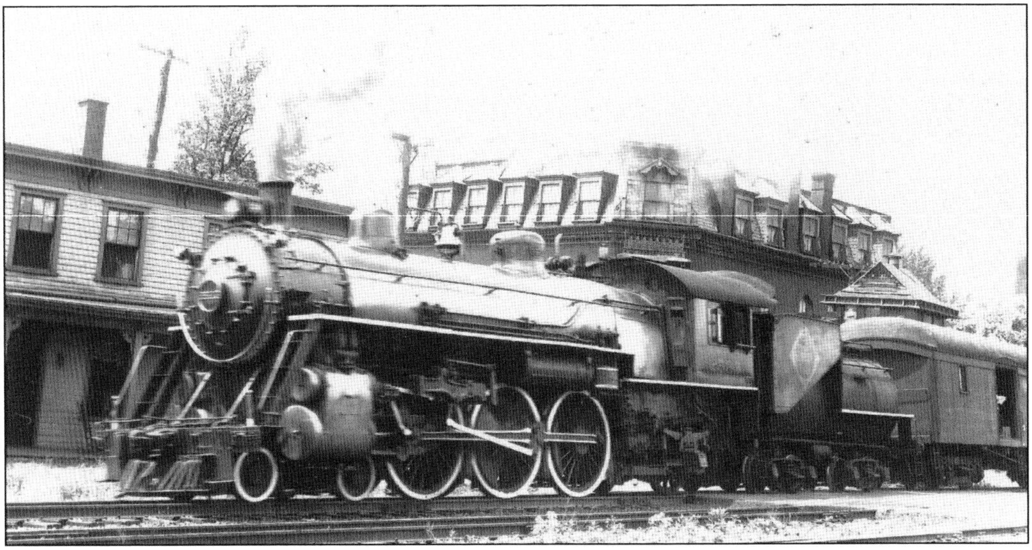

Erie K1 Pacific 2533 is eastbound crossing East Main Street on July 27, 1940. Note the Switch Inn to the left of the 2533 and the absence of the Erie East Main Street depot. Above the cab of the 2533 is Hannon's Hotel with the roof of EM tower peeking over the combine car. (John Stellwagen Collection.)

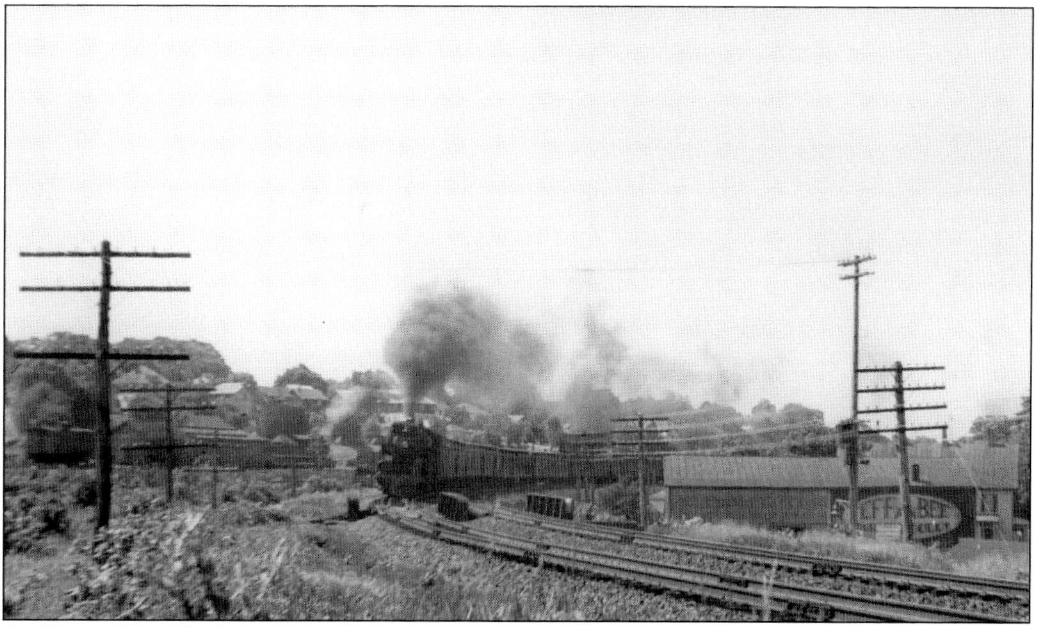

An Erie K5 Pacific leads the westbound Erie Limited into Middletown during 1941. The K5 is about to pass over the Sprague Avenue bridge and East Main Street crossing. In the background is the M&U right-of-way. Caboose 50 is in the left background and M&U No. 7 is just to the left of the Erie Pacific. (Railroad Avenue Enterprises Collection.)

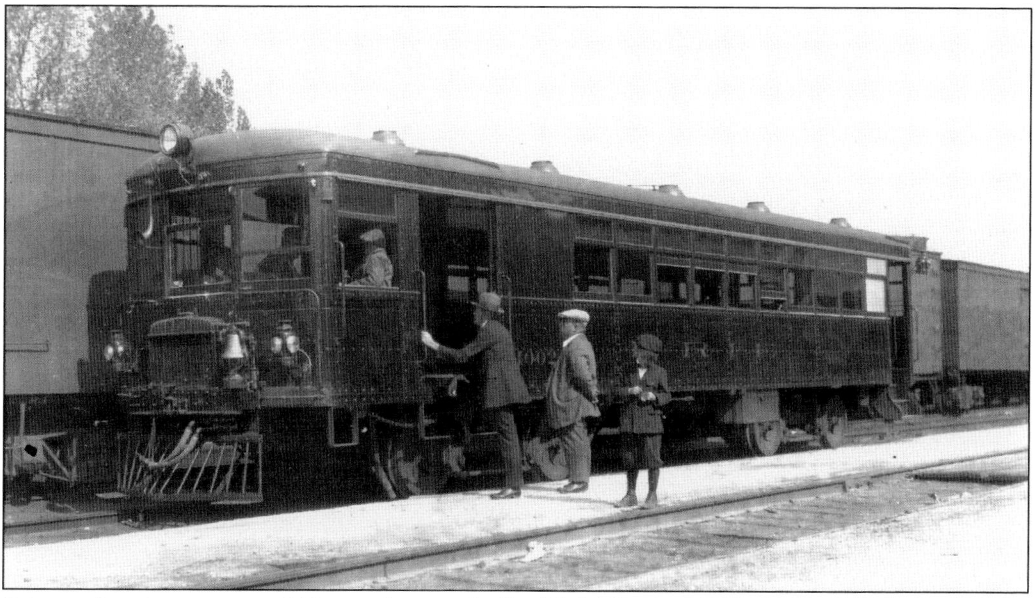

Erie gas electric motor car 4002, seen here at the Erie's Middletown depot during the 1920s. This was the type of motor car used in the final years of passenger service on the Erie's Pine Bush branch that was reached by a run over the M&U main line next to the depot at East Main Street to access the NYO&W by the long crossover for the trip to Crawford Junction. (John Stellwagen Collection.)

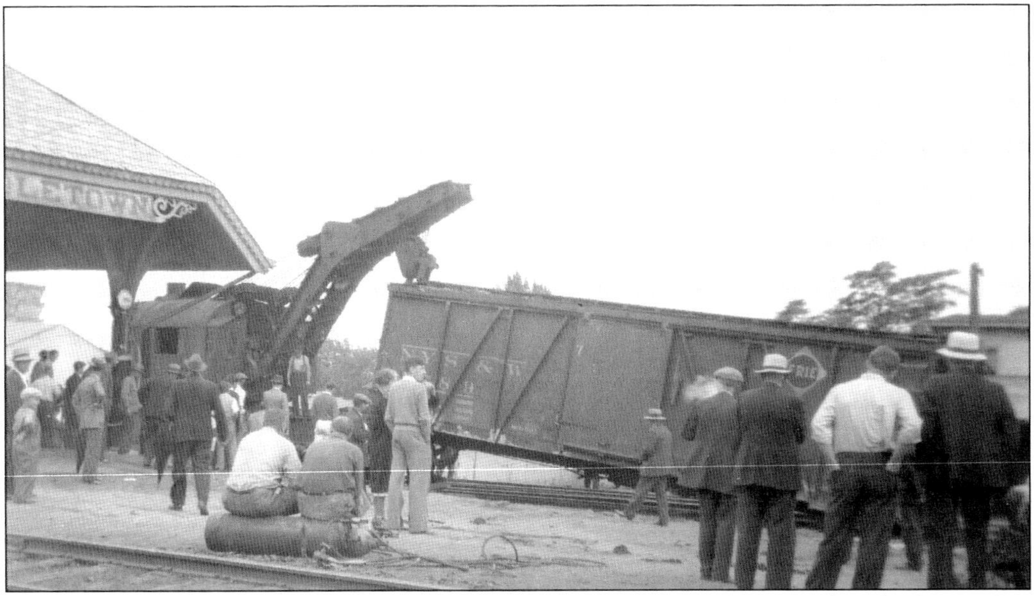

All the spectators are watching as a boxcar is lifted back on its trucks. Note that the boxcar has the Erie diamond logo on the right portion of the car, but New York, Susquehanna, and Western markings on the left. After the Erie took control of the NYS&W in 1898 most equipment used thereafter on the NYS&W was Erie. (Ray Brown Collection, M&NJRHS Archives.)

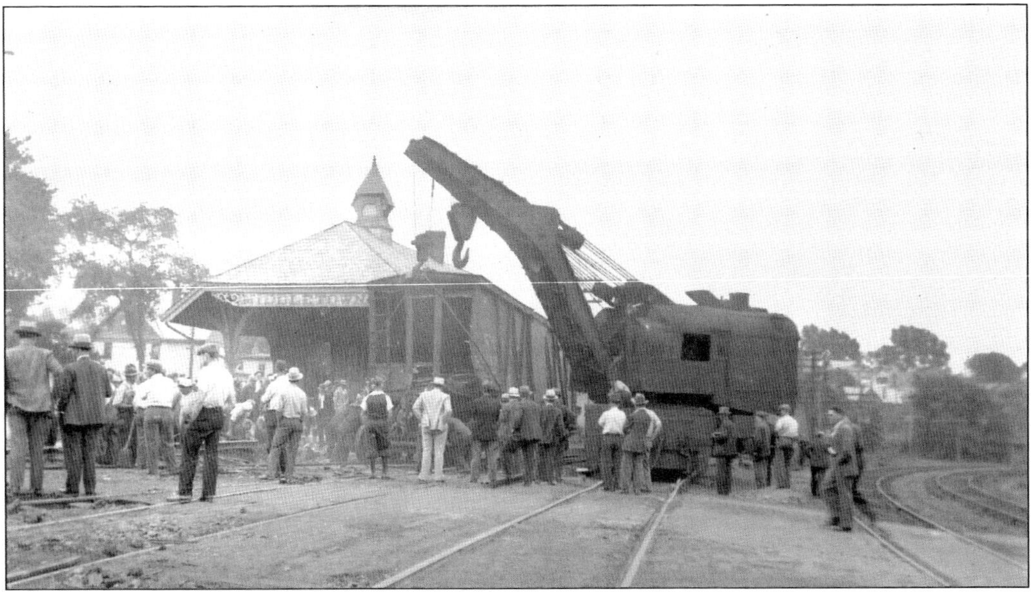

This photograph taken directly across East Main Street at the M&U depot captures the Erie steam derrick lifting the outside-braced Erie boxcar that was damaged and derailed on the long crossover to the NYO&W. This effectively stopped any interchange between the Erie, M&U, and the NYO&W. The Erie westbound and eastbound main tracks are to the right. (Ray Brown Collection, M&NJRHS Archives.)

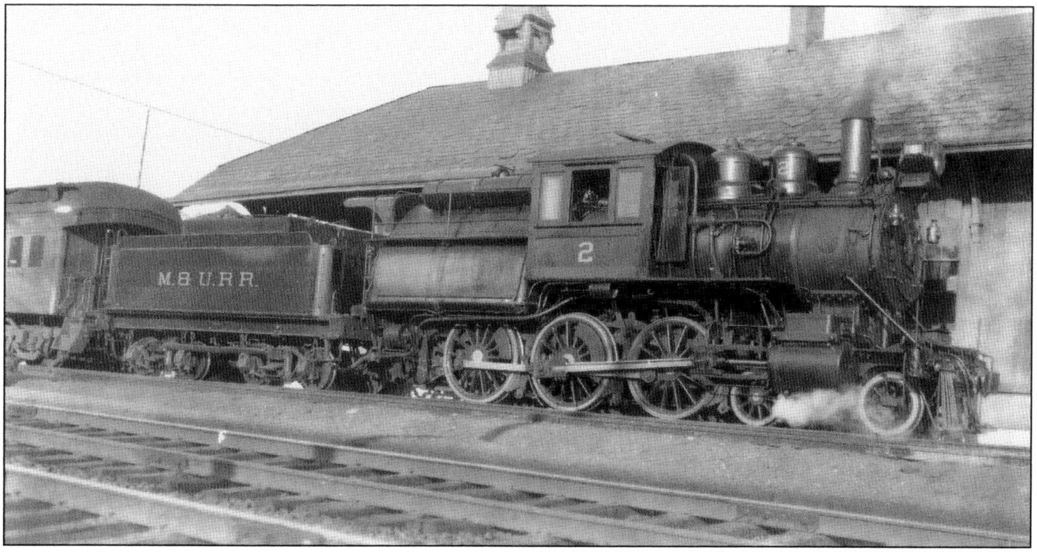

Middletown and Unionville No. 2, a former Lehigh and Hudson River Railway 4-6-0 camelback locomotive, heads an eastbound passenger train at the M&U's Middletown depot. The tracks in the foreground are the Erie Railroad's main line. (Harold Fagerberg Photograph, Ray Brown Collection, M&NJRHS Archives.)

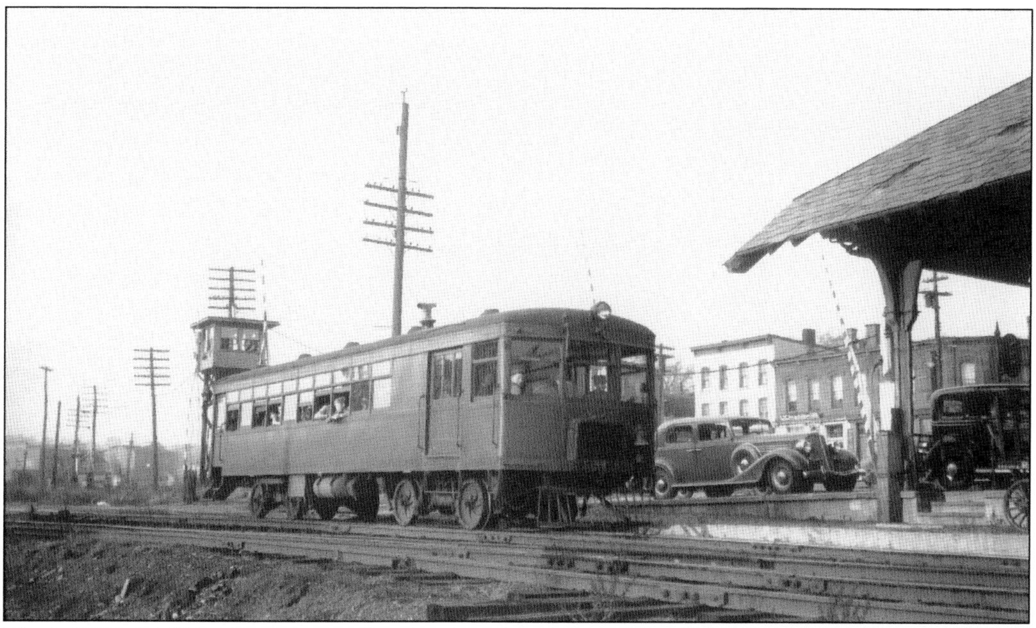

The M&U's M-55 Brill car has high school students aboard for the return trip home after classes. On the M&U, this service included taking children from Unionville, Westtown, Johnson, and Slate Hill to the Middletown High School. The M&U depot is to the right, the O&W gate tower protecting the East Main Street crossing is behind the M-55, and the Railroad Avenue crossing is in the left background. (Rasmussen Family Collection.)

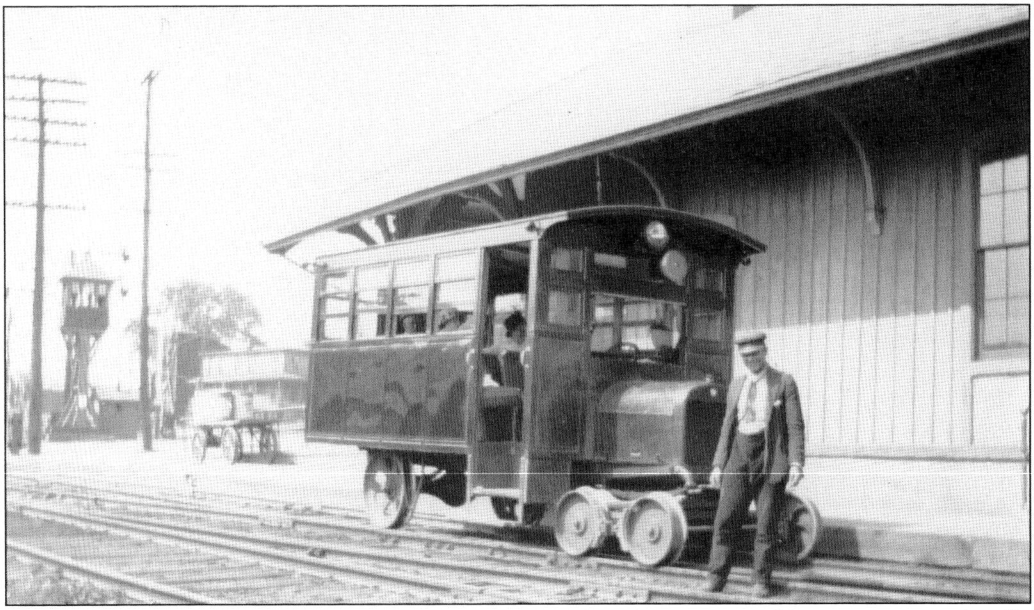

The Reo rail bus No. 11 carried a maximum of 20 people. The No. 11 and her operator are kindly allowing the photographer to take this very rare image by the Middletown depot. No. 11 operated from February 1921 until being traded in to the Brill Company for the M-55 in 1926. (Ray Brown Collection, M&NJRHS Archives.)

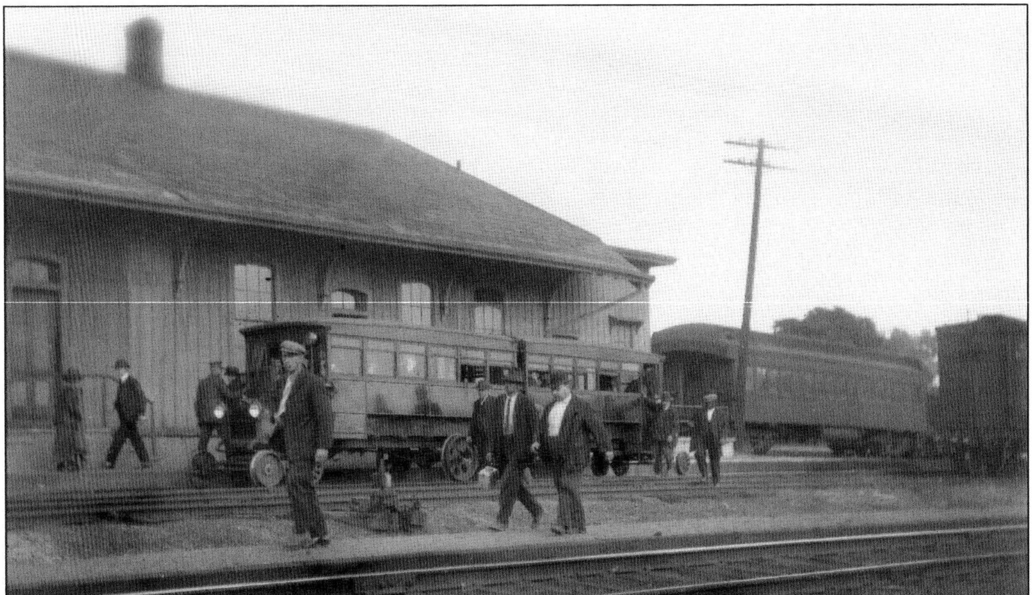

The Reo rail bus and trailer have arrived in Middletown. This was essentially two Reo rail buses operated back-to-back. Note the passenger car behind the depot. This is where the rail bus shed would be built for the Brill car. The tracks in the foreground are the Erie west and eastbound main lines. (John Stellwagen Collection, M&NJRHS Archives.)

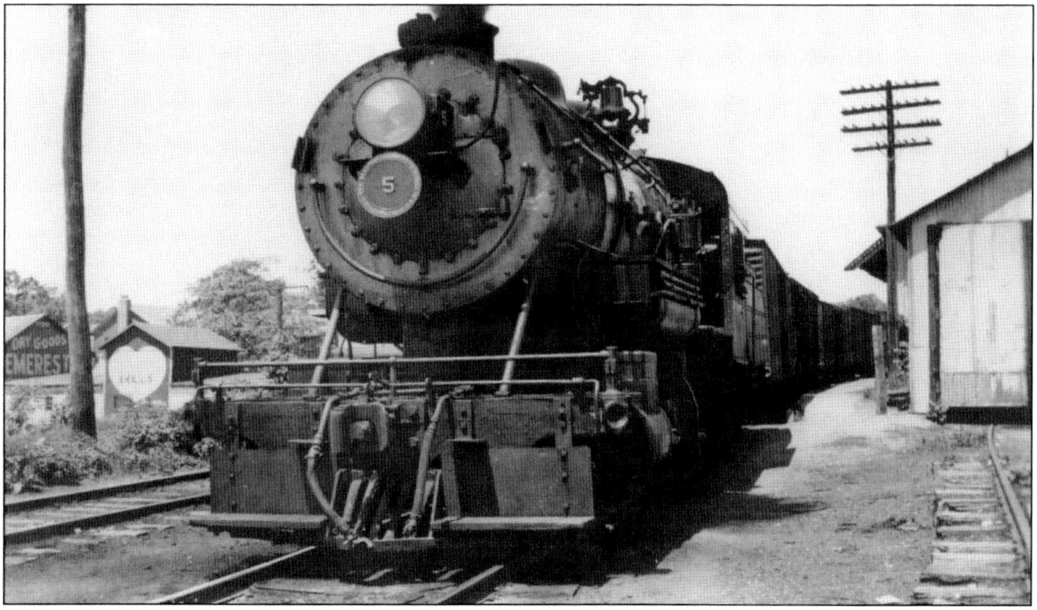

M&U No. 5 has at least six cars in tow on the long crossover track from the NYO&W. While normally the NYO&W would bring cars to the M&U interchange and pick up any in return, sometimes the roles needed to be reversed. The rail bus engine house doors are perhaps 2 feet above the rails. Compare this to the earlier picture with Erie K-2 Pacific 2715. (Ray Brown Collection, M&NJRHS Archives.)

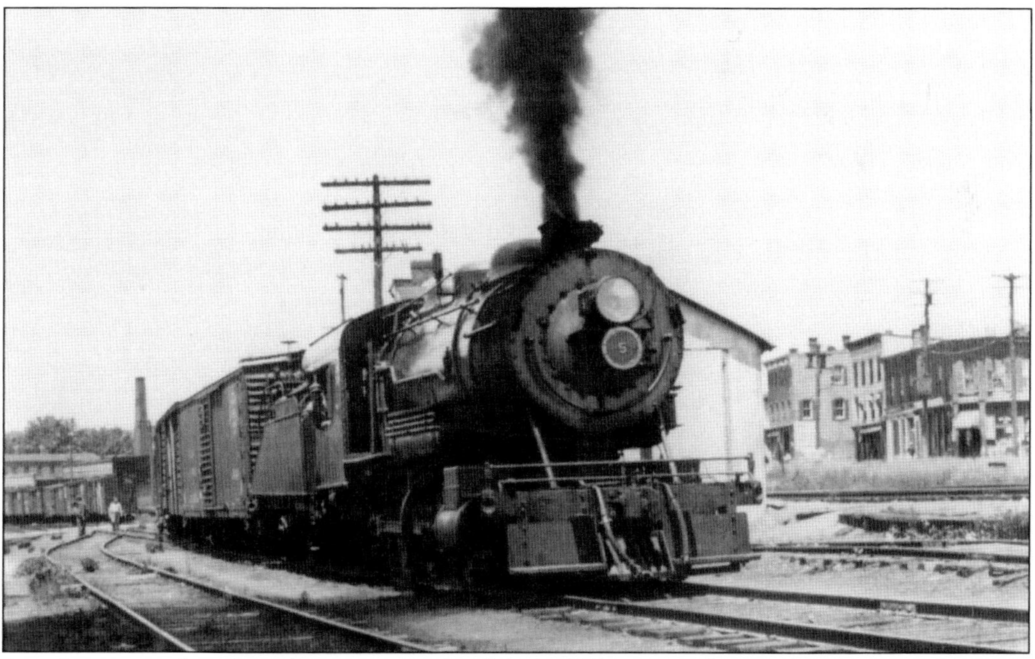

Another view taken from the opposite side of the M&U main as the No. 5 moves past the depot and rail bus engine shed. Note all the cars in the distant left background to be interchanged with the Erie Railroad. The NYO&W main tracks are visible to the right of the rail bus engine shed. (Ray Brown Collection, M&NJRHS Archives.)

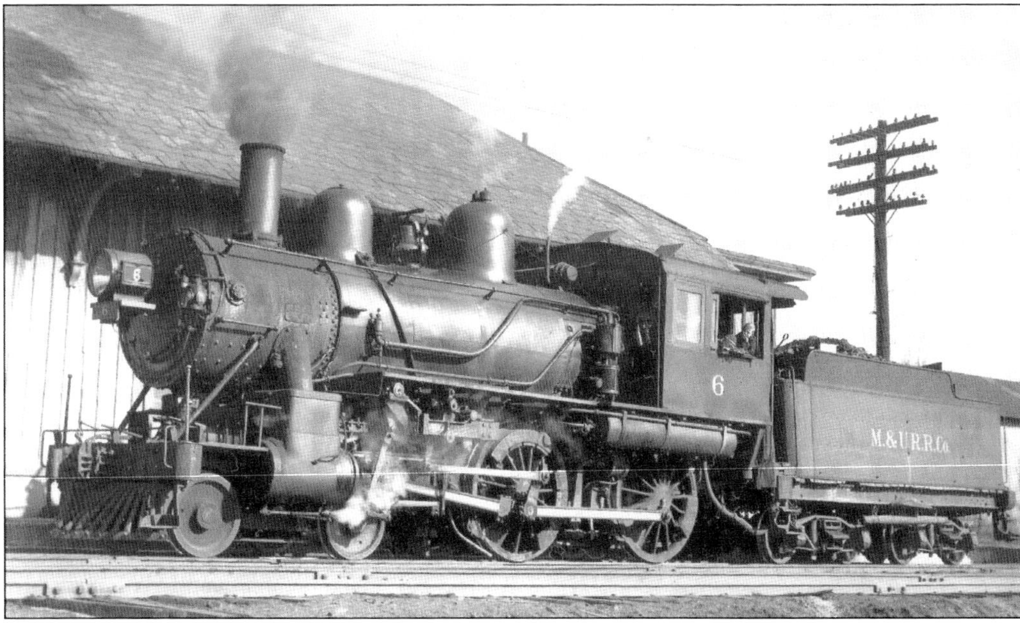

M&U No. 6 lays over next to the East Main Street depot on February 26, 1938, waiting for new orders. As the milk traffic went to trucks, the M&U would suffer great financial hardship that would continue through the later years of World War II. (Robert Morris Photograph, Peter Hasler Collection.)

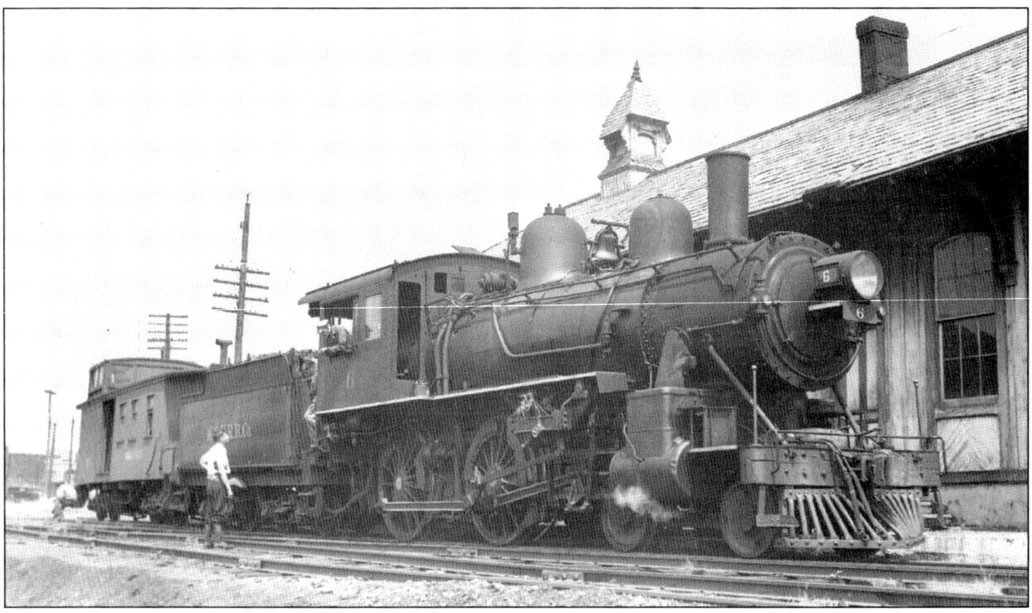

M&U No. 6 and caboose 51 are at the East Main Street depot on August 16, 1936. The engineer and fireman seem to be conversing with a boy who may be one of the high school students who rode the M&U. The conductor may be in the station picking up his orders and train list for the next eastbound run along the line to Unionville. (Jack Farrell Photograph, Ray Brown Collection, M&NJRHS Archives.)

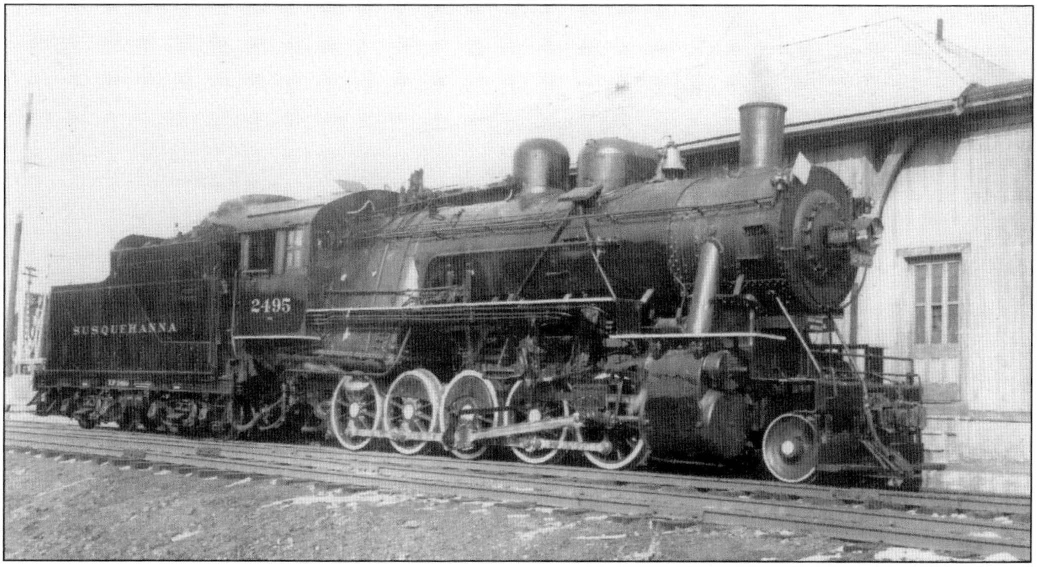

During January 1942, the New York, Susquehanna, and Western J2 2-10-0 2495 is at the M&U Middletown depot. The engine was repaired in the NYO&W's Middletown shops and is headed eastbound to Hanford Junction and Susquehanna home rails. An M&U pilot boarded the 2495 at Hanford Junction for the trip to Middletown and will board 2495 at Middletown for the return to the state line at Hanford, New Jersey. (Ray Brown Collection, M&NJRHS Archives.)

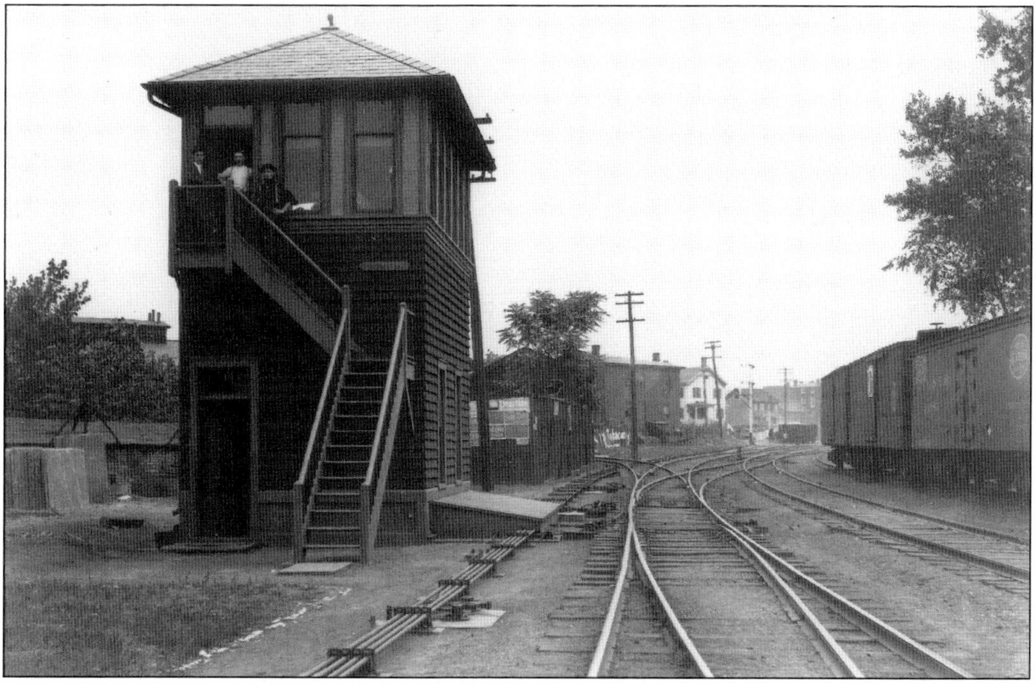

NYO&W's Main Street tower was located just off Railroad Avenue. This was a 28-lever mechanical interlocking tower that controlled nine switches along with various signals and permitted the Erie to use trackage rights on the NYO&W for 3 miles to RF tower at Crawford Junction to reach their Pine Bush branch. In addition, Main Street controlled the interchanges between the Erie, NYO&W, and the M&U via the long crossover switch. (O&WRHS Collection.)

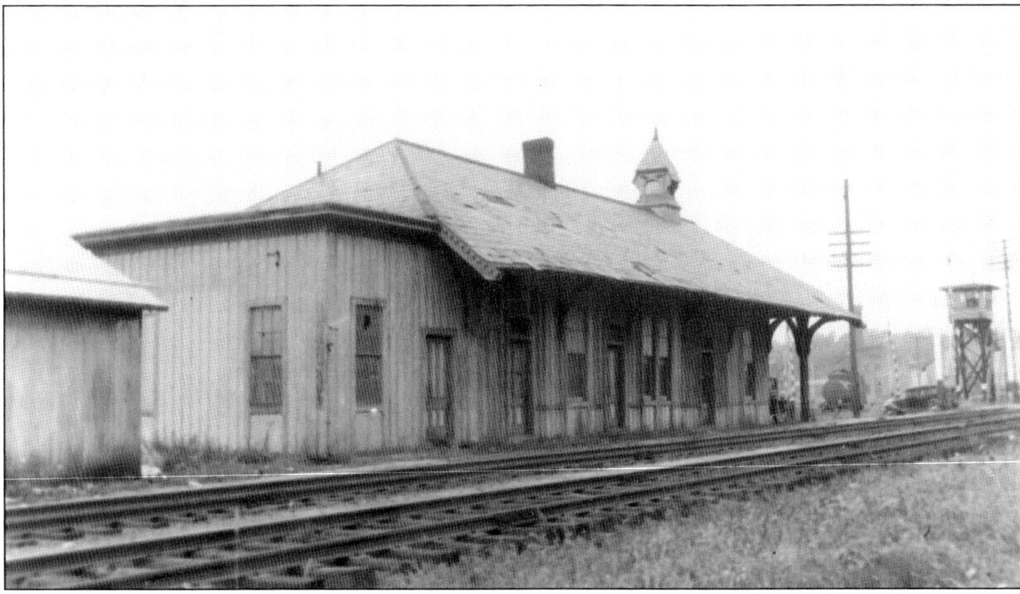

This view taken during the mid-1930s on the NYO&W side of the M&U's Middletown depot was before the eves on the depot were cut down. The NYO&W's East Main Street gate tower is also visible. It was erected after Main Street interlocking tower was taken down in 1932. (Ray Brown Collection, M&NJRHS Archives.)

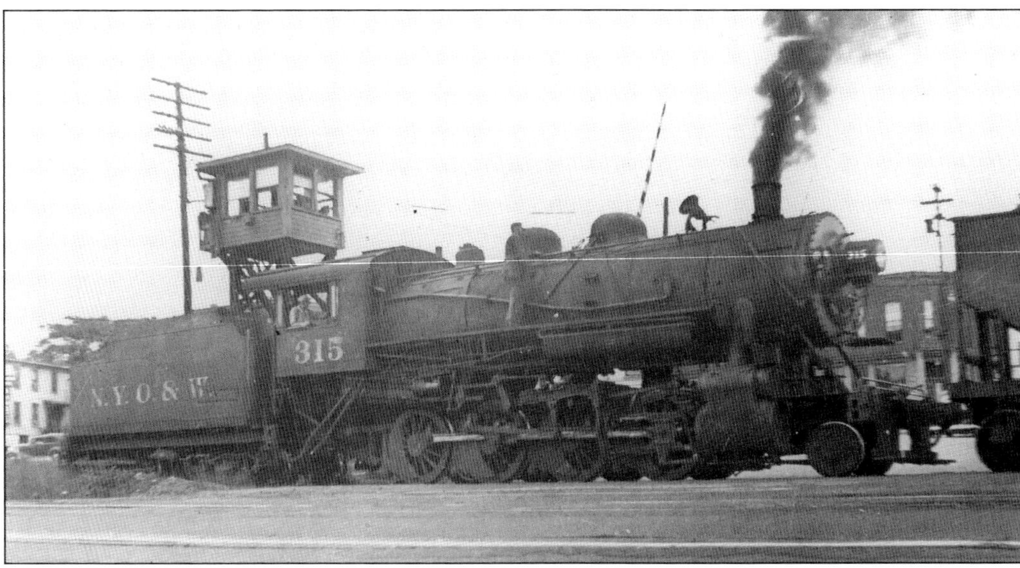

NYO&W W class 2-8-0 315 is delivering a number of cars of coal to the M&U during the mid-1930s. The 315 is on East Main Street grade crossing with the NYO&W crossing gate tower looming above the cab. As detailed in NYO&W employee timetables, all coal and freight trains were restricted to a speed less than the 15 mph between East Main Street and Wisner Avenue in Middletown. (O&WRHS Collection.)

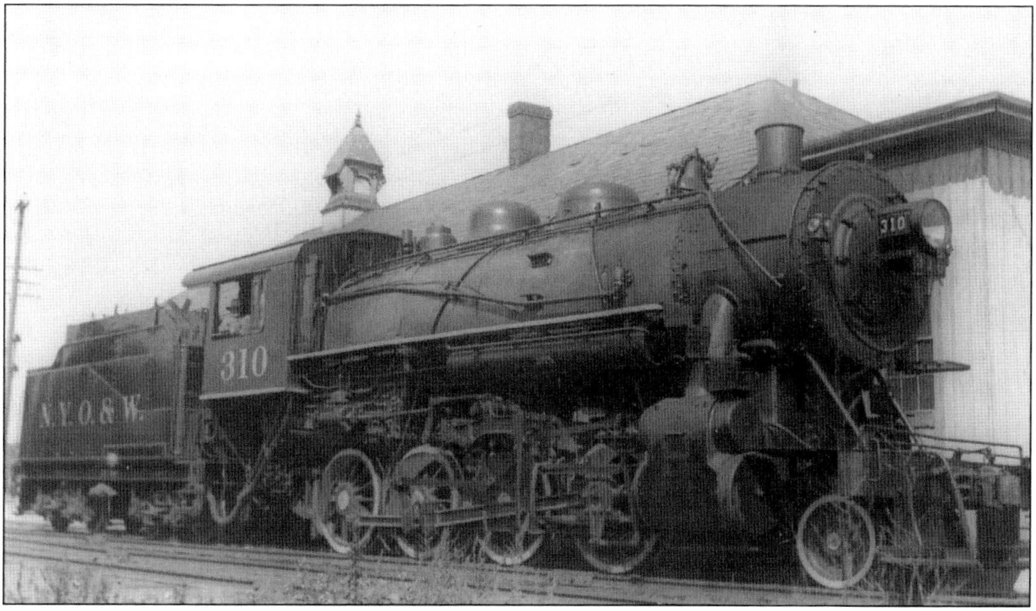

The engineer in the cab of NYO&W 310, a recently shopped W class 2-8-0, waits by the M&U's Middletown depot after delivering a cut of cars to the M&U. The crew is most likely waiting for clearance to enter the long crossover track in order to access their home rails and proceed back to AV yard for further switching duties of the day. (Peter Brill Collection.)

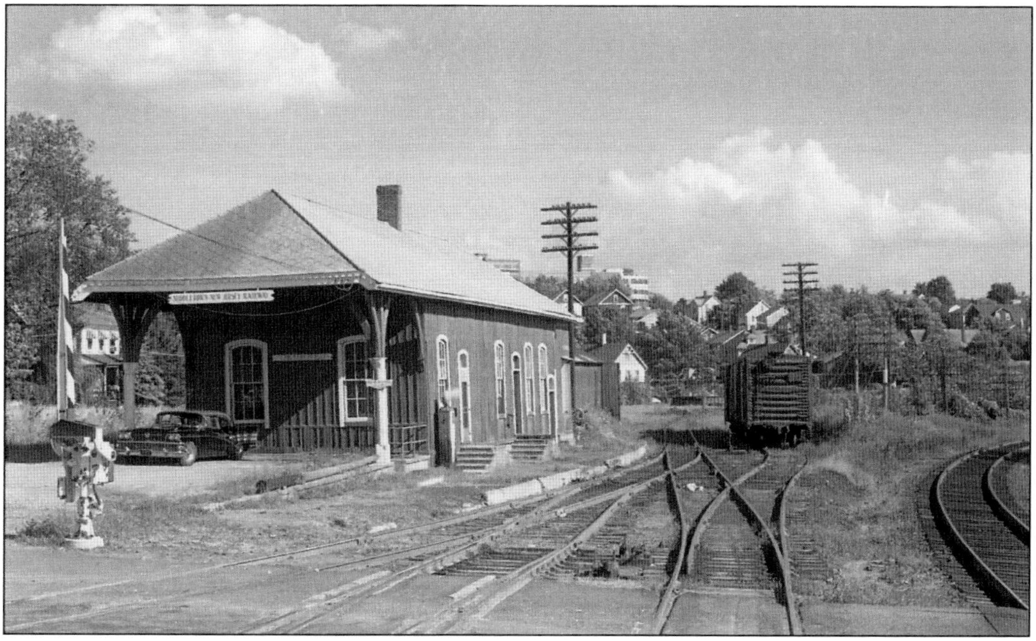

John Stellwagen photographed the movement of a westbound Erie Pine Bush train from the caboose backing across East Main Street. The freight will pass through the switch for the "loop" track that holds two boxcars, reaching the M&U/M&NJ main past the depot. This switch will be aligned for the long crossover track to the far left along the depot allowing access to the NYO&W main. The depot's eves were cut back during the late 1930s. (John Stellwagen Photograph, M&NJRHS Archives.)

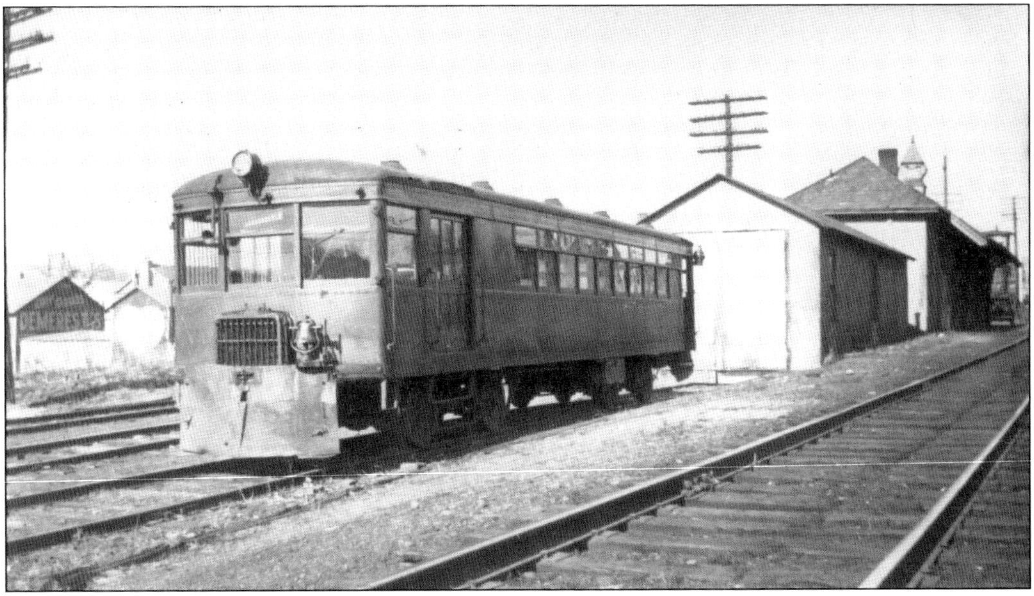

The M&U M-55 Brill car is idling outside the rail bus engine house. Looking into the front right window, the silhouette of the Brill car operator can be seen as he gets ready for his run to Unionville. The O&W is in the lower right foreground. (Ray Brown Collection, M&NJRHS Archives.)

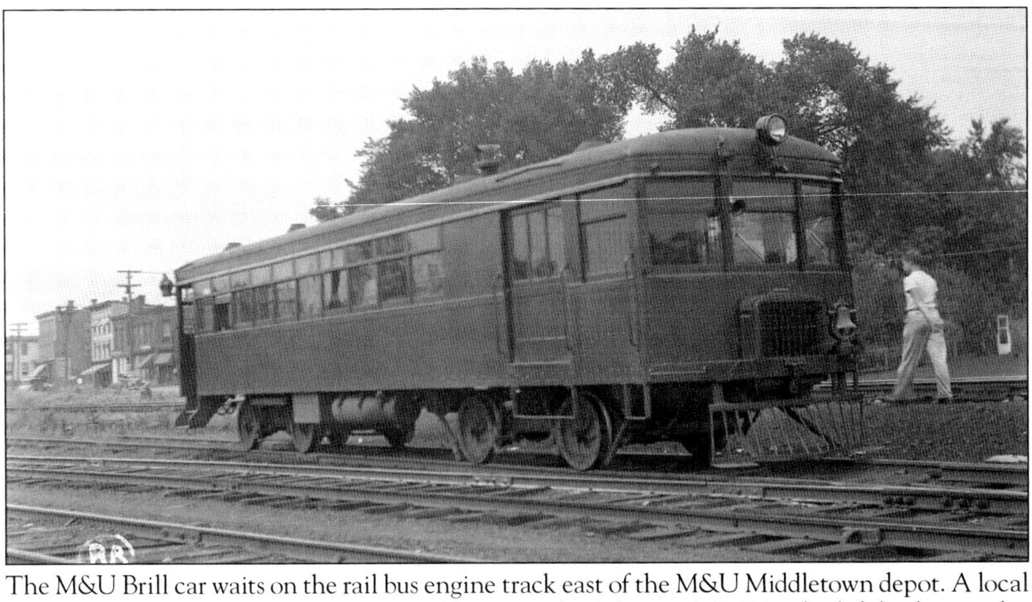

The M&U Brill car waits on the rail bus engine track east of the M&U Middletown depot. A local resident is walking along the southbound main track of the NYO&W. In the left background is the intersection of East Main Street and Railroad Avenue. (M&NJRHS Archives.)

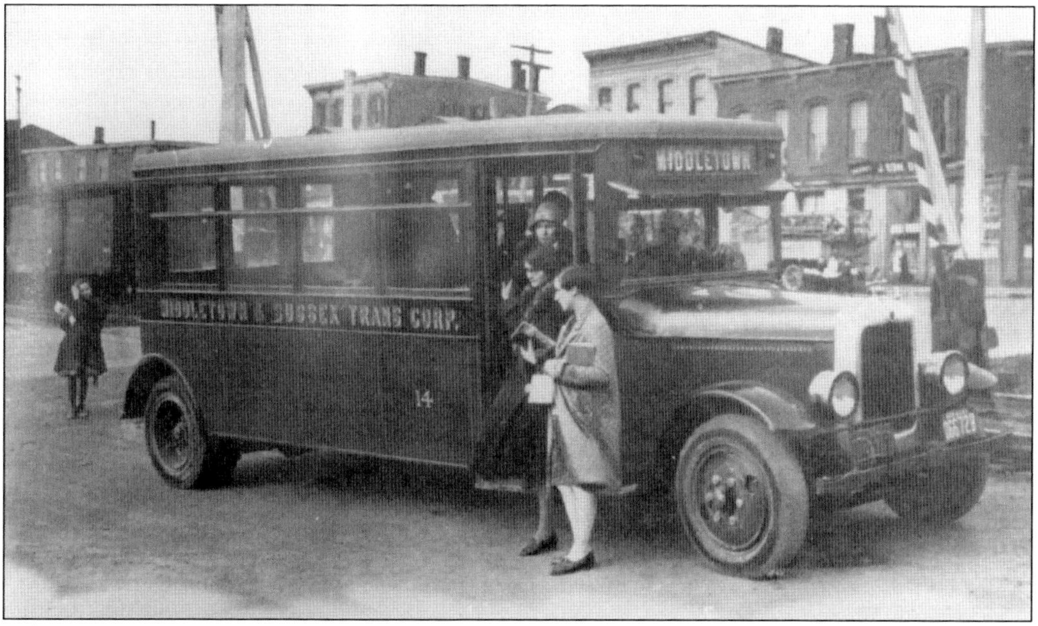

When competing bus companies threatened the M&U's passenger service, the M&U started the Middletown and Sussex Transit Company. This company won the franchise for the bus service between Middletown and Sussex, New Jersey, and connected with the M&U at all its stations to ensure the passenger traffic, however small, stayed with the M&U. (Ray Brown Collection, M&NJRHS Archives.)

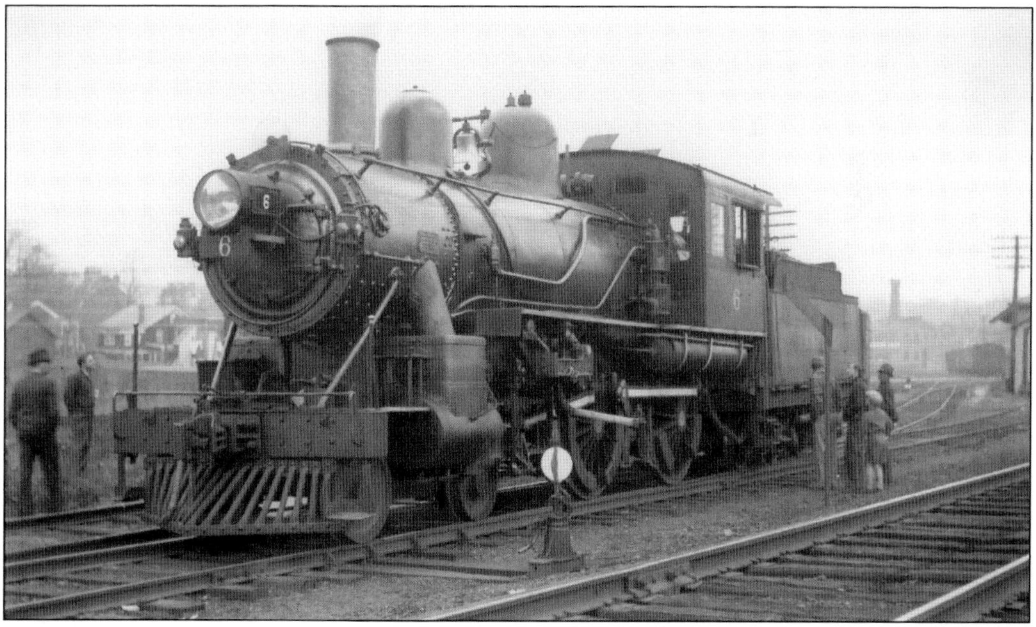

M&U No. 6, former NYO&W No. 24, is seen on the M&U main track in Middletown. The large number of people looking at the No. 6 suggests it is perhaps railroad fan day. The interest in the No. 6 was shared by the M&U engine crews who would state after steam had left the M&U that old No. 6 was their favorite M&U locomotive. (John Stellwagen Collection, M&NJRHS Archives.)

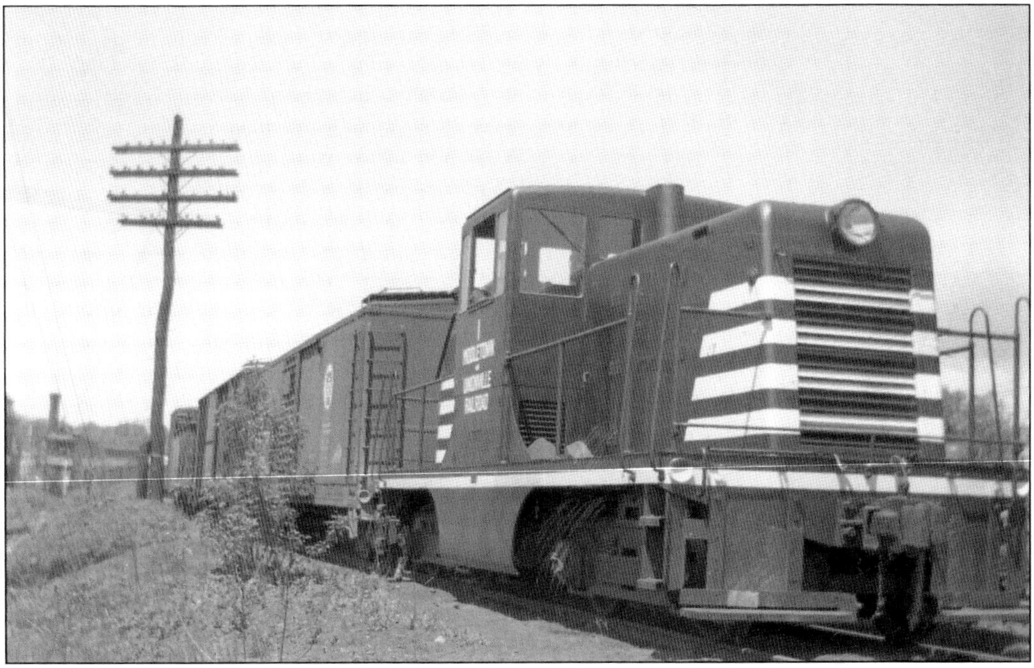

The only new locomotive the Middletown and Unionville Railroad ever operated was this General Electric 44-ton diesel-electric center-cab switcher. Shortly after its arrival the caboose was no longer used since the entire crew fit in the spacious cab. The second engine to be designated M&U No. 1 would run for well over 20 years, longer than any steam locomotive on the old M&U. (Ray Brown Photograph, M&NJRHS Archives.)

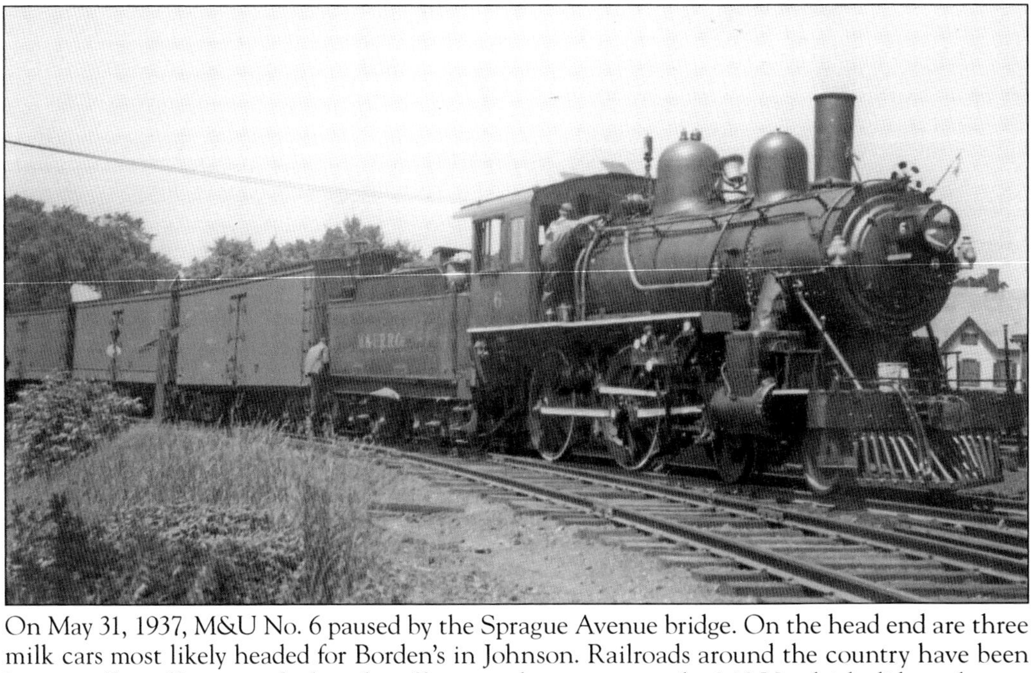

On May 31, 1937, M&U No. 6 paused by the Sprague Avenue bridge. On the head end are three milk cars most likely headed for Borden's in Johnson. Railroads around the country have been losing milk traffic to trucks but the effect was far greater on the M&U, which did not have a diverse traffic base. (Ray Brown Collection, M&NJRHS Archives.)

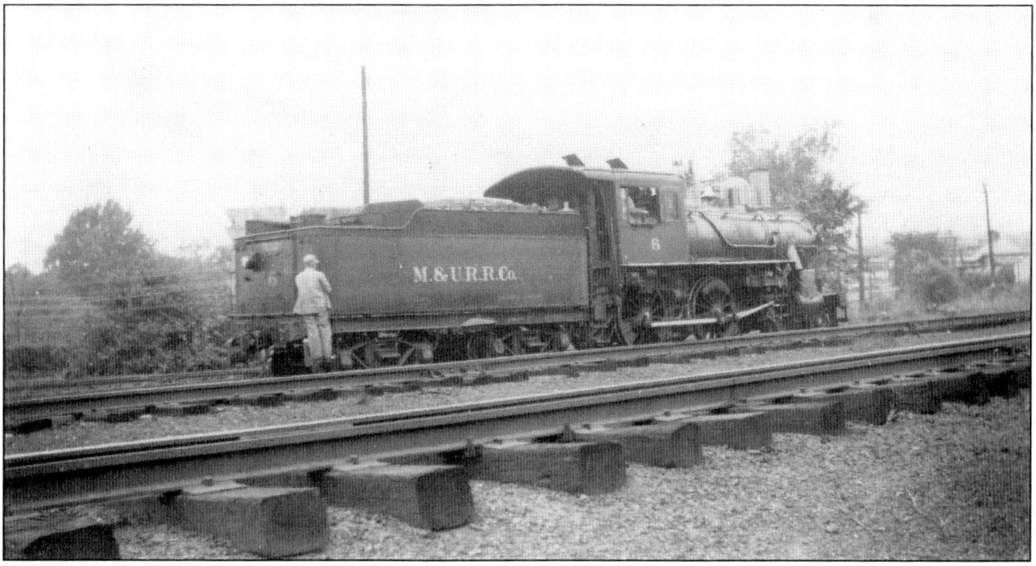

M&U No. 6 moves slowly westbound through DG yard toward the M&U Middletown depot where a cut of cars as well as the station can be seen in the distant right. The No. 6 and crew may then drill the NYO&W and Erie interchanges, work DG yard, then assemble a train before striking out eastward to Unionville and Hanford Junction once again. (Ray Brown Collection, M&NJRHS Archives.)

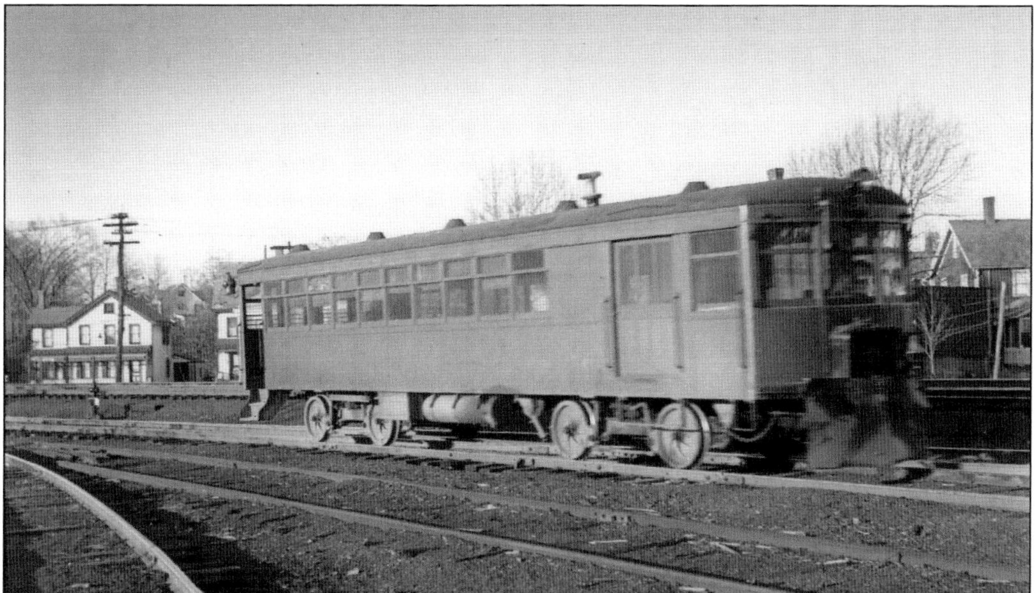

The M&U M-55 Brill car rolls west to the East Main Street depot through the M&U's Middletown yard to pick up the high school students for their return trip home along the M&U. The O&W main line is in the background. (John Stellwagen Collection, M&NJRHS Archives.)

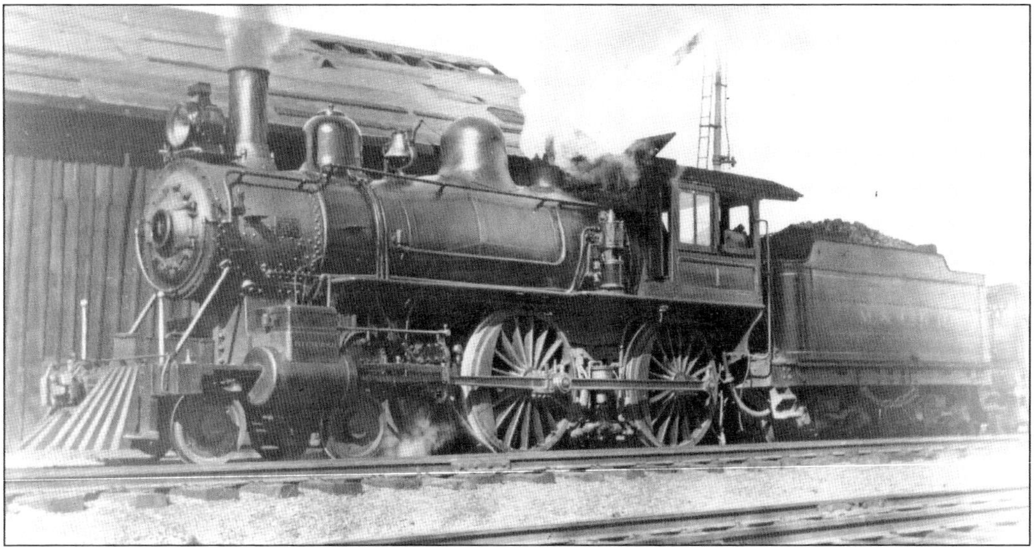

The first locomotive the M&U purchased was this 4-4-0 American numbered, of course, No. 1. The engine appears to be next to the original engine house. The many years of NYS&W control of the Middletown, Unionville, and Water Gap may be reflected in the extreme deterioration of the roof. On April 11, 1915, a severe storm destroyed the water tank and damaged the engine house beyond repair. (Ray Brown Collection, M&NJRHS Archives.)

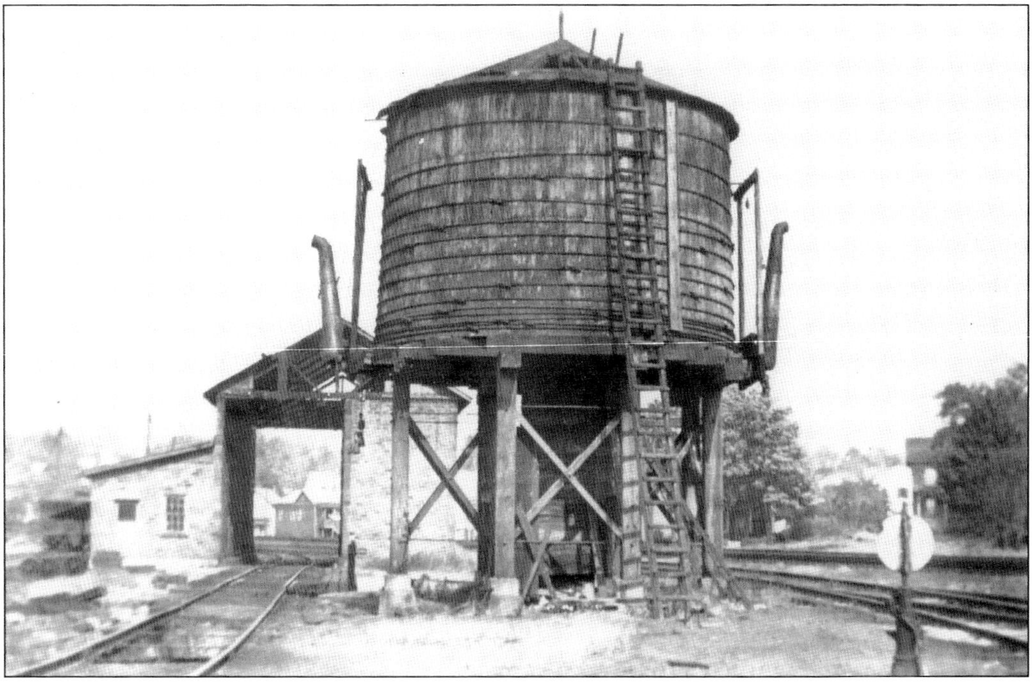

The M&U rebuilt its water tank in 1915 and constructed a new engine house and coal facility south of Houston Avenue during 1917. This view around 1937 of the DG yard engine facilities shows the water tank with the ash pit to the left and the turntable and the engine house directly behind it. The M&U main is to the right of the water tank. (Ray Brown Collection, M&NJRHS Archives.)

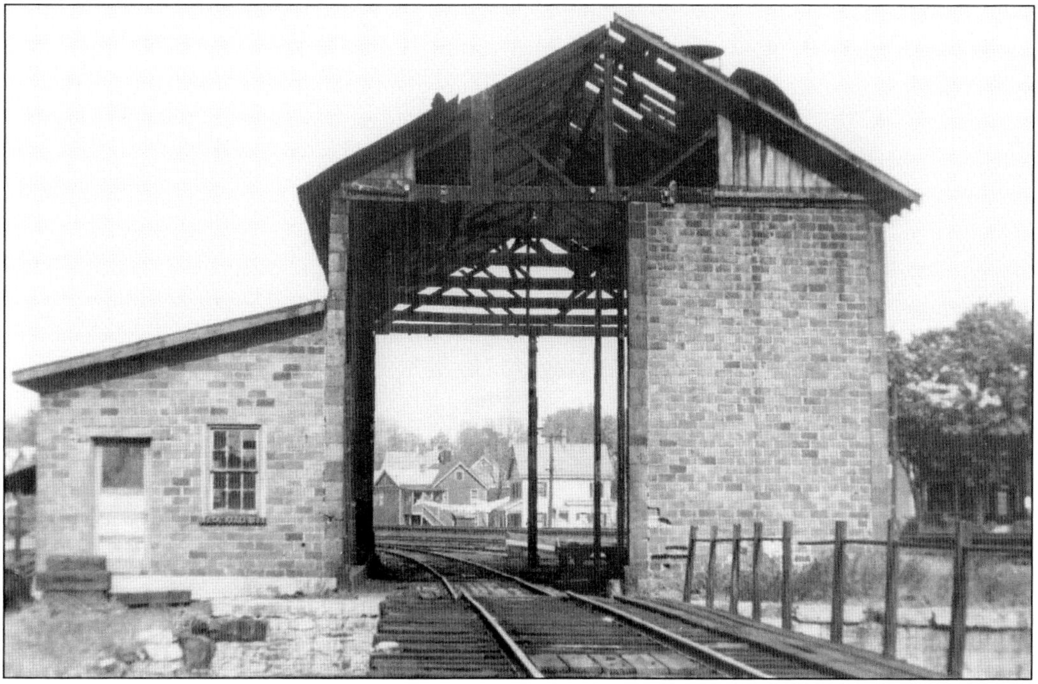

Above is a close-up of the turntable and the two-stall engine house. The deterioration on the right side of the roof due to the acrid smoke of the locomotives is quite apparent. On the left adjoining the building is what was known as the oil house. The M&U main line and the double-track NYO&W main line are visible through the rear of the building. (Ray Brown Collection, M&NJRHS Archives.)

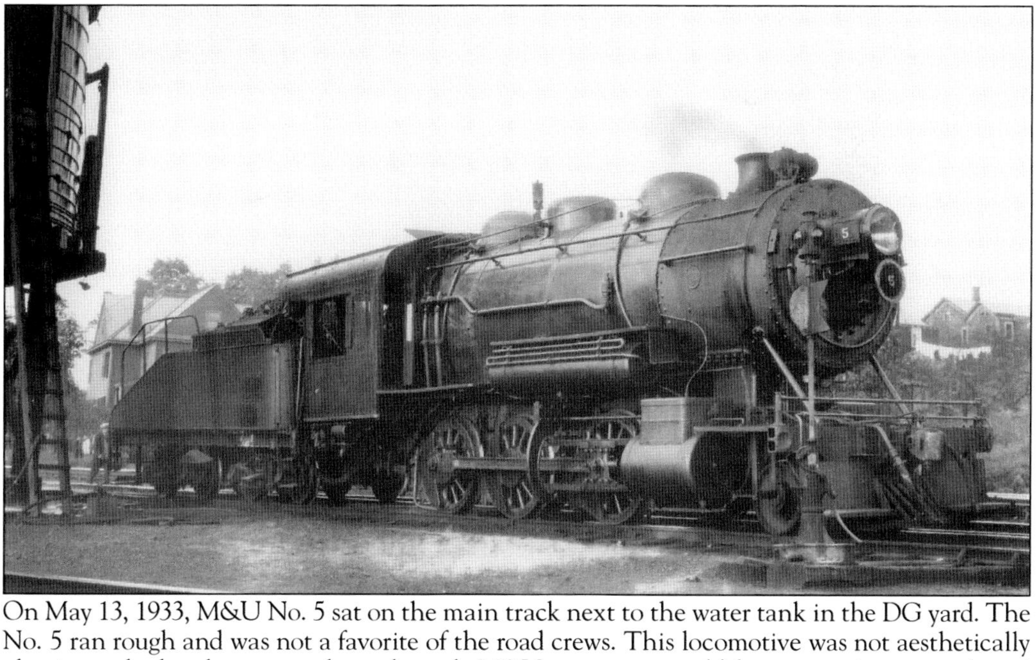

On May 13, 1933, M&U No. 5 sat on the main track next to the water tank in the DG yard. The No. 5 ran rough and was not a favorite of the road crews. This locomotive was not aesthetically pleasing to look at but was perhaps the only M&U steamer not sold for scrap as it was purchased by the West Pittston and Exeter. (Harold Fagerberg Photograph, M&NJRHS Archives.)

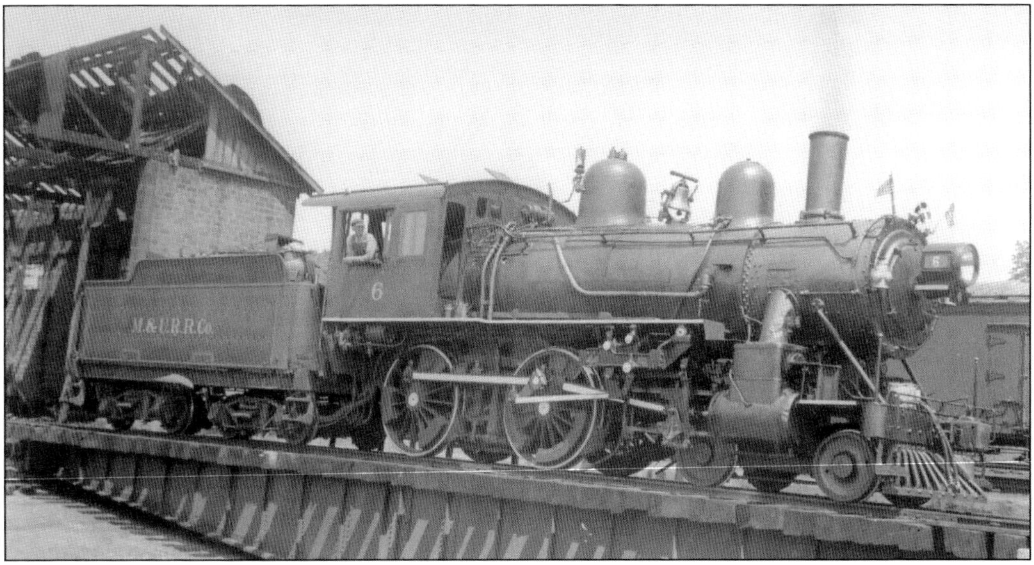

In a pre-1938 photograph, M&U No. 6 has just been turned on the turntable for the daily freight to Unionville and Hanford Junction. The locomotive looks to be in fine shape, unlike the engine house in the rear. The acrid smoke from the locomotives has slowly been eating away at the roof. Having to make difficult financial decisions, especially during the Depression, perhaps explains why this was in disrepair. (Allen Seebach Collection.)

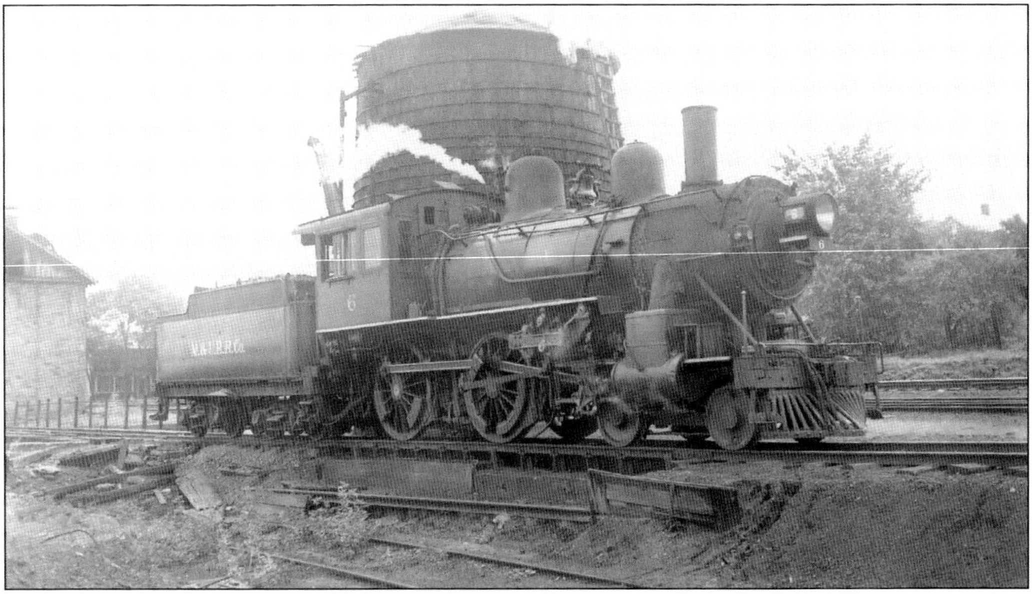

No. 6 is seen on the ash pit at the M&U's Middletown engine terminal. The cinders enjoyed a long life on the M&U and M&NJ as they were used as cheap track ballast. The hostler will coal the engine if needed, rebuild the fire, then monitor the engine until the No. 6 is ready to carry out the duties of the day. (Ray Brown Collection, M&NJRHS Archives.)

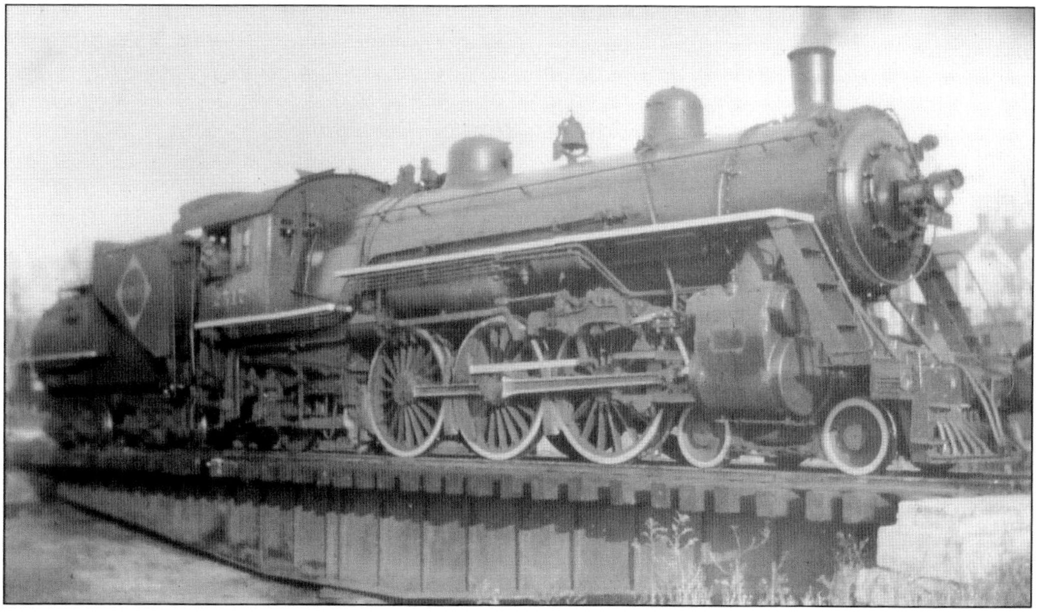

Erie Pacific No. 2517, a class K-1 4-6-2, takes a spin on the M&U turntable in DG yard. The Erie used this turntable more than the M&U. All Erie locomotives assigned to passenger trains originating or terminating in Middletown, the Middletown Yard Drill, and the Middletown Drill were turned daily on the M&U turntable. (Ray Brown Collection, M&NJRHS Archives.)

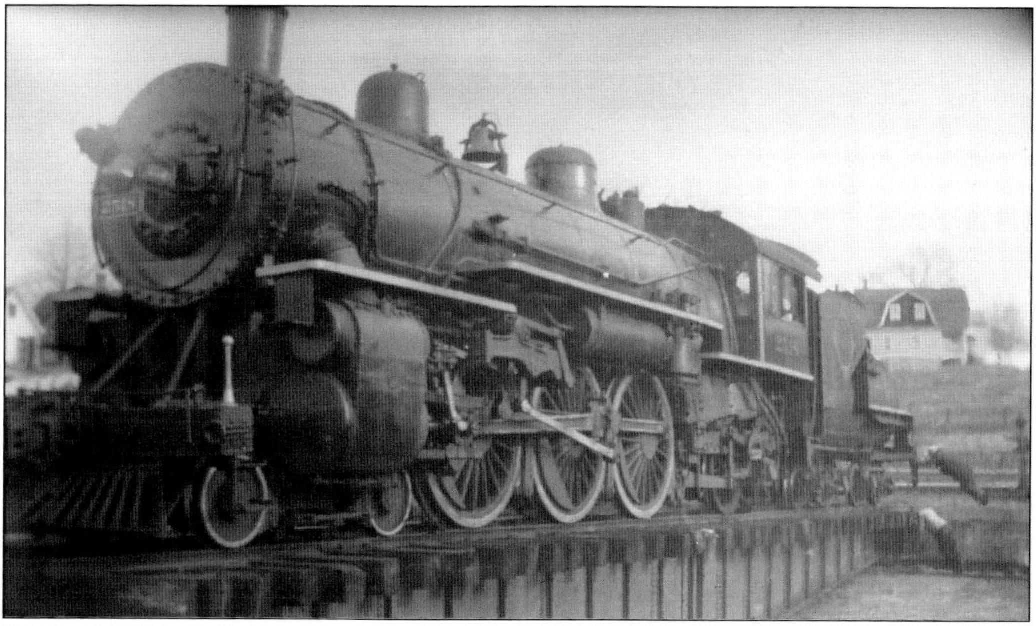

K-1 Pacific 2518 was the last Erie steam locomotive to use the M&U turntable on May 7, 1949. The turntable was never electrically powered but instead was of the "armstrong" variety. Note in the background one crewman is in the turntable pit while another pushes on the handle as they literally use strong arms and legs to turn the engine! (Carl Detwyler Collection, M&NJRHS Archives.)

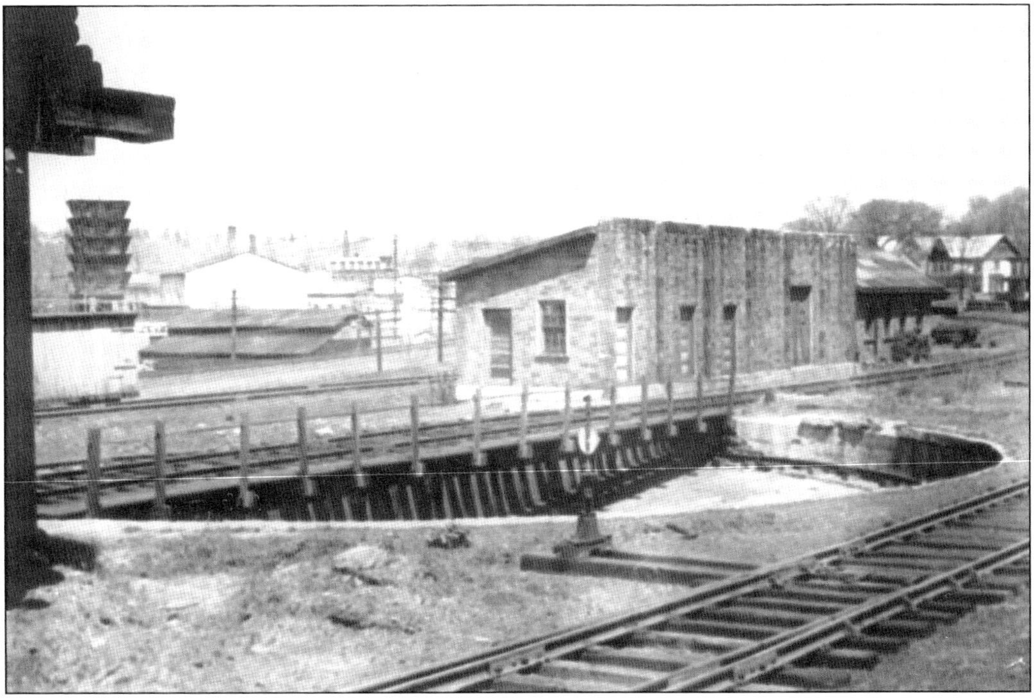

This photograph taken around 1938 reveals the remains of the two-stall engine house that was known as the "oil house." The water tank is to the left. In the left background is the coach track and beyond that the double-track main line of the Erie Railroad. The M&U main track is in the bottom foreground. (Ray Brown Collection, M&NJRHS Archives.)

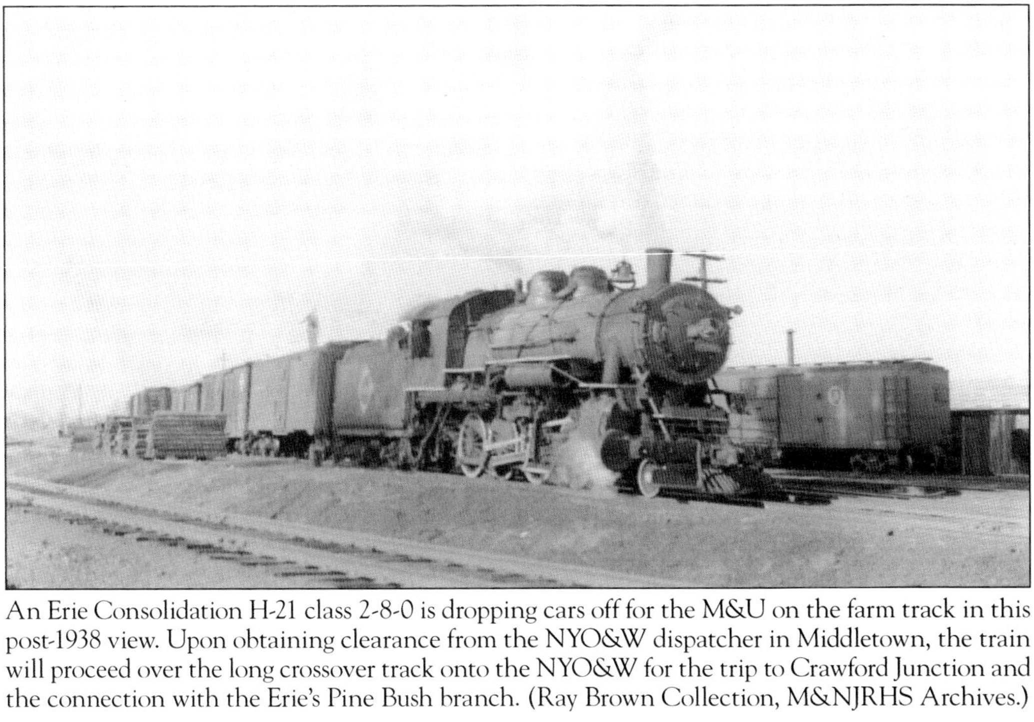

An Erie Consolidation H-21 class 2-8-0 is dropping cars off for the M&U on the farm track in this post-1938 view. Upon obtaining clearance from the NYO&W dispatcher in Middletown, the train will proceed over the long crossover track onto the NYO&W for the trip to Crawford Junction and the connection with the Erie's Pine Bush branch. (Ray Brown Collection, M&NJRHS Archives.)

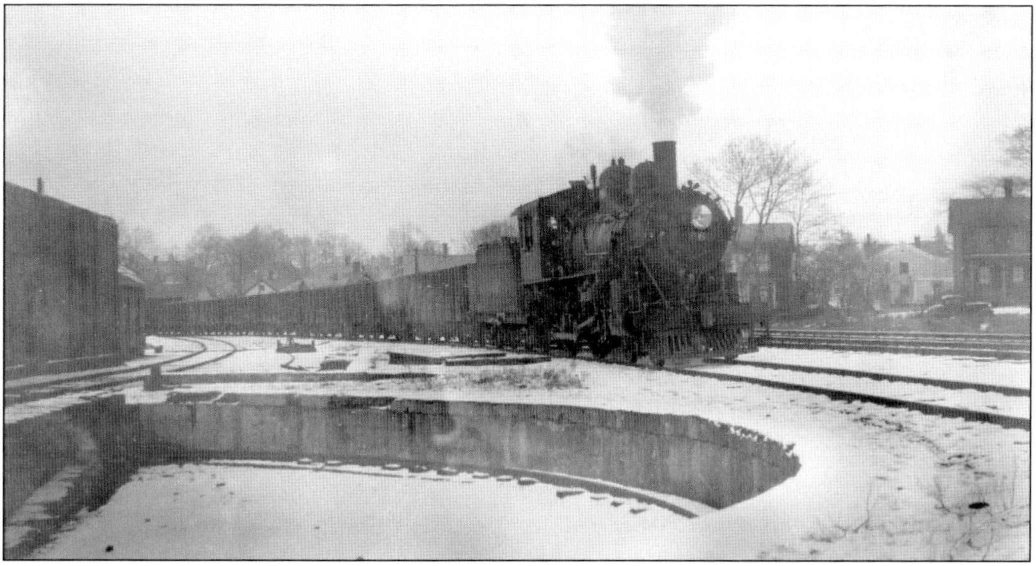

During early 1940, M&U No. 6 leads a long coal train eastbound past the DG yard turntable on the 14.5-mile journey to the NYS&W at Hanford Junction. This overhead coal traffic began on December 30, 1939, with the NYO&W delivering coal cars to the M&U's Middletown yard. This heavy traffic brought the career of the No. 6 to an early end with her last run on March 26, 1940. (John Stellwagen Collection, M&NJRHS Archives.)

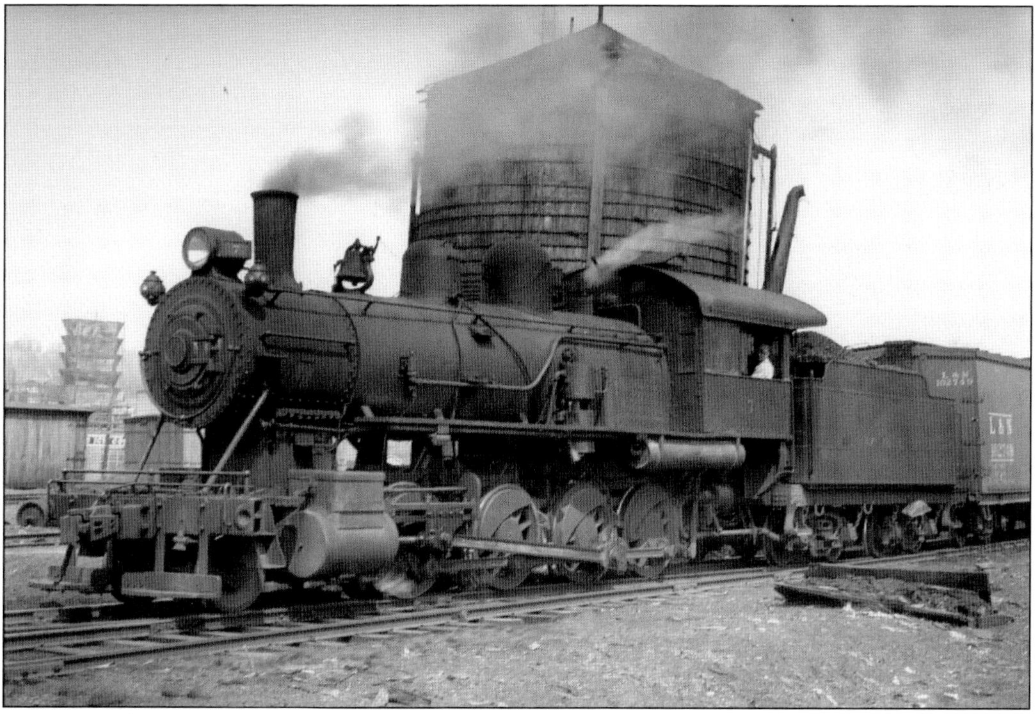

On April 14, 1941, M&U No. 7 steams eastbound by DG yard's engine terminal heading to Unionville and a connection with the NYS&W at Hanford Junction M&U. No. 7 was the last steam locomotive owned by the M&U. Note the refrigeration tower of the Vass Ice Company in the distance. (Steven Maguire Photograph, M&NJRHS Archives.)

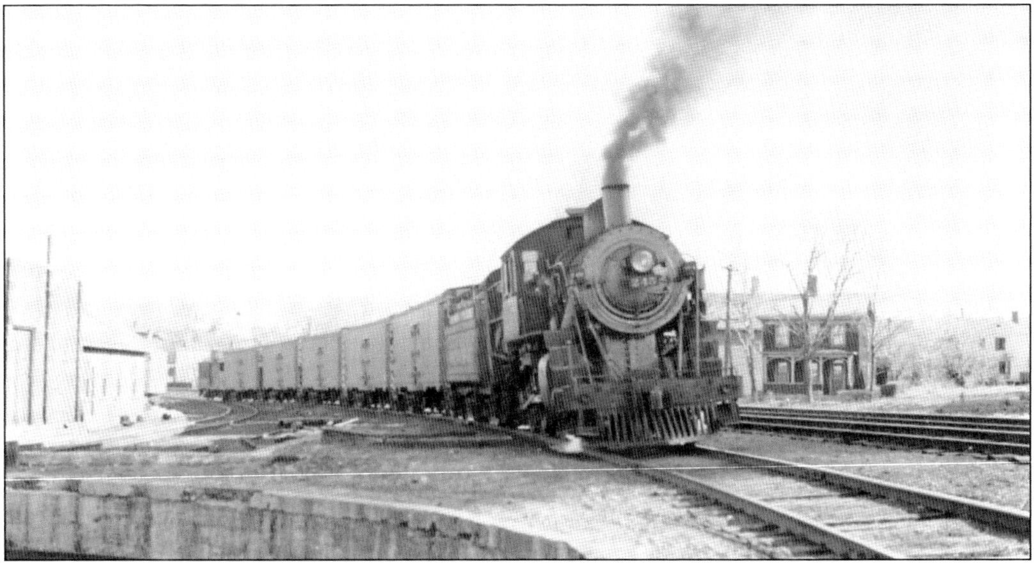

Around 1938 or the early 1940s, NYO&W U-1 class 4-6-0 No. 245 is headed eastbound through the DG yard with five Erie milk cars. At this late date for milk traffic, these cars must be bound for Borden's in the village of Johnson. The turntable pit is in the lower left while the NYO&W main lines are to the right of the 245. (Ray Brown Photograph, M&NJRHS Archives.)

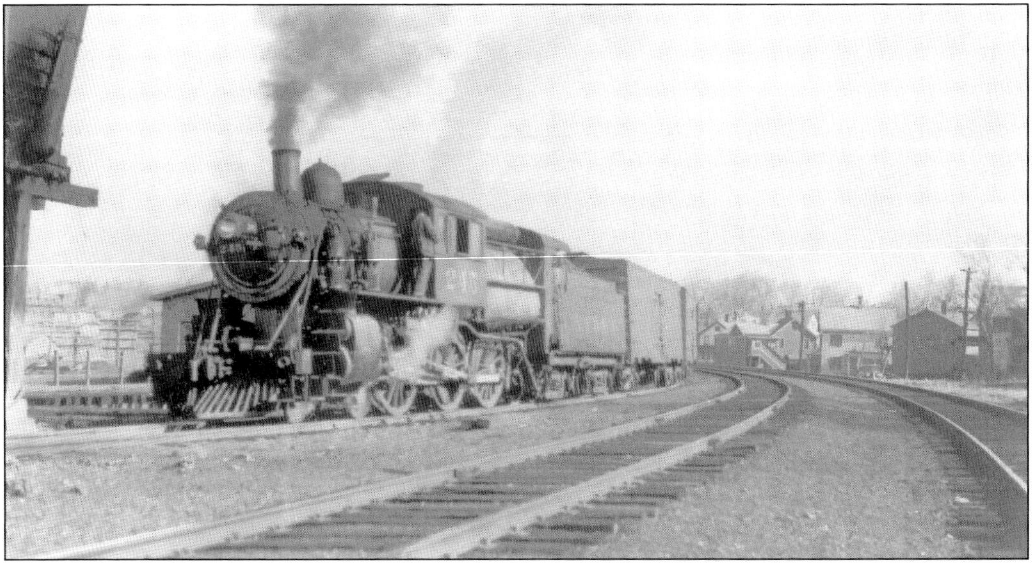

Slightly east of the last picture, the 245 is just about to pass the M&U water tank. According to an agreement between the NYO&W and the M&U that was made on December 22, 1913, all heavy repairs to steam locomotives and rolling stock were contracted to the NYO&W's Middletown shops. In return, the NYO&W would allow the M&U to rent a steam locomotive when the railroad was short of power. (Ray Brown Photograph, M&NJRHS Archives.)

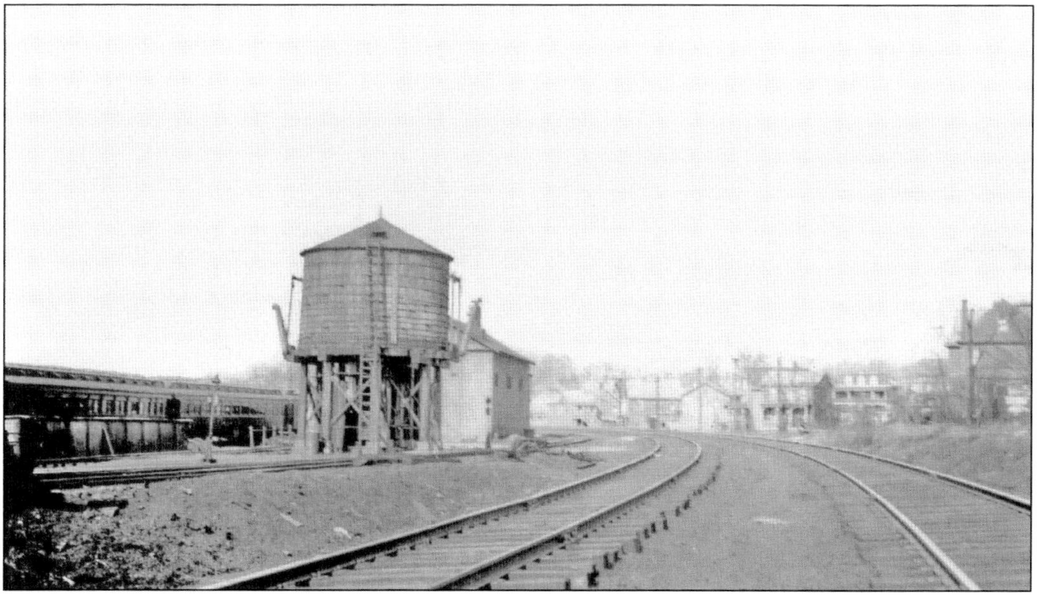

In this early 1930s view, the M&U engine house and water tank are in excellent condition. From East Main Street to Genung Street, the M&U and the NYO&W railroads were side by side mirroring their close business relationship and shared history. To the left of the M&U water tank, Erie commuter coaches can be seen on the M&U loop track being serviced and readied for the next eastbound trip to Jersey City. (O&WRHS Collection.)

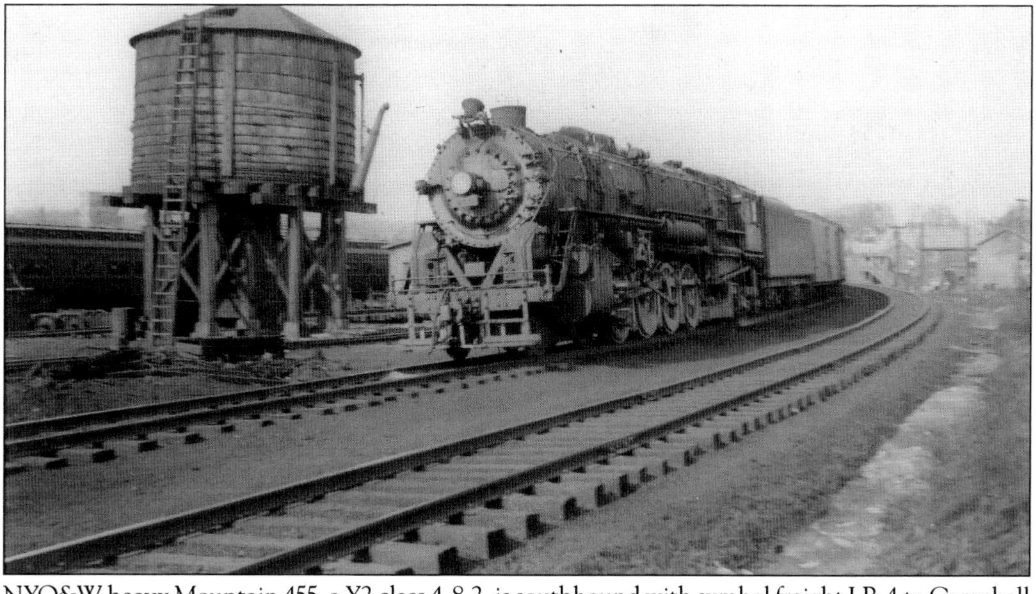

NYO&W heavy Mountain 455, a Y2 class 4-8-2, is southbound with symbol freight LB-4 to Campbell Hall and to the New Haven's Maybrook Yard during 1933. LB-4 forwarded perishable traffic from the Lehigh Valley at Coxton, Pennsylvania, as well as tonnage from the Delaware, Lackawanna, and Western at Cayuga Junction, just north of Scranton, Pennsylvania. (O&WRHS Collection.)

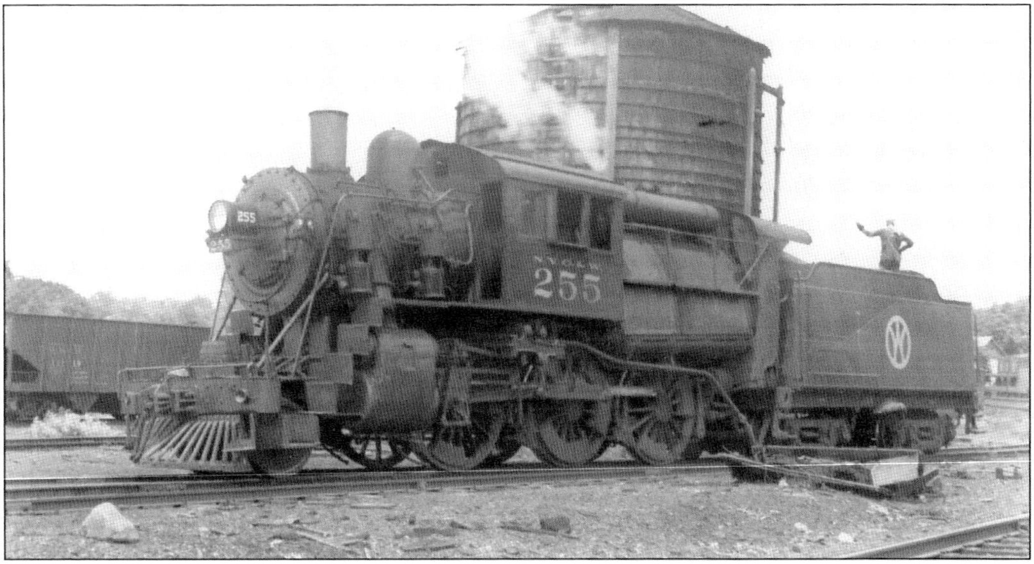

On July 13, 1940, NYO&W U class 2-6-0 255 is being rented by the M&U. The fireman is filling the water tank in the coal tender for today's trains on the main line and for drilling DG yard. An O&W coal car seen on the coach track to the left of the 255 definitely indicates that there are other coal hoppers in the yard bound for the NYS&W at Hanford Junction. (O&WRHS Collection.)

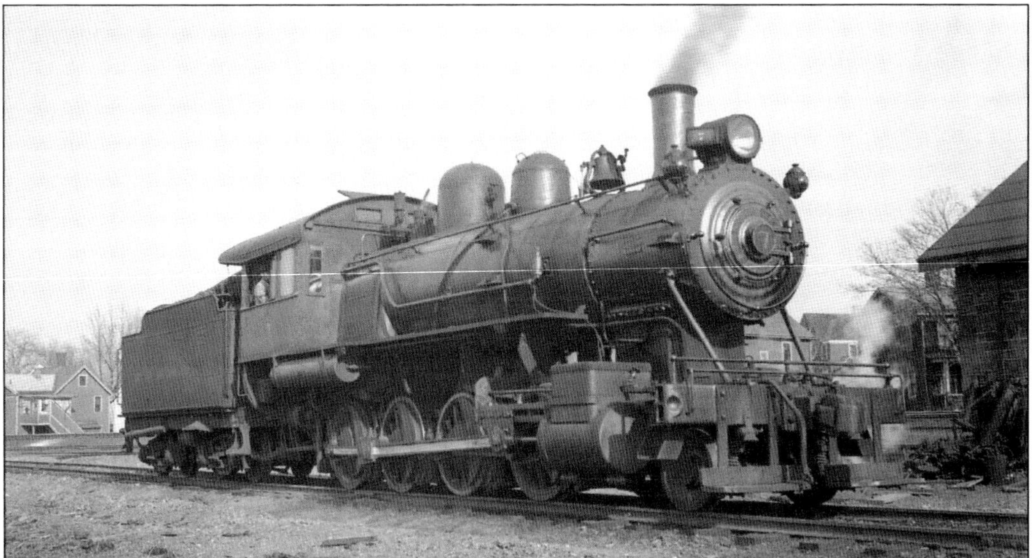

On July 11, 1941, M&U No. 7 backs down to the East Main Street depot with her crew. They will pick up caboose 51 on the house track, get their train orders and drill sheet at the East Main Street depot, and switch out the yard for their eastbound consist. (Robert Collins Photograph, M&NJRHS Archives.)

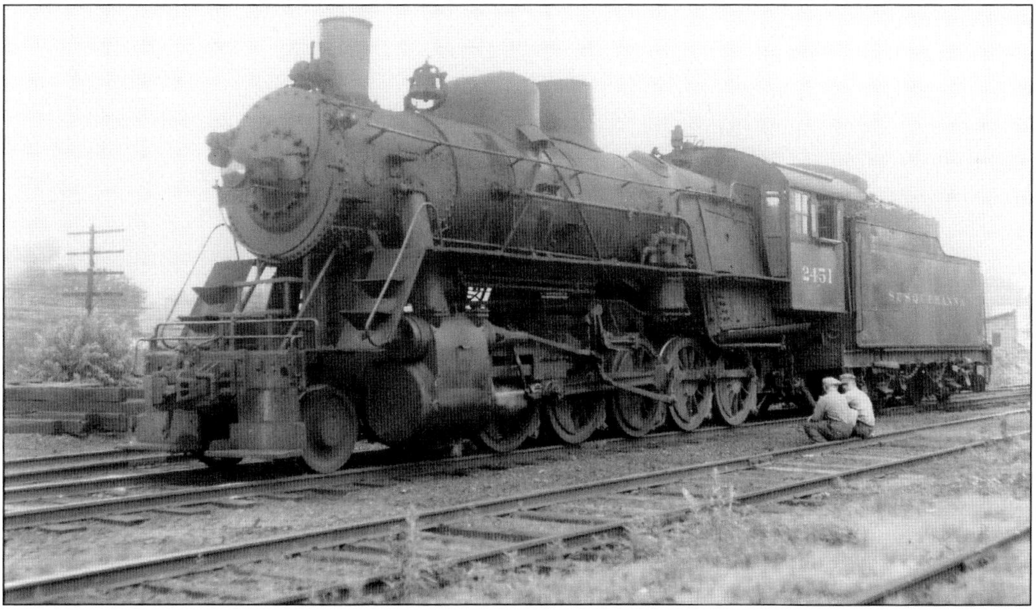

Near Houston Avenue, NYS&W 2451 and her crew are taking it easy between runs on July 25, 1945. While short on speed, the J2 Class 2-10-0 had a tractive effort of 51,000 lbs, more than any other locomotive owned or leased by the M&U. It could easily handle any assignment on the M&U and had no trouble with any grade on the railroad. (Bob's Photos Collection, M&NJRHS Archives.)

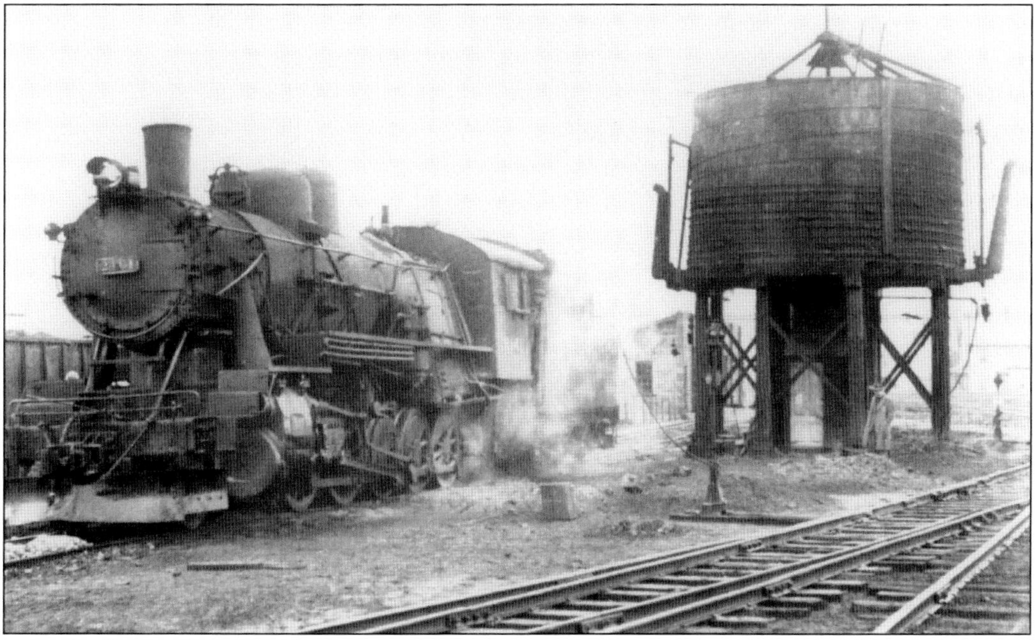

The M&U leased NYS&W J2 decapods from July 22, 1945, until April 19, 1946. The 2461 shown here was leased three times: October 5 to November 3, 1945; December 22, 1945, to March 23, 1946; and from April 8 to April 19, 1946. When the 2461 made her last eastbound trip to Hanford Junction, the M&U's brand-new GE 44-ton diesel No. 1 was delivered by the NYS&W. (Ray Brown Collection, M&NJRHS Archives.)

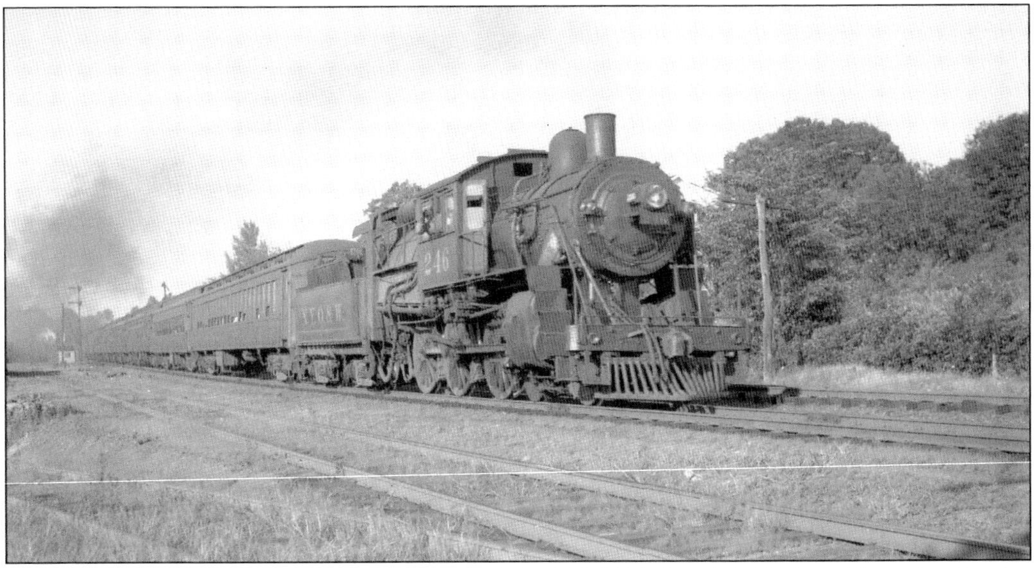

On August 11, 1940, Robert Collins photographed NYO&W U-1 class 4-6-0 246 southbound with eight cars of train 36. The 246 has crossed Houston Avenue and is approaching Washington Street. The M&U main line is to the left of the 246. (Robert Collins Photograph, O&WRHS Collection.)

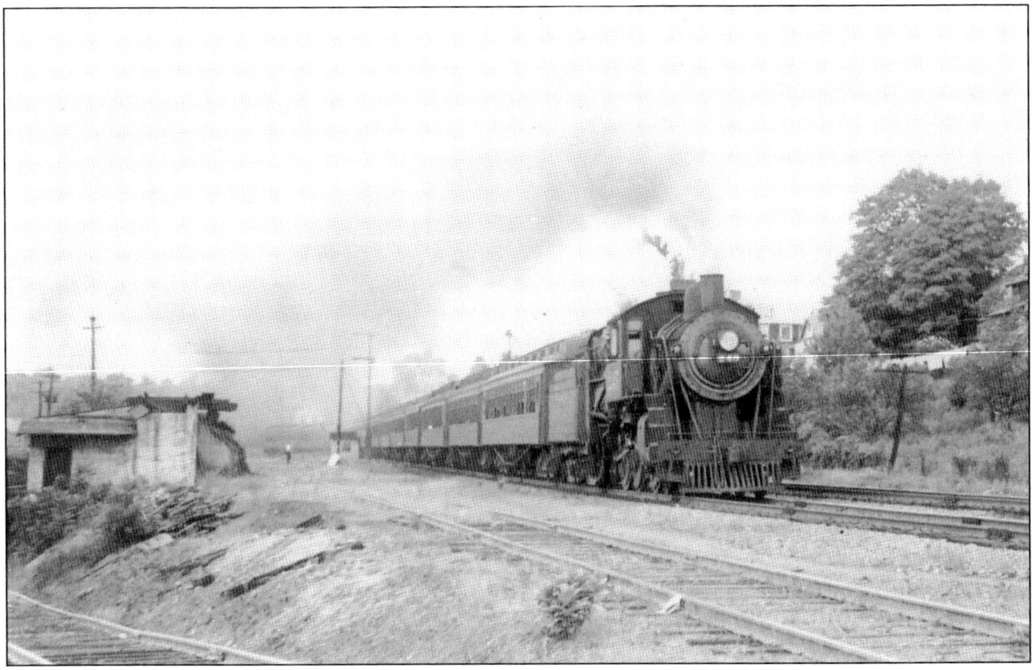

NYO&W U-1 class 4-6-0 245 is leading the second section of train 2 across Houston Avenue to Weehawken, New Jersey. The M&U main is to the left of the 245 along with the primitive M&U coal facility. Note the crossing guard in the distance on Houston Avenue. The signals next to the passenger train are for the NYO&W southbound main track. (Jack Farrell Photograph, Walter Kierzkowski Collection.)

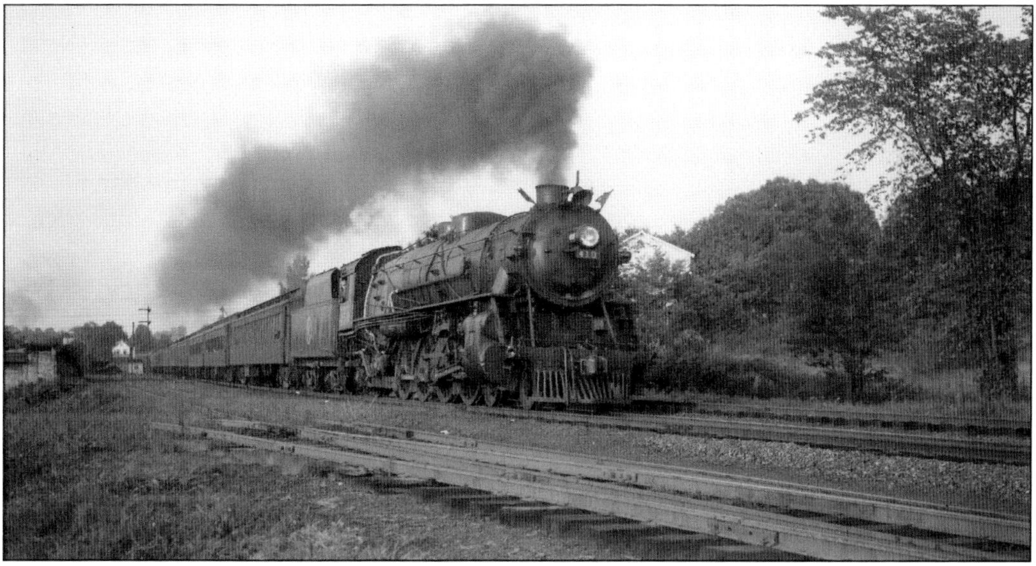

NYO&W Y class 410 leads the fourth section of train 4 southbound on September 2, 1940. This is the Labor Day rush home for the families vacationing in the Catskill Mountains. The M&U main line is again to the left with the switch leading to the "coal hole" track. (Robert Collins Photograph, O&WRHS Collection.)

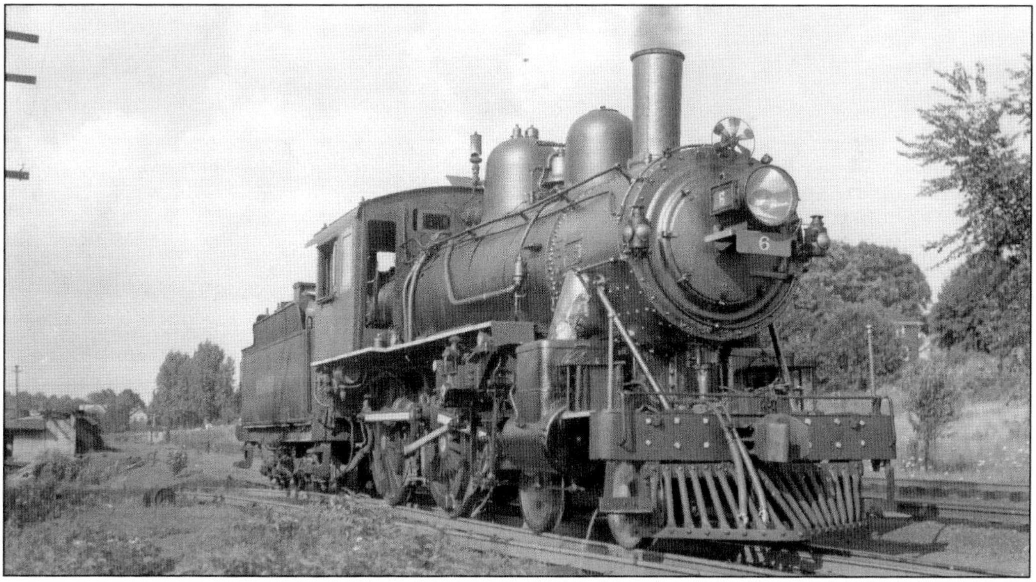

Halsey L. Tilton photographed M&U No. 6 idling near Washington Street on August 13, 1939. The locomotive appears to be in fine shape. However, in little over seven months she will suffer a cracked flue sheet due to the M&U's heavy coal traffic. The switch for the "coal hole" can be seen leading down to the coaling facility in the background. (Halsey L. Tilton Photograph, M&NJRHS Archives.)

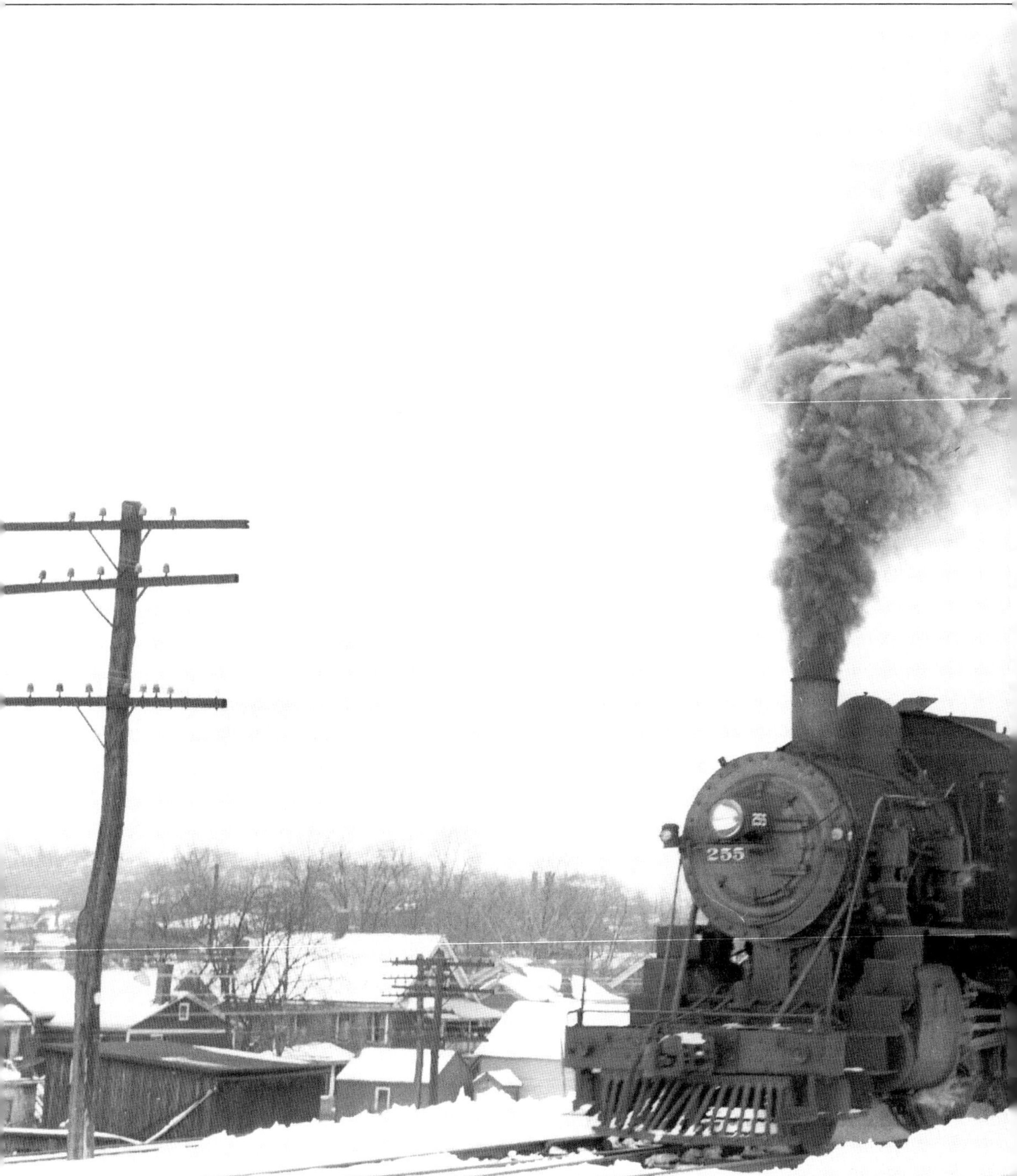

On January 25, 1941, NYO&W 255 nears Washington Avenue leading a 14 car M&U train eastbound to the NYS&W at Hanford Junction. M&U No. 7 is in the NYO&W Middletown shops for repair forcing the M&U to rent the 255 per the agreement of December 13, 1913. The NYS&W, as of January 1, 1940, became independent from the Erie and was considering a merger with the NYO&W to form the New York, Susquehanna, and Ontario. Instead the NYO&W and

the NYS&W agreed to cooperate to reduce costs by deciding to reroute coal traffic via the M&U instead of by the New York Central to Edgewater, New Jersey. The M&U found it necessary from December 30, 1939, to March 22, 1941, to run three freight trains daily to handle this surge in coal traffic. (A.V. Neusser Photograph, O&WRHS Collection.)

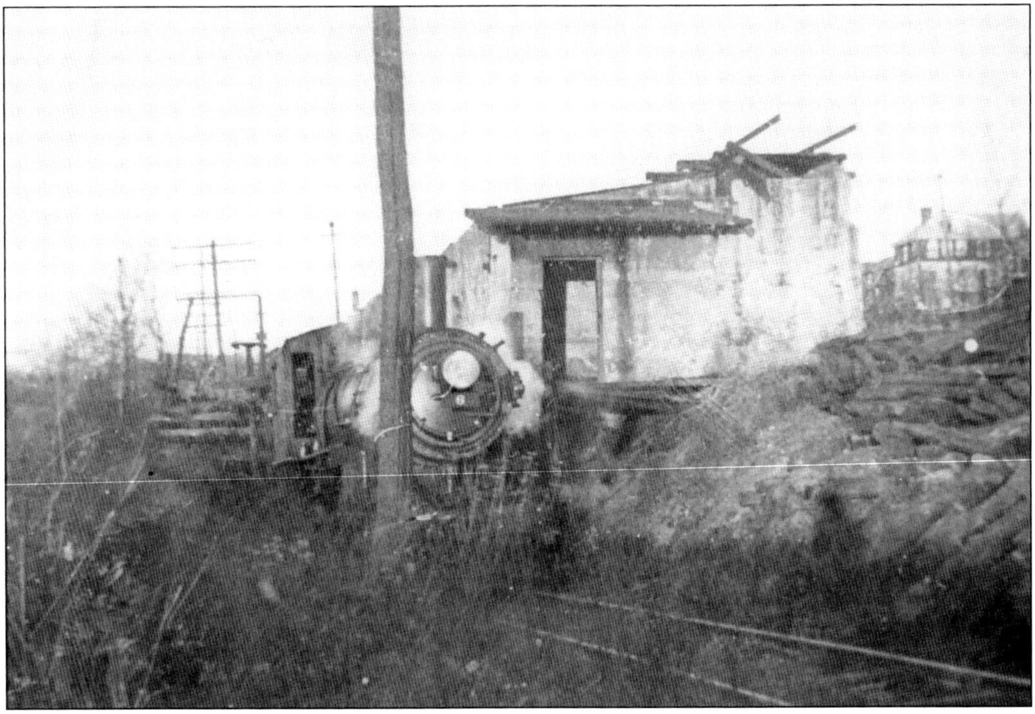

The No. 6 is in the coal hole for refueling. The facility was not constructed for engines with coal tenders as high as the No. 6 or many of the leased O&W locomotives the road would use. As a result, a platform had to be built over the old coal chutes as seen below. The coal had to be first shoveled into a wheelbarrow then dumped into the coal tender. This greatly increased the time required to coal an engine. This was not a job for extreme weather as it took a number of wheelbarrows to fill the coal tender. Conventional coal towers or loading facilities used pockets of coal leading to a coal chute that allowed rapid loading. Until steam left the M&U in 1946, this was how their engines were refueled. (Both photographs, Ray Brown Collection, M&NJRHS Archives.)

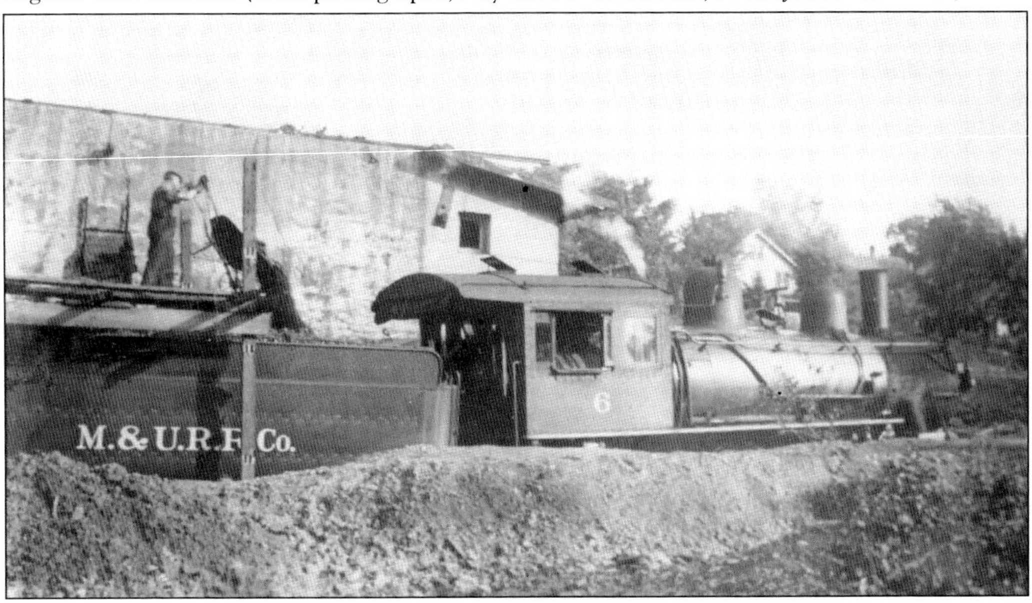

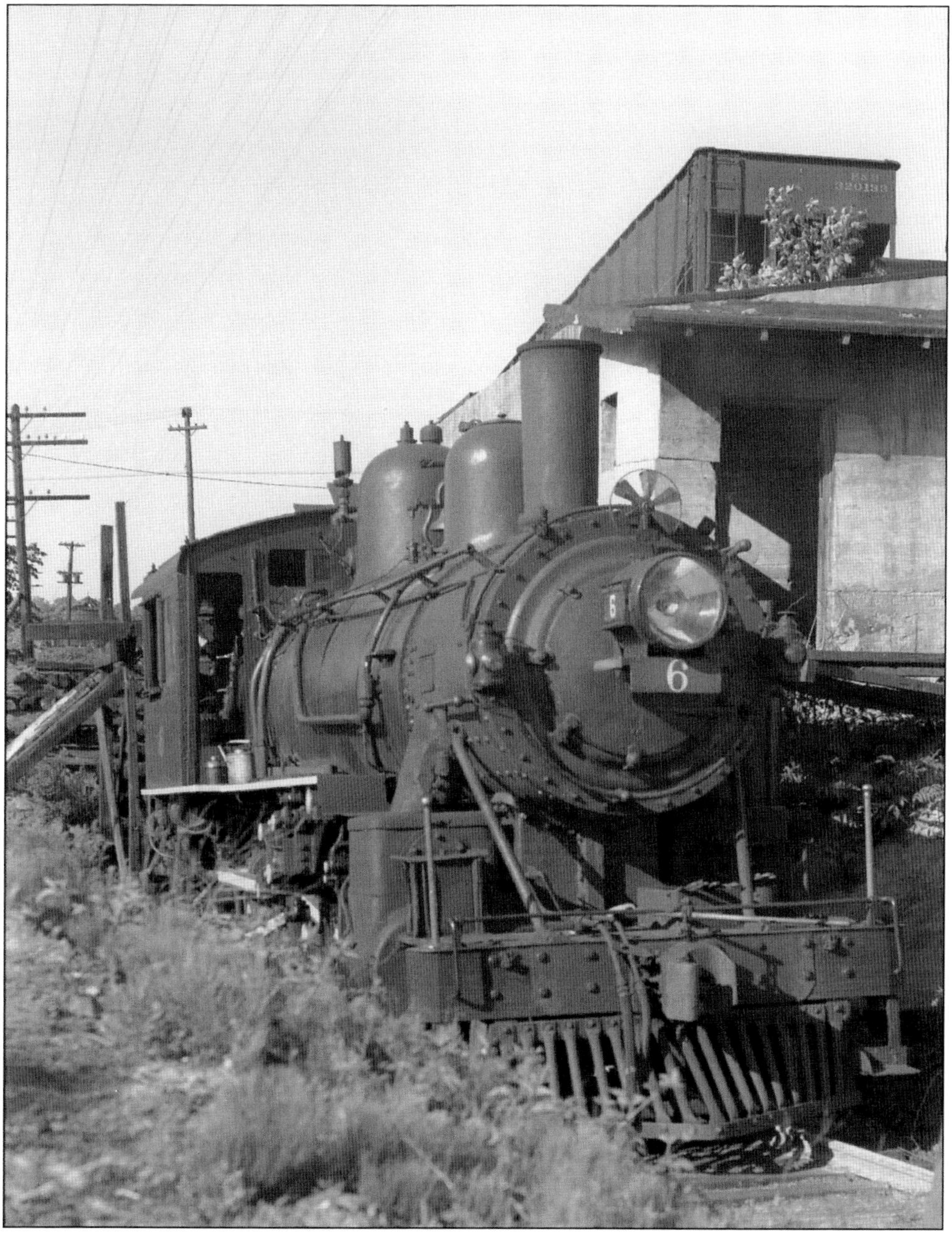

On May 30, 1939, the No. 6 is in the coal hole track for coal for the round-trip train to Unionville and Hanford Junction. The coal facility has one coal car providing bituminous coal for refueling the No. 6. Due to the grade that is quite apparent it was not uncommon for any engine being used by the M&U to damage the rear coupler on the coal tender if the engineer or hostler was not extremely careful. Water pooling on this track was also a problem, especially during the winter. One evening during late winter or early spring, the hostler left the No. 6 at the bottom of the coal-hole track. Snow melting had pooled with the water rising over the rails and covering the lower portion of the drivers. That evening, the temperature dropped below freezing encasing the drive wheels in ice. Finding an icebound No. 6, the M&U was forced to use blowtorches to melt the ice to free the locomotive. (John Schrade Photograph, M&NJRHS Archives.)

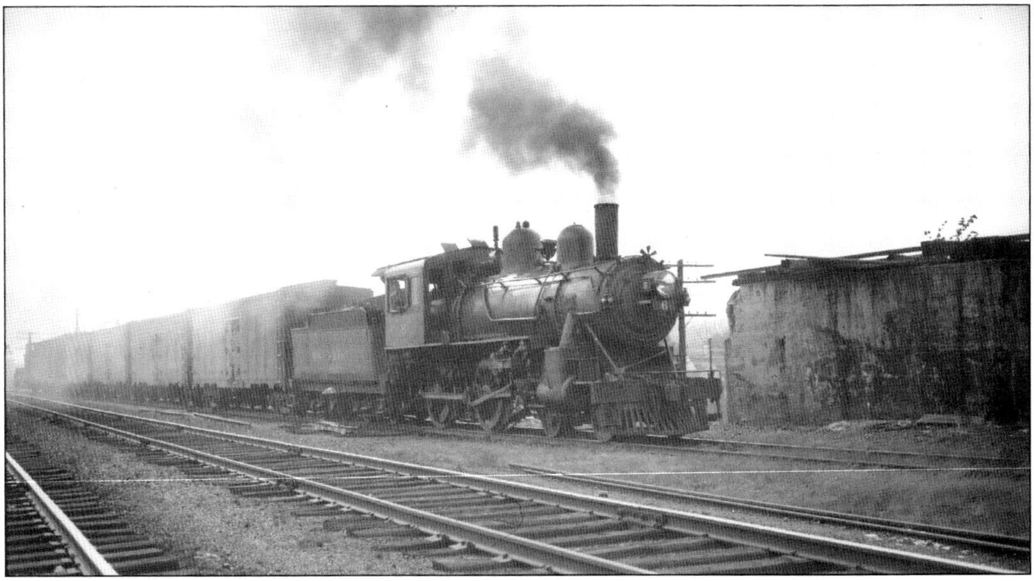

On October 21, 1939, Robert Collins captured M&U No. 6 leading a westbound freight across Washington Street and past the railroad's primitive coal dock. The four milk cars will be interchanged with the Erie to be delivered to Jersey City. The milk traffic on the M&U is being lost to trucks that pick up the milk directly from the creamery to deliver to New York City markets. (Robert Collins Photograph, M&NJRHS Archives.)

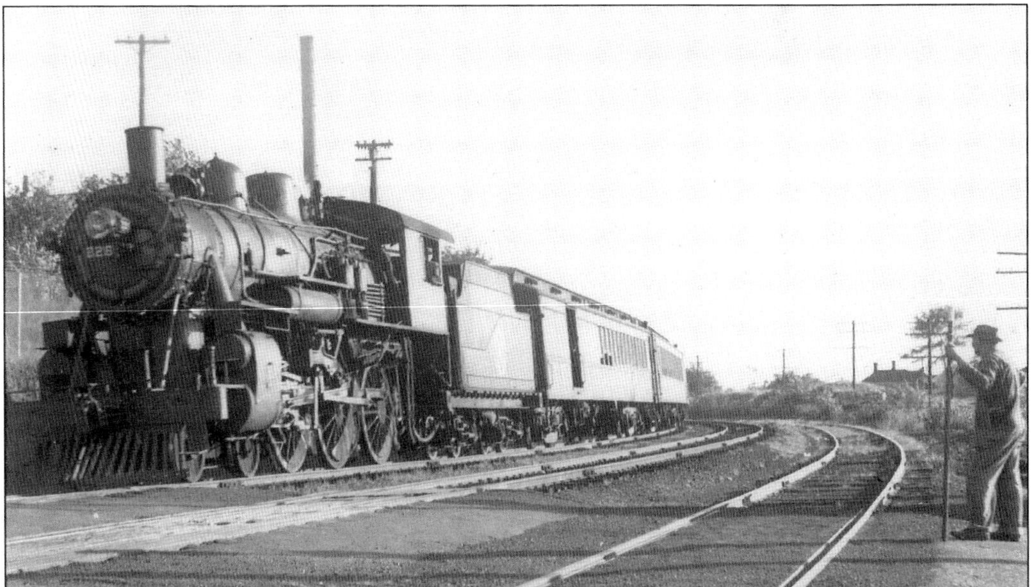

On September 1, 1941, NYO&W E class 4-6-0 226 leads northbound train 7 at Washington Street. The M&U main line is on the right next to the grade crossing guard. The proximity of both railroads here resulted in both railroads sharing the salary of this employee. (Jack Farrell Photograph, Walter Kierzkowski Collection.)

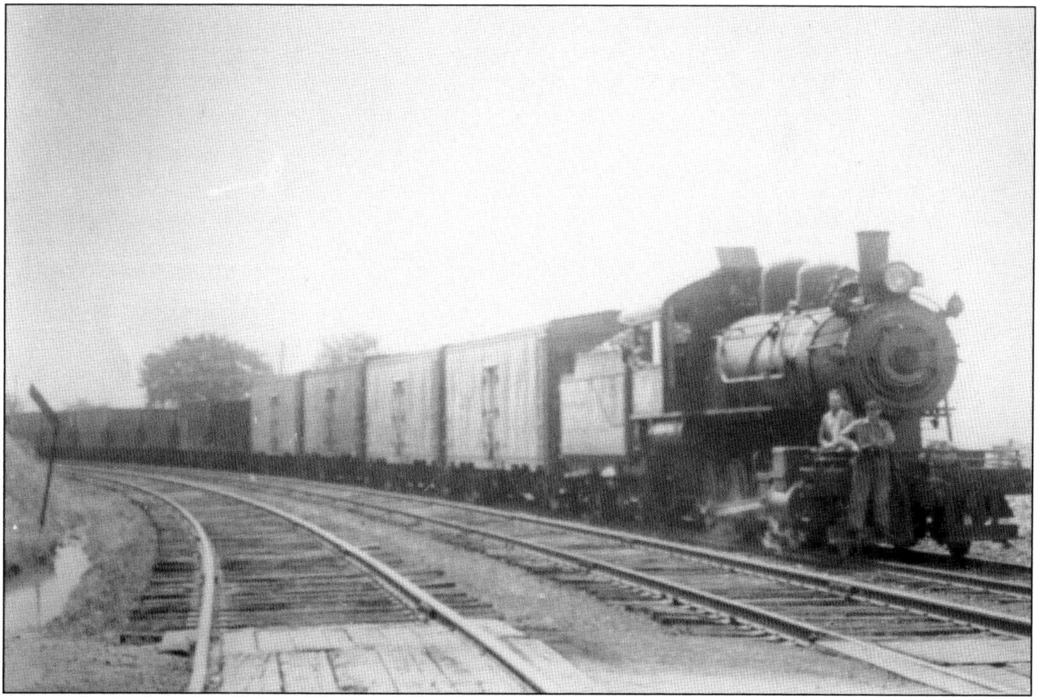

Jack Farrell photographed M&U No. 7 returning to Middletown at Washington Street. The M&U westbound has four milk cars from Borden's in Johnson along with more than eight empty coal cars from the NYS&W. The NYO&W transported the empty hopper cars to the anthracite coalfields near Scranton, Pennsylvania. (Jack Ferrell Photograph, Ray Brown Collection, M&NJRHS Archives.)

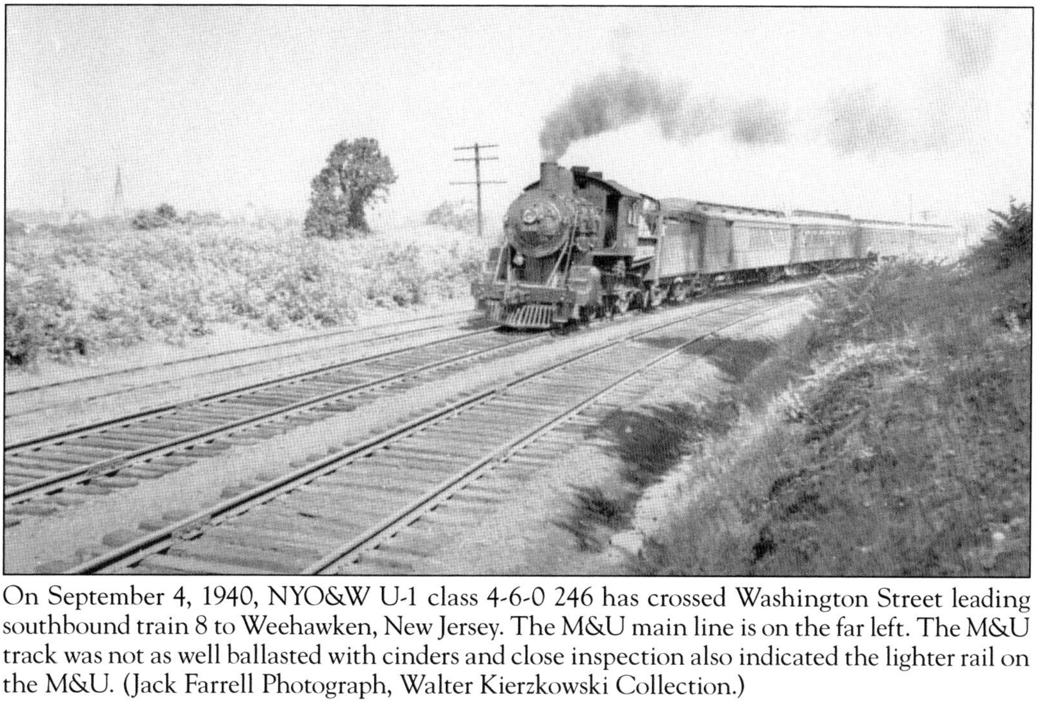

On September 4, 1940, NYO&W U-1 class 4-6-0 246 has crossed Washington Street leading southbound train 8 to Weehawken, New Jersey. The M&U main line is on the far left. The M&U track was not as well ballasted with cinders and close inspection also indicated the lighter rail on the M&U. (Jack Farrell Photograph, Walter Kierzkowski Collection.)

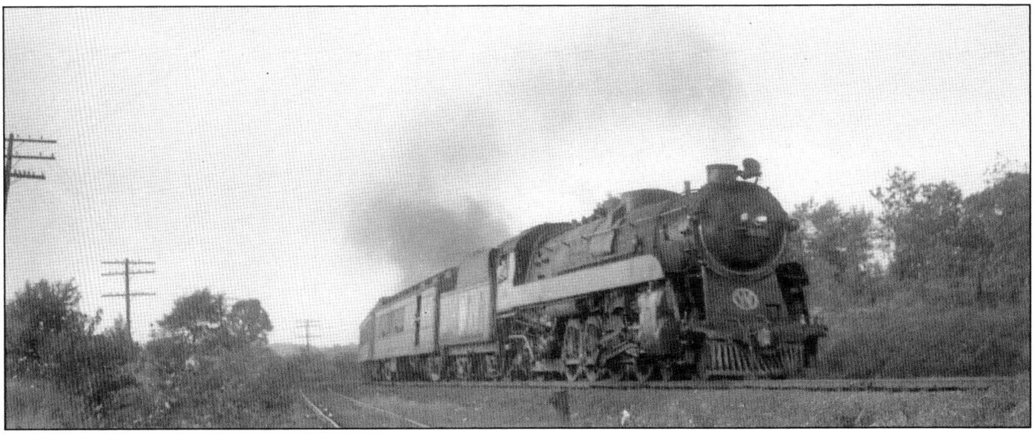

On September 7, 1942, NYO&W 405, known as the Mountaineer leads the second section of train 2 south to Weehawken, New Jersey. The NYO&W is curving out of the City of Middletown on a 180-degree turn nicknamed for a house of ill repute. The M&U, to the left, is parting company for Unionville and the New Jersey State line. The NYO&W tracks are upgrade here to cross the Phillips Street overpass. (Jack Farrell Photograph, Walter Kierzkowski Collection.)

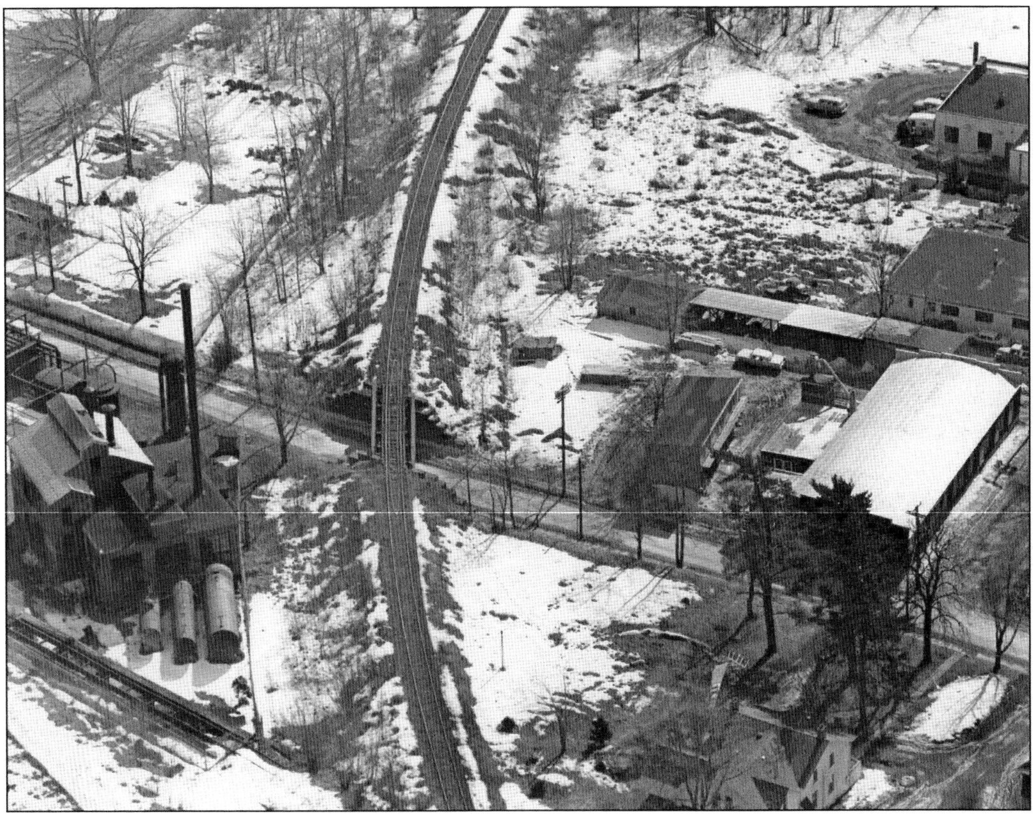

This aerial view of the former M&U taken during the era of the M&NJ in early 1960s shows the Genung Street bridge and the curve toward Dolson Avenue. In the lower left is Rockland Power and Light's coal gas facility serviced by NYO&W until the 1946 single tracking of the railroad. The M&U then was allowed to connect to the trestle to provide the service to this utility. (Middletown Historical Society and the Wallkill Precinct Collection.)

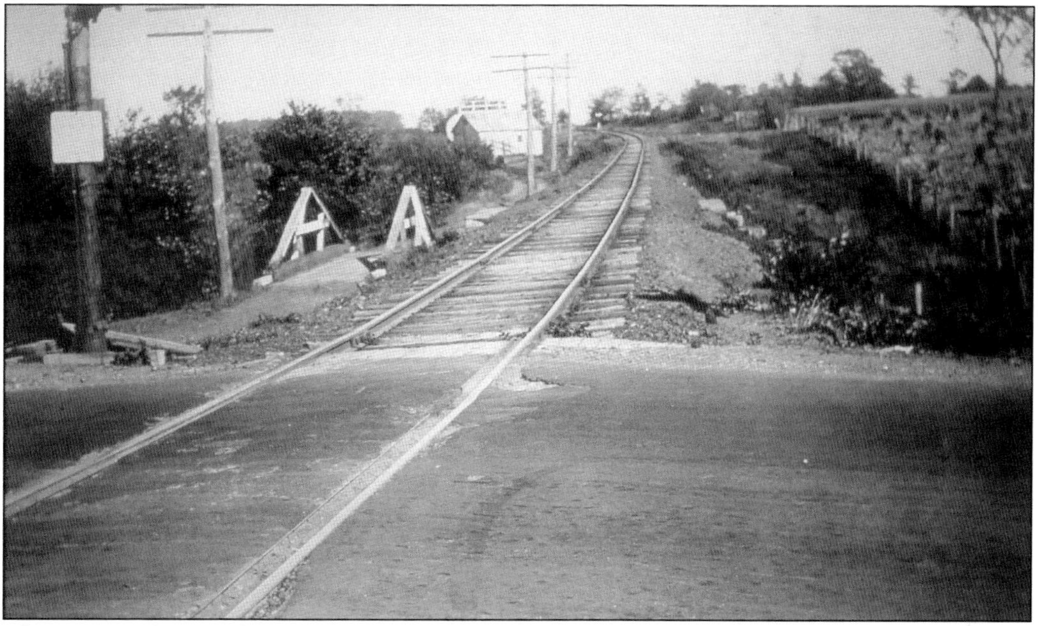

This view is from Dolson Avenue looking up the grade that was built by the New York and Oswego Midland. Ownership of these 1.1 miles to East Main Street was passed to its successor the NYO&W. The original connection to the Erie Railroad was approximately where the building appears to the left of the track. (Carl Detwyler Collection, M&NJRHS Archives.)

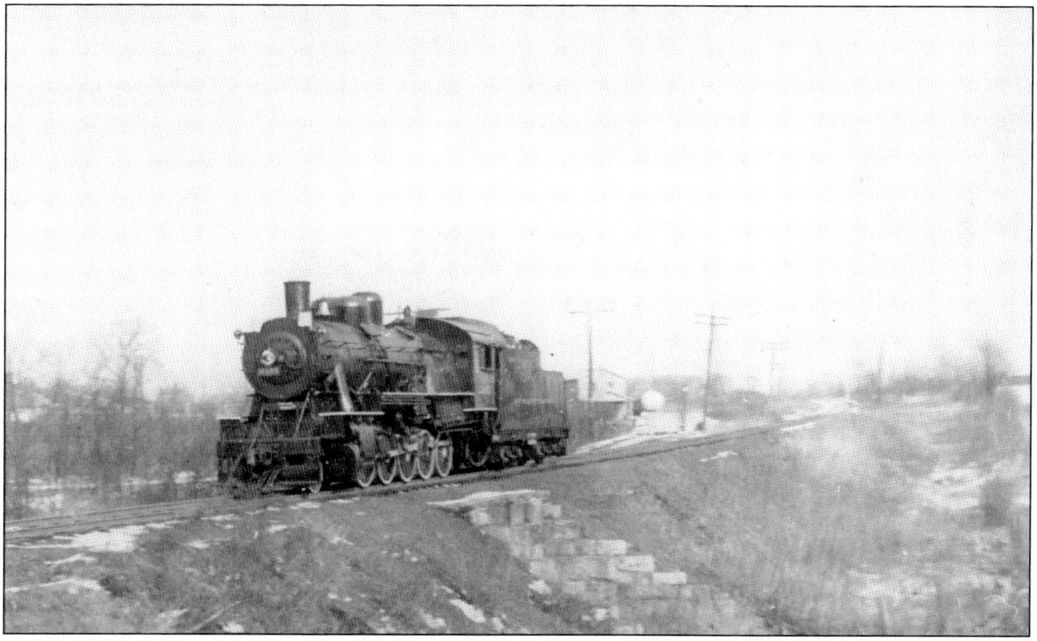

NYS&W J2 2495 is eastbound crossing over the Monhagen Creek stone arch bridge approaching Dolson Avenue during January 1942. The 2495 is returning from repairs at the NYO&W Middletown shops to home rails at Hanford Junction. The building in the background is the location of Barney's Go Gas that eventually moved to the north yard of the NYO&W. (Stephen Maguire Photograph, Ray Brown Collection, M&NJRHS Archives.)

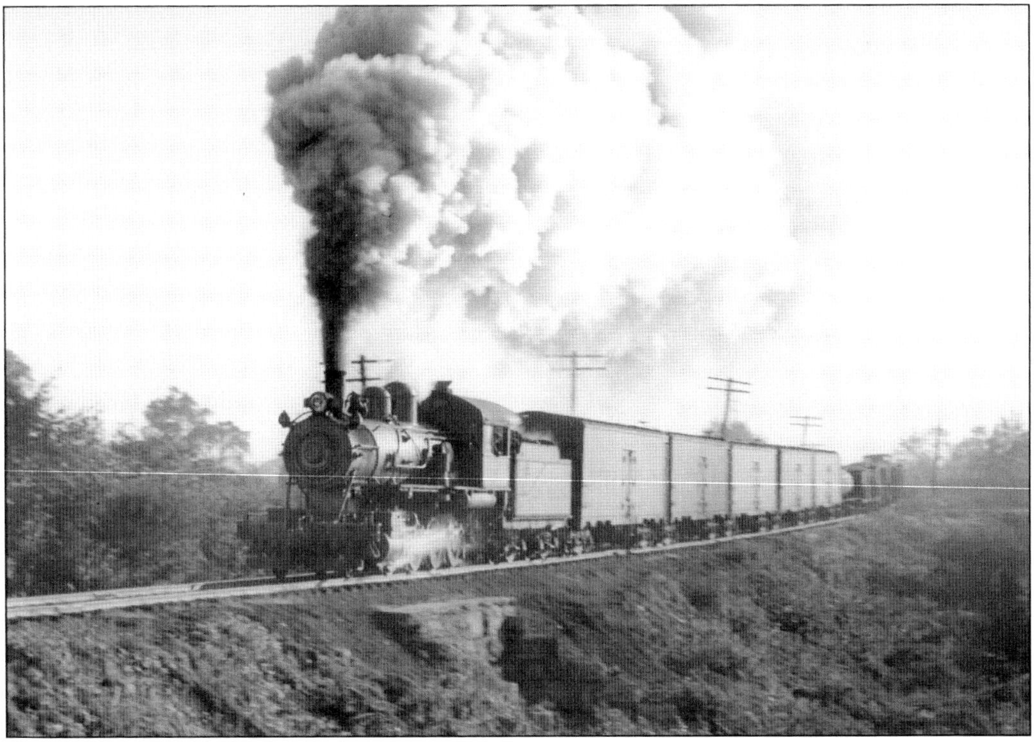

M&U No. 7 is just about to cross the stone arch bridge over Monhagen Creek with a 10-car train as it approaches Dolson Avenue. It will then head up the stiff grade to Pounds station at Webb Road. Note the five milk cars on the head end, empties returning to the creameries, most notably Borden's at Johnson. (Stephen Maguire Photograph, Ray Brown Collection, M&NJRHS Archives.)

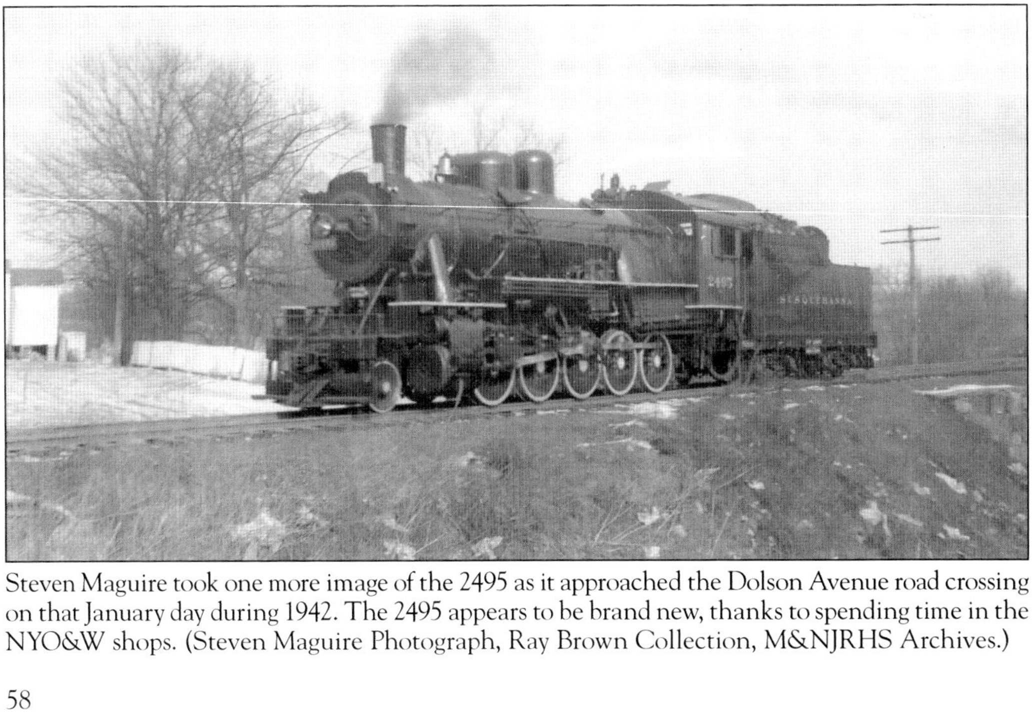

Steven Maguire took one more image of the 2495 as it approached the Dolson Avenue road crossing on that January day during 1942. The 2495 appears to be brand new, thanks to spending time in the NYO&W shops. (Steven Maguire Photograph, Ray Brown Collection, M&NJRHS Archives.)

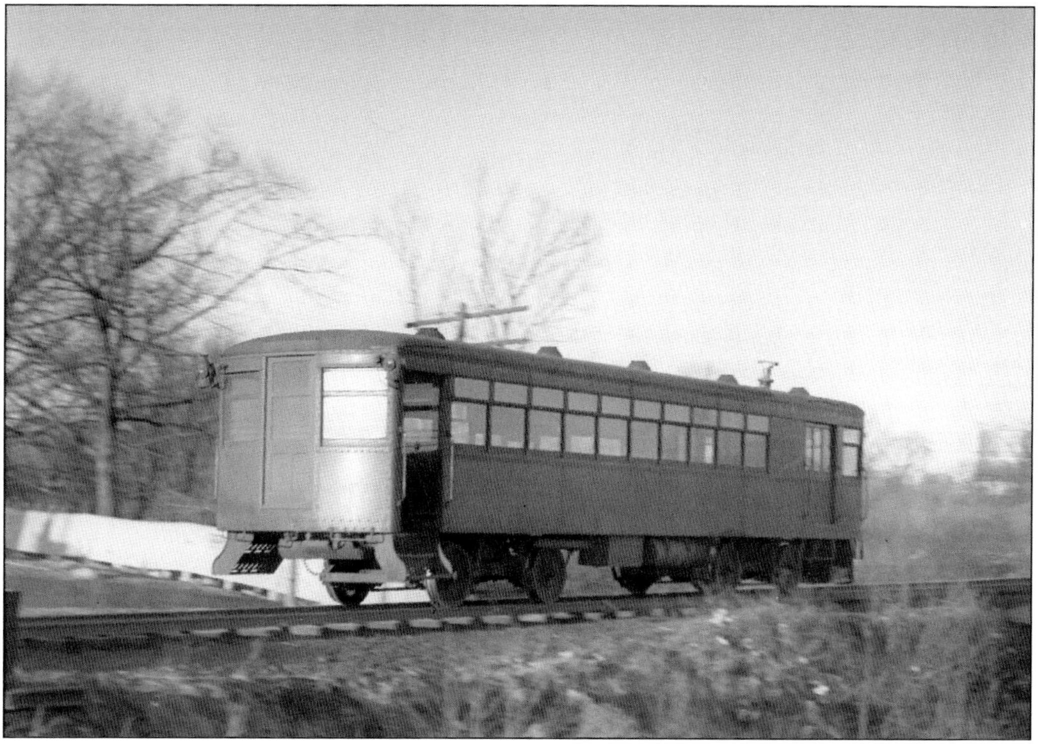

The M&U's M-55 Brill rail car has just crossed Dolson Avenue headed west to the East Main Street depot in Middletown on March 2, 1940. In the distance on the right, one of Rockland Power and Light's coal-gas storage tanks towers over its surroundings. (Robert Collins Photograph, M&NJRHS Archives.)

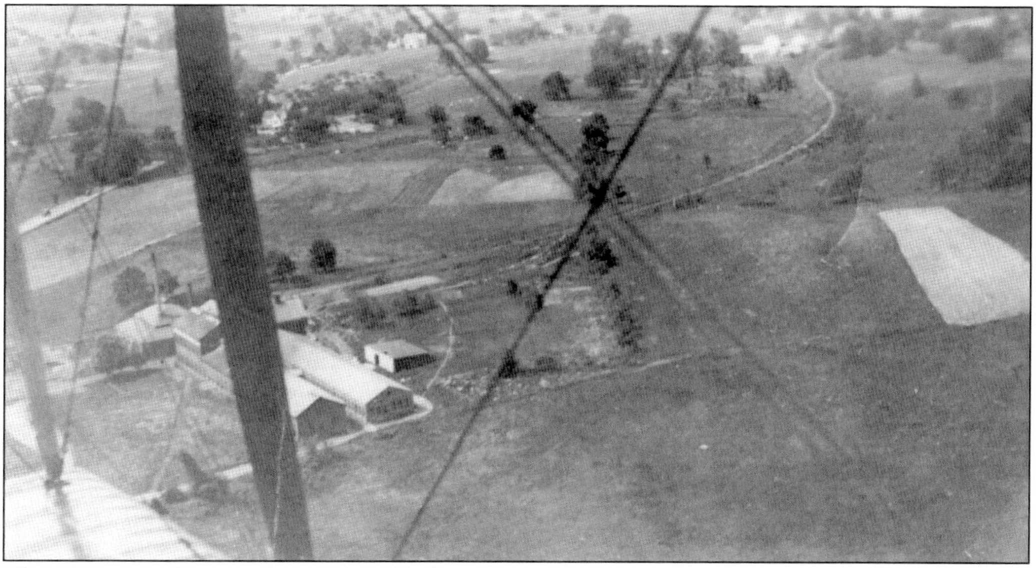

This photograph was taken from a biplane during 1920 capturing the Madden and Morrison File Shop in the lower left. The M&U right of way is visible climbing and winding up to Pounds Creamery at the upper right of the photograph. (Ray Brown Collection, M&NJRHS Archives.)

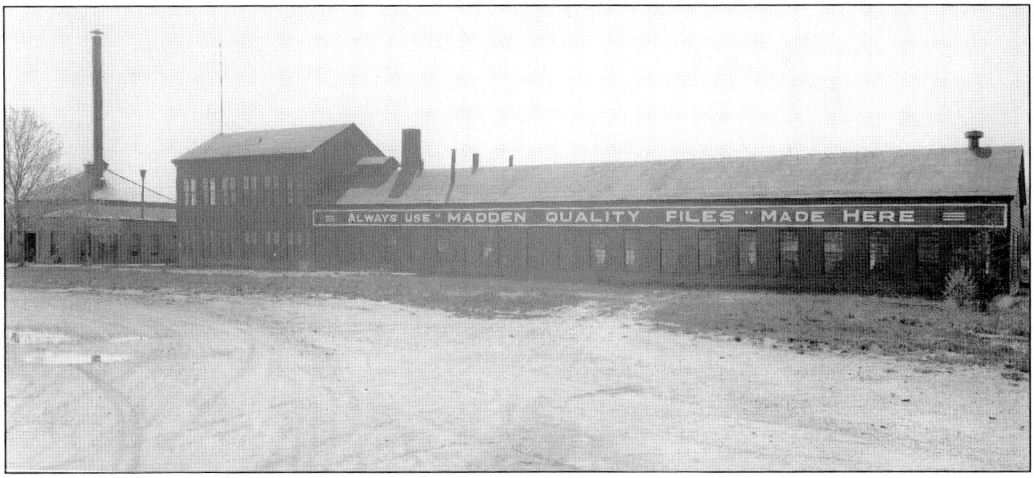

Prior to being the Madden File shop, this facility was the Hogan Boiler Works. This photograph of Madden File shop was taken from Dolson Avenue. The M&U is to the extreme left of the picture. (Middletown Historical Society and Wallkill Precinct Collection.)

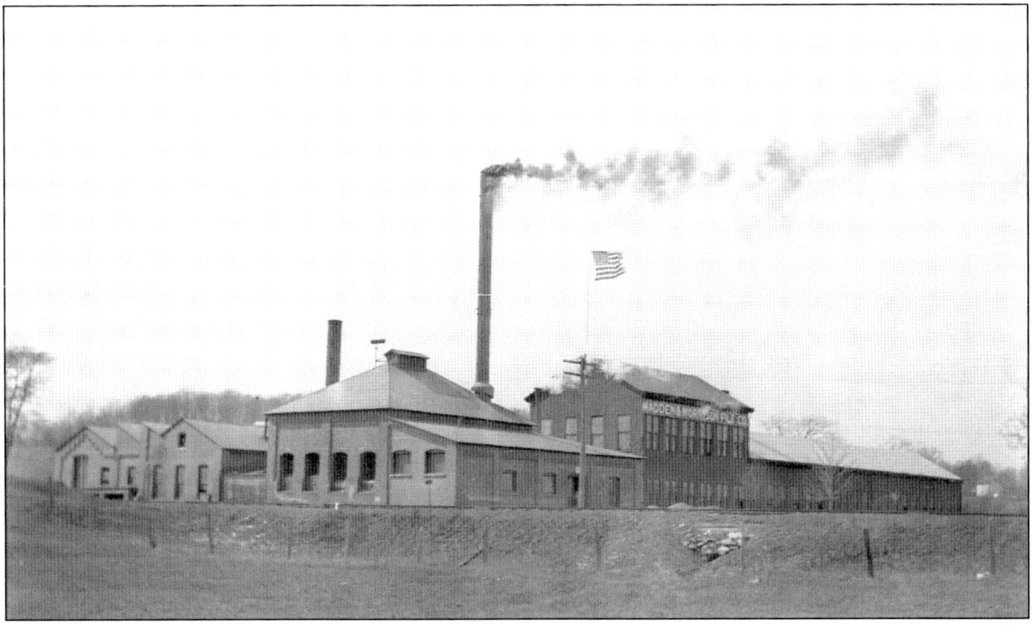

The M&U main line runs east to west from left to right in front of the Madden and Morrison file shop around 1911. This photograph was taken during the Middletown, Unionville, and Water Gap era, predecessor to the M&U, that was under NYS&W control. (Middletown Historical Society and Wallkill Precinct Collection.)

Three

SLATE HILL

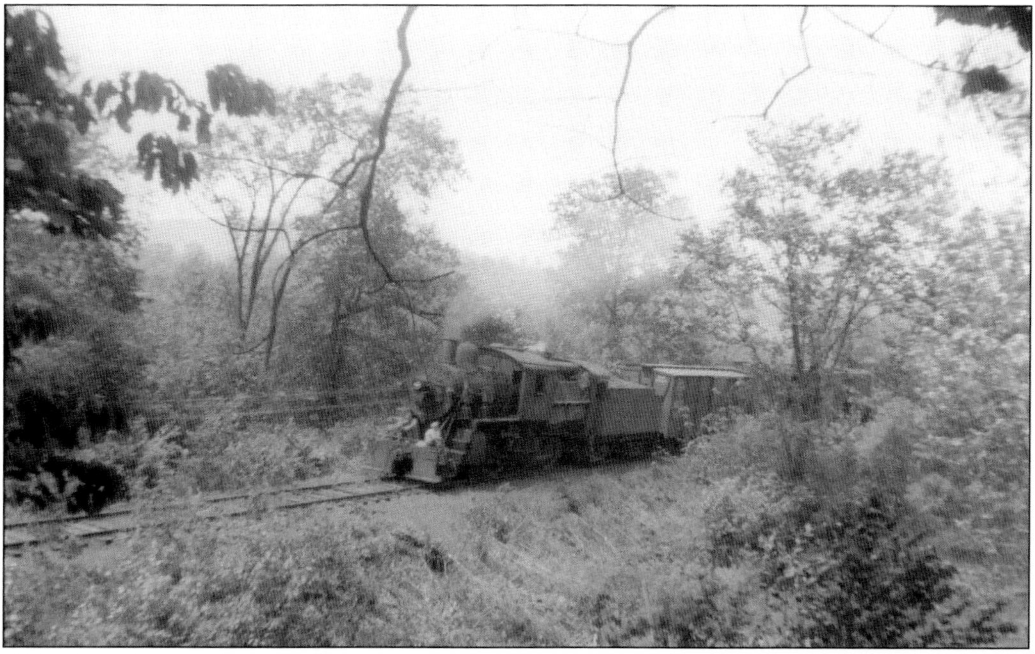

O&W No. 245 is eastbound during August 1944. During the period from April 23, 1944, when M&U No. 7 was retired, until July 17, 1945, the M&U relied exclusively on rented O&W locomotives. A closer inspection of the 245 reveals two members of the train crew enjoying the trip as they ride on the pilot. (John Stellwagen Collection, M&NJRHS Archives.)

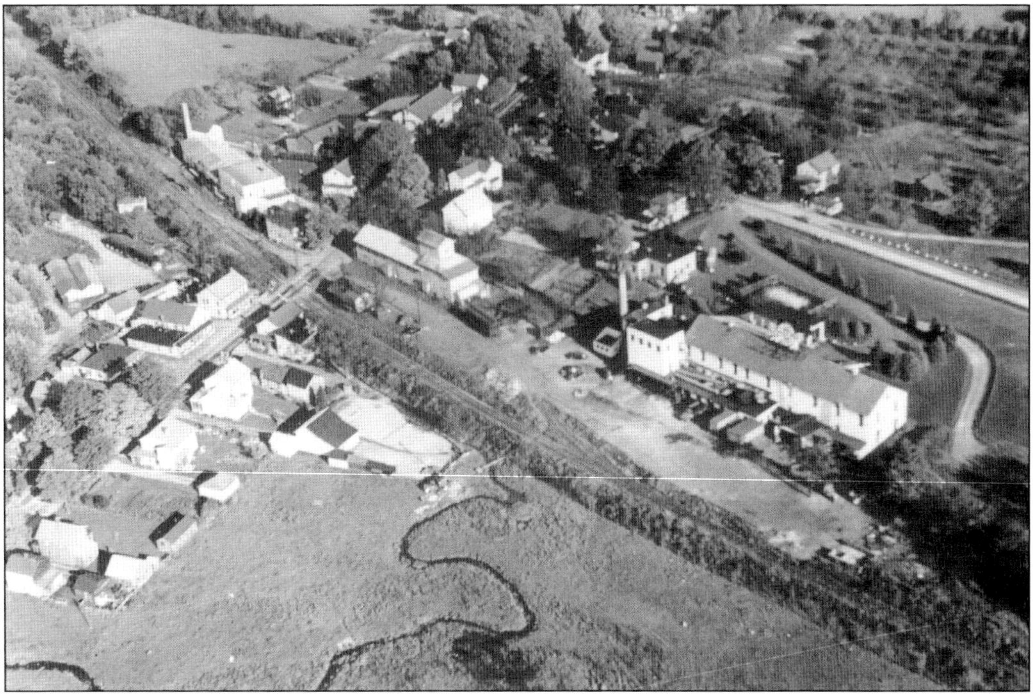

From left to right along the M&U are the A plant creamery and runaround track, the Slate Hill depot in front of Martins Feed Mill, and the B plant creamery. The first creamery was located between the depot and the switch to the feed mill. The water tank stood about where the meandering stream intersects the M&U main line. (Ray Brown Collection, M&NJRHS Archives.)

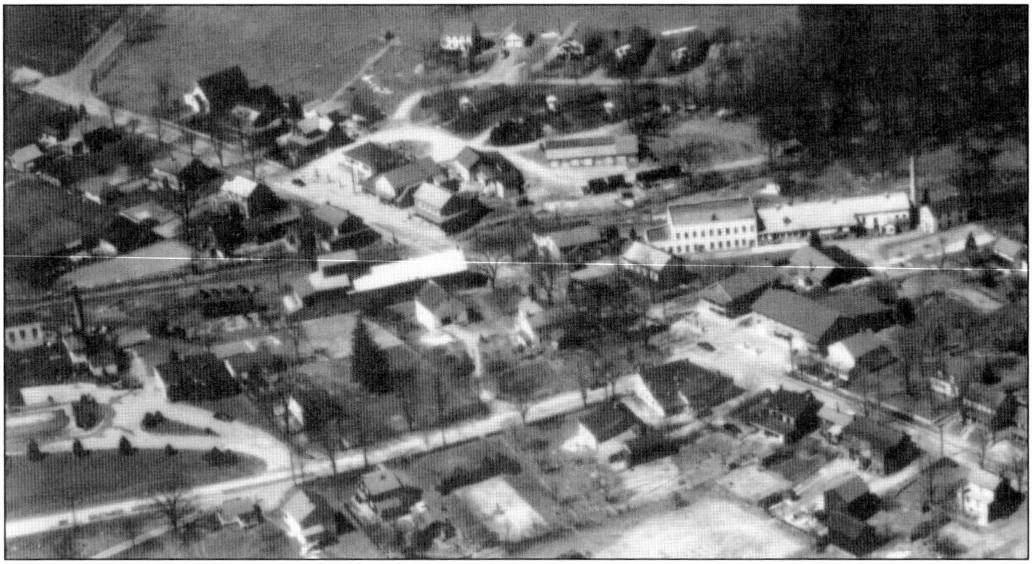

Looking at a southwesterly view of Slate Hill, the M&U right-of-way runs east to west from left to right revealing a portion of the B plant creamery, Martins Feed Mill and the A plant creamery to the right. The A plant was built by Middletown Milk and Feed in 1922, became Middletown Milk and Cream in 1924, and closed during the early 1940s, when operations were consolidated in the B plant. (Town of Minisink Museum Collection.)

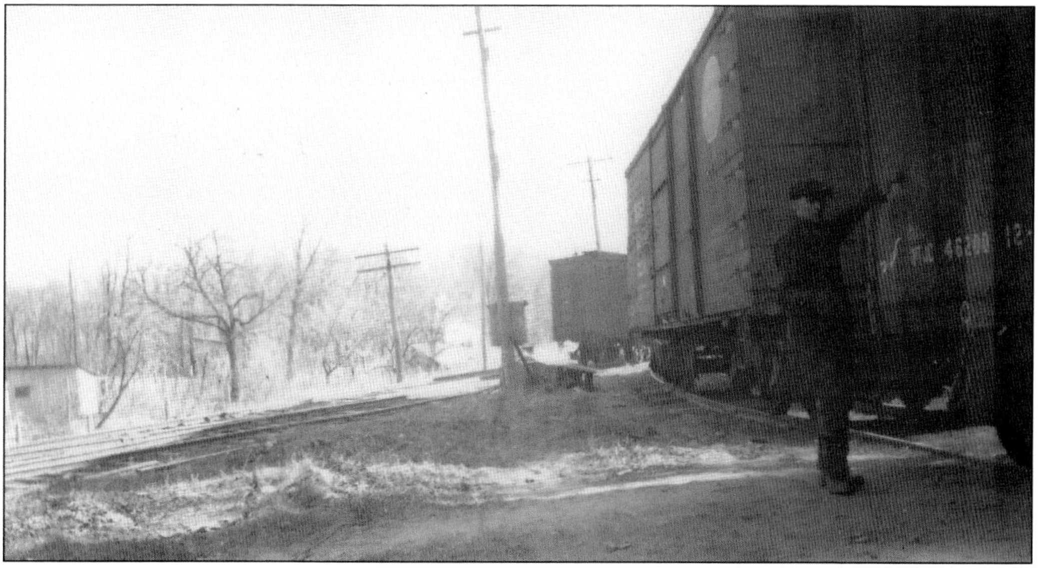

Around 1922, an M&U brakeman is on the siding to the feed mill, behind the photographer, that at this time has been connected to the A plant creamery runaround track that is visible to the lower left extending to the milk car in the center background. When the runaround track was built for the A plant in 1922, the switch to the feed mill was moved from the main line to the runaround track. (Ray Brown Collection, M&NJRHS Archives.)

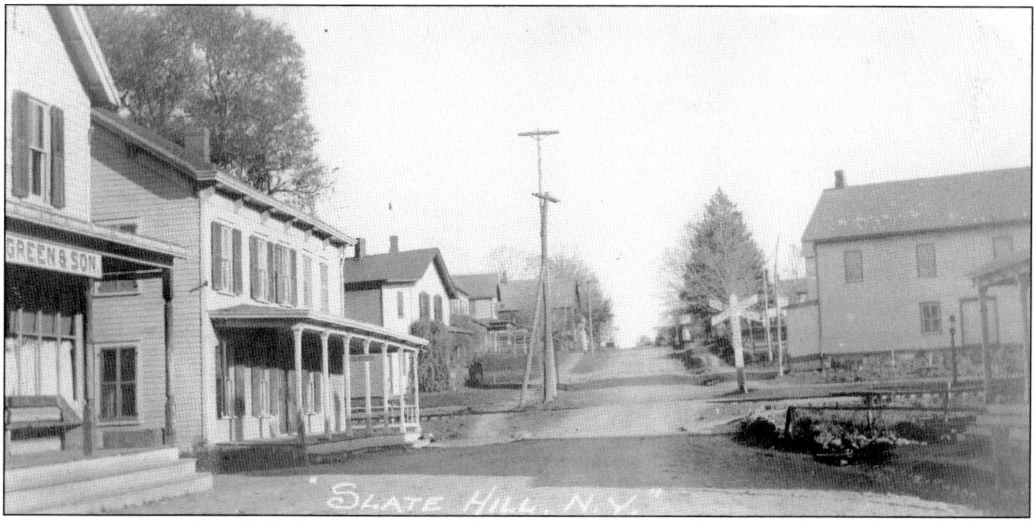

Looking east in Slate Hill along U.S. Route 6, the M&U main line runs west to east, from left to right, in the middle of this photograph. To the right of the railroad crossbuck is Slate Hill Feed and Coal, successor to a series of companies extending back to Castle Flour and Feed around 1881. Their siding was behind the large telephone pole crossing the highway in order to reach the mill. (Ray Brown Collection, M&NJRHS Archives.)

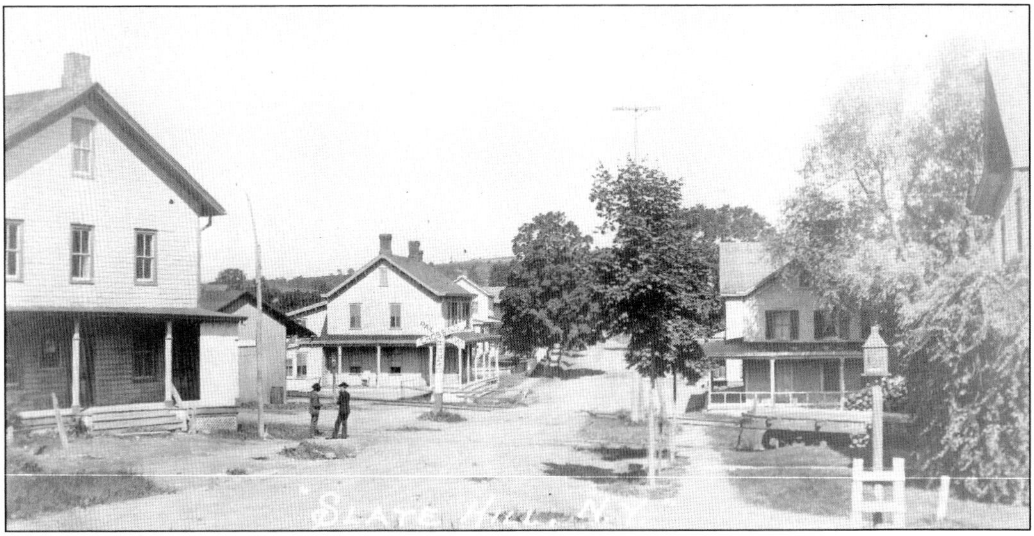

Looking west across the M&U grade crossing on the left is the Slate Hill Feed and Coal dealer with the Slate Hill depot behind it. A portion of a flat car can be seen on the siding to the right that was used to deliver carloads for the feed mill. (Ray Brown Collection, M&NJRHS Archives.)

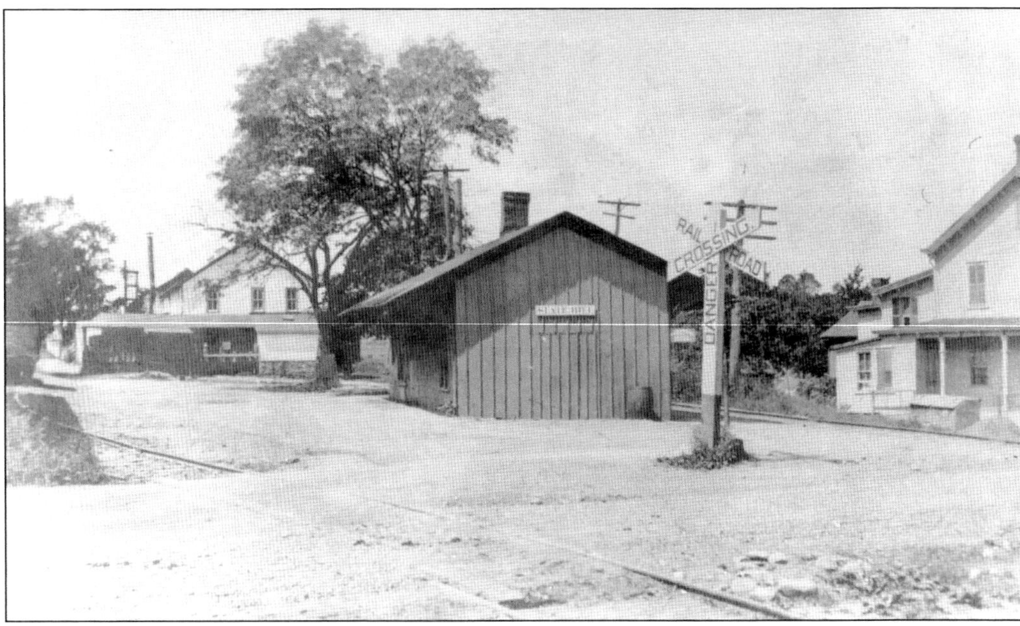

Looking across the highway eastward along the M&U, the feed mill siding runs to the left with the Slate Hill depot visible in the center next to the main line. In the background is the first creamery along the M&U in Slate Hill, Clover Farms Dairy built in 1895. Clover's construction of a new creamery in 1915–1916, later known as the B plant, permitted eventual demolition of the original creamery by 1923. (Ray Brown Collection, M&NJRHS Archives.)

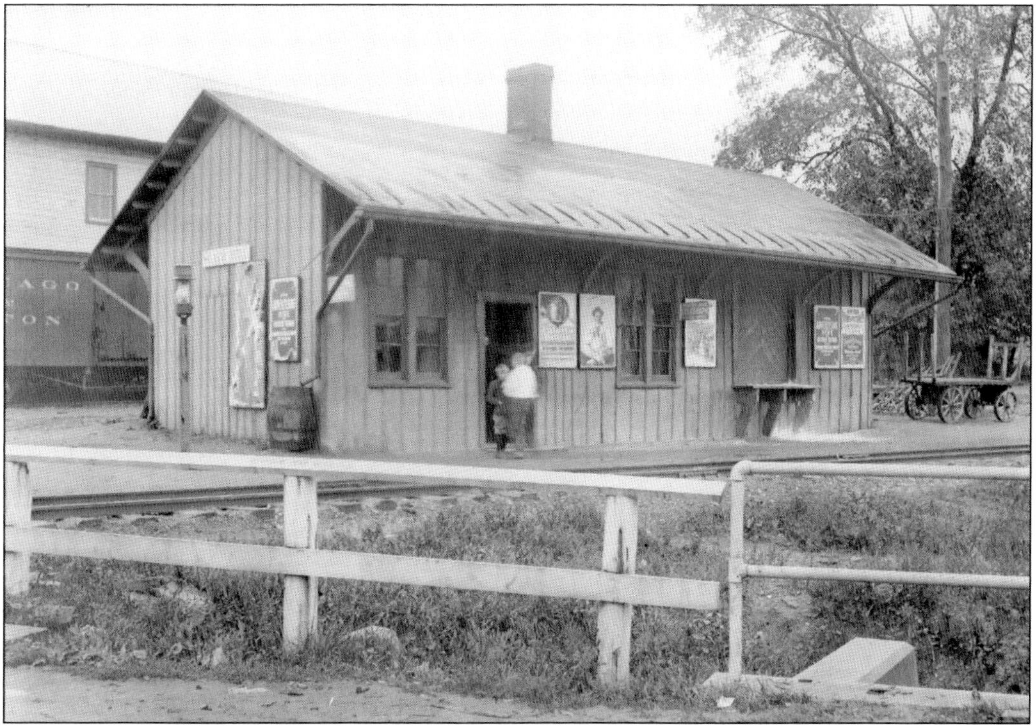

The Slate Hill depot as it was in the early 1900s under the management of the NYS&W when it controlled the MU&WG. The advertisements on the depot walls are typical of that era of railroad transportation prior to the automobile. The depots at Slate Hill, Johnson, and Westtown were identical structures. (New Jersey Midland Railroad Historical Society Collection.)

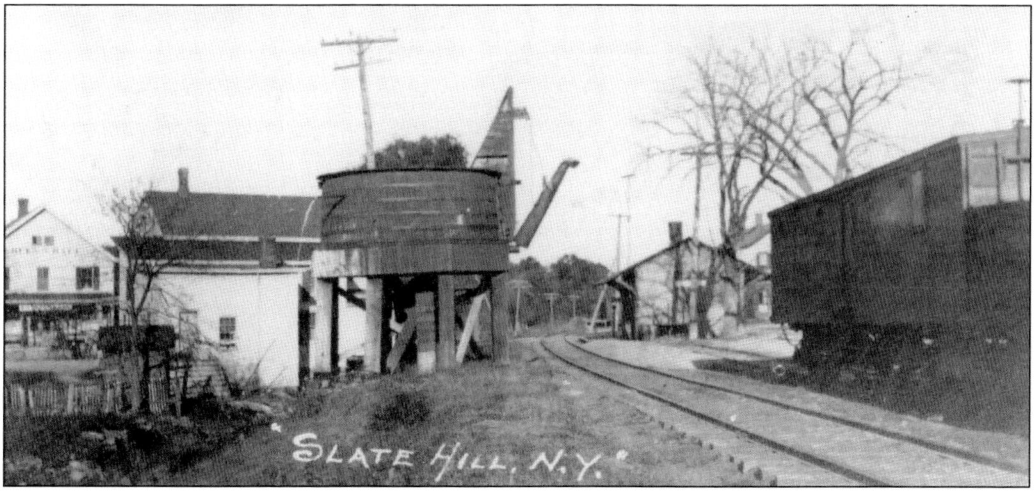

The Slate Hill water tank can be seen in this westerly view of the M&U main looking toward Middletown. The water tank was directly across the track from the original Clover Farms creamery that is to the right of the milk car. The water tank was gravity fed from the nearby stream and required an overflow pipe to expel excess water as can be seen in this picture. (Ray Brown Collection, M&NJRHS Archives.)

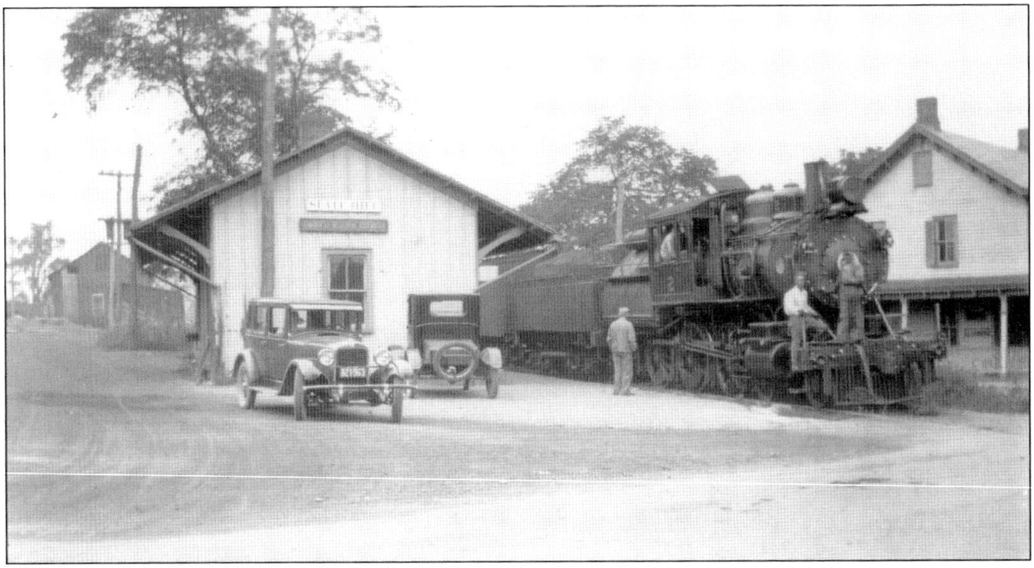

M&U No. 2 is westbound at the Slate Hill depot on August 8, 1927. No. 2 will cross present-day U.S. Route 6 on the 5.5-mile journey back to the East Main Street depot in Middletown. The original Clover Farms creamery has been taken down as only the icehouse can be seen in the distance to the left of the depot. (James Speer Photograph, M&NJRHS Archives.)

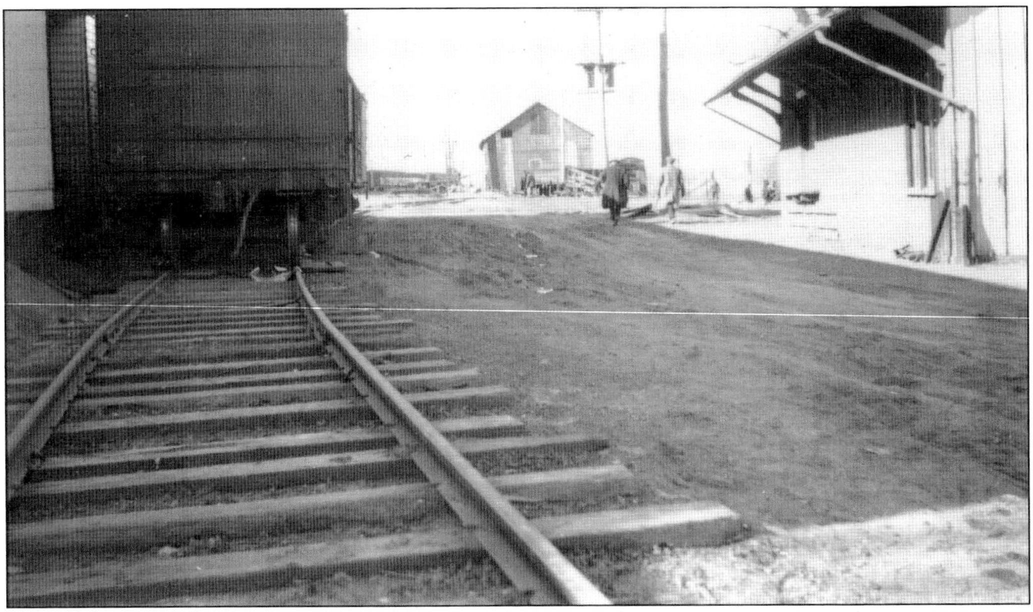

The feed mill siding hosts several cars that were delivered over the new siding during 1928 after the track and switch had been moved to the east side of the depot through the footprint of the original Clover Farms Creamery. This siding is barely visible in the background running between the icehouse and small cattle pen used by dairy farmers to receive new cows for their herds. (Ray Brown Collection, M&NJRHS Archives.)

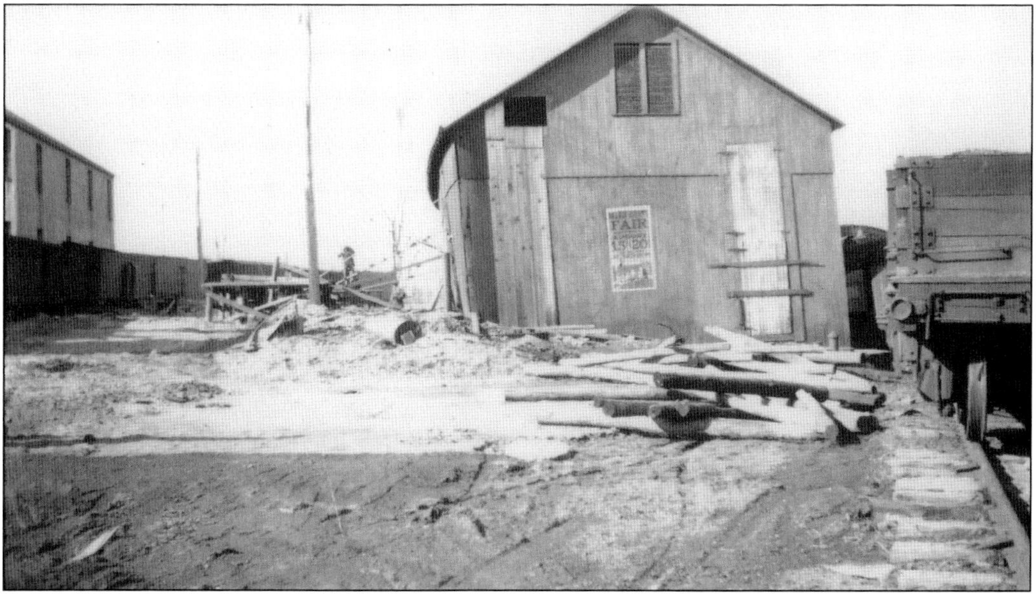

Removal of the original Clover Farms creamery in 1923 and icehouse in 1928 allowed construction of the new feed mill siding. This required relocation of the siding for the B plant creamery to a site several hundred feet behind the icehouse. The presence of six milk cars along the B plant creamery and the siding to the right of the icehouse remnants indicates that part of this project was completed. (Ray Brown Collection, M&NJRHS Archives.)

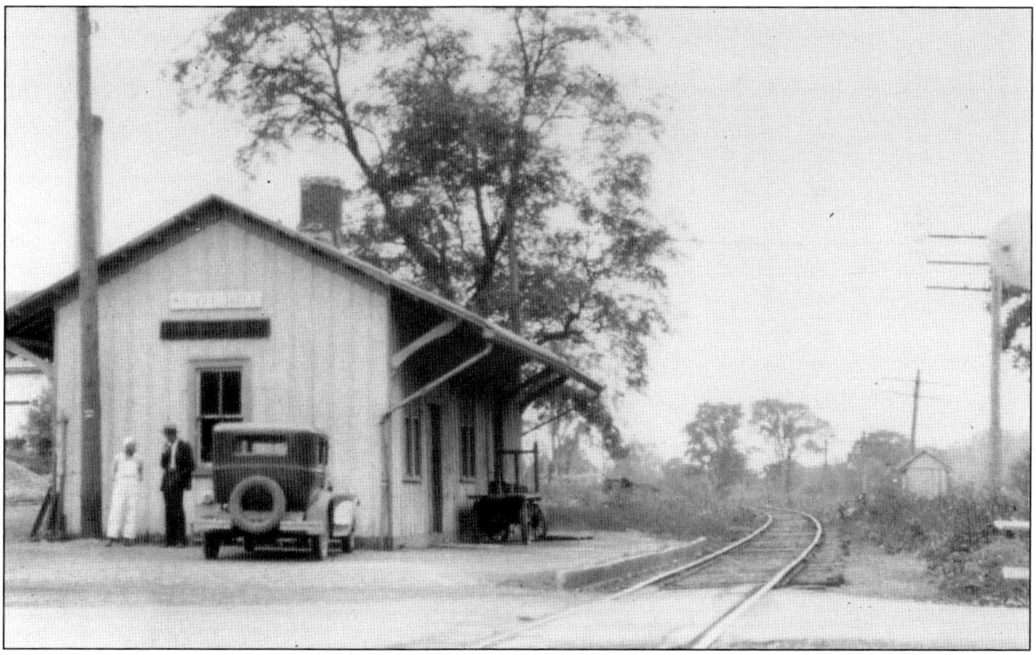

This post-1928 image of the Slate Hill depot is important for what is not seen in the picture. The original Clover Farms creamery, icehouse, and water tank are now distant memories. The side-track relocation projects are now complete leaving the Middletown Milk and Cream A plant and Slate Hill Milk and Cream B plant as the operational creameries in Slate Hill. (Carl Detwyler Collection, M&NJRHS Archives.)

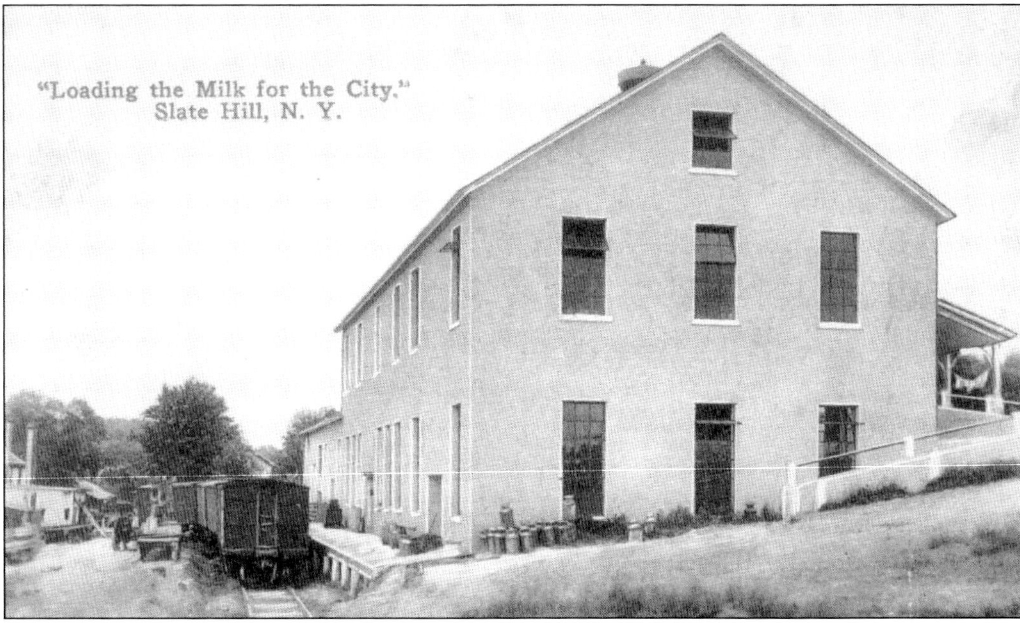

The B plant was the second Clover Farms creamery but it was soon sold and re-opened by Hires on March 1, 1916. Hires sold the facility to Nestles in August 1919. The plant was later sold to Slate Hill Milk and Cream, which operated it between September 1925 and 1940. The Middletown Milk and Cream Company purchased the creamery in 1940 and soon closed the A plant, consolidating all operations in the B plant during the early 1940s under the new name "Creami Rich." Below, the author photographed the altered cheese factory building with the M&U right-of-way off to the left of the facility. The cheese factory was located approximately 500 yards east of the B plant from which it purchased milk for cheese processing. (Above photograph, Ray Brown Collection, M&NJRHS Archives.)

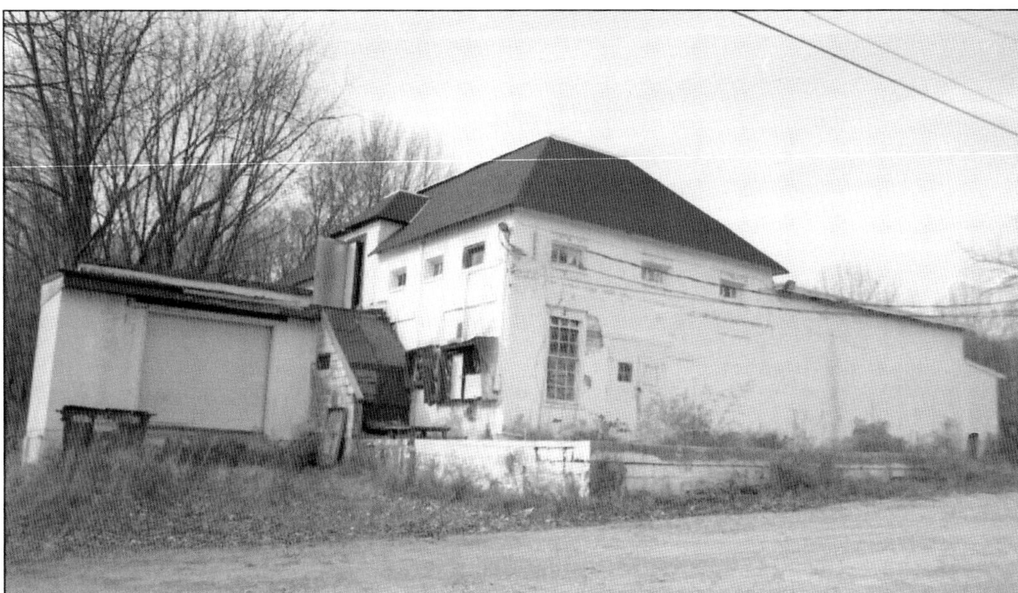

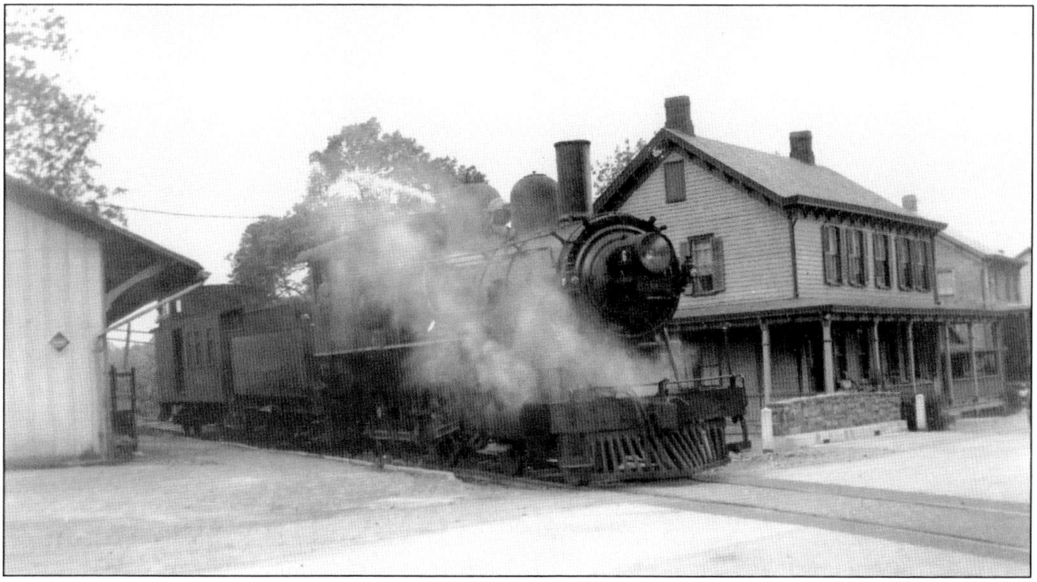

Until 1940, the M&U operated only one freight train eastbound to Hanford Junction and the westbound return trip to Middletown each day. M&U No. 6 is seen westbound at the Slate Hill depot from 1935 to 1940 with a "caboose hop." The caboose was used to carry less-than-carload freight shipments (LCL) and also served as the conductor's office while out on the road. (Cal's Classics Collection.)

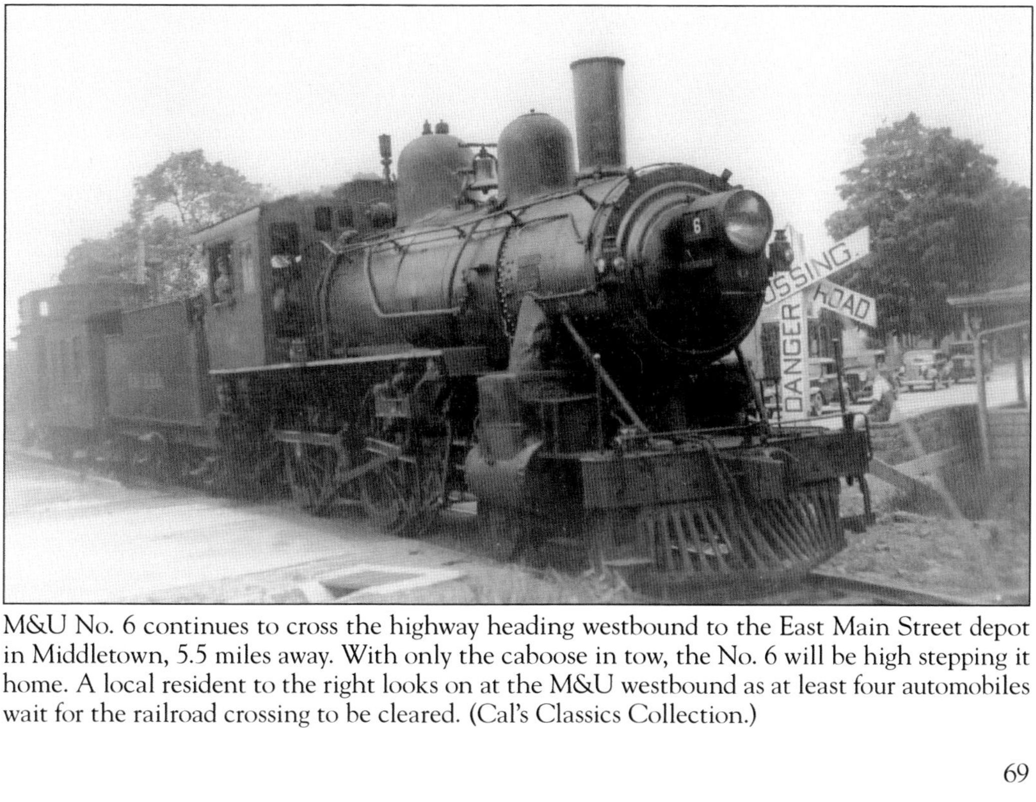

M&U No. 6 continues to cross the highway heading westbound to the East Main Street depot in Middletown, 5.5 miles away. With only the caboose in tow, the No. 6 will be high stepping it home. A local resident to the right looks on at the M&U westbound as at least four automobiles wait for the railroad crossing to be cleared. (Cal's Classics Collection.)

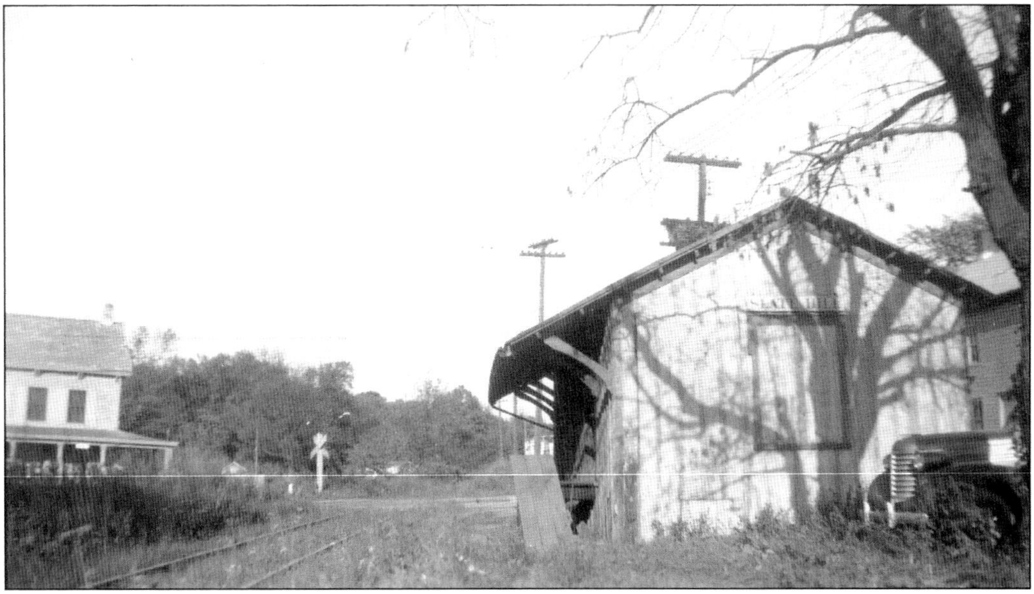

It is 1941 looking west toward Middletown and at the Slate Hill depot. By this time, all the operational creameries along the M&U were shipping milk by trucks and all passenger traffic had ceased. The depot telegraph call letters were "SH." (Ray Brown Photograph, M&NJRHS Archives.)

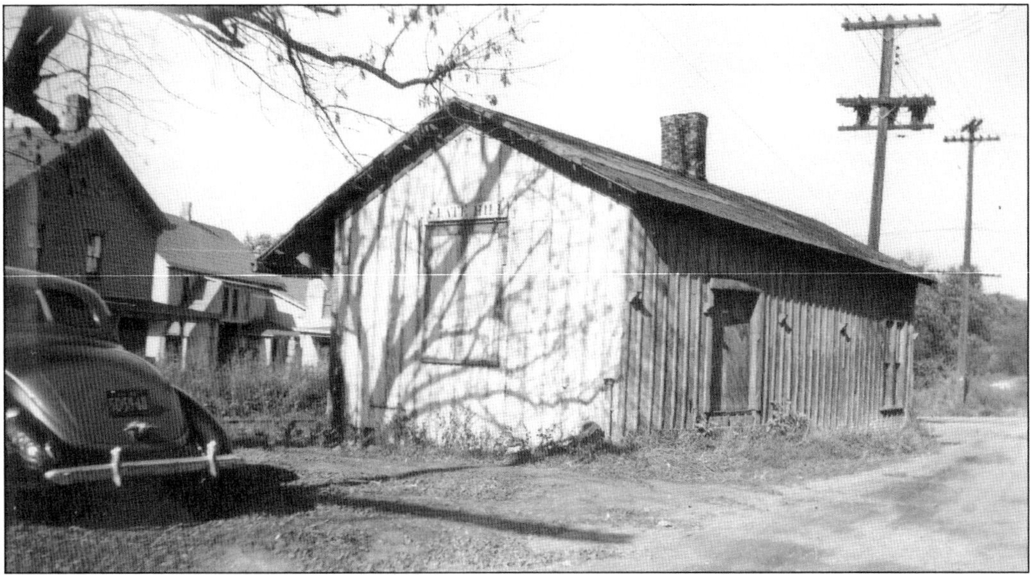

This rear view of the Slate Hill depot was taken on the same day in 1941 as the previous photograph. This view clearly shows the rear roofline has been shortened. The roof was damaged so often by milk trucks serving the B plant creamery, it was finally cut back to avoid the continuous damage and volumes of accompanying paperwork documenting the accidents. (Ray Brown Photograph, M&NJRHS Archives.)

Four

JOHNSON

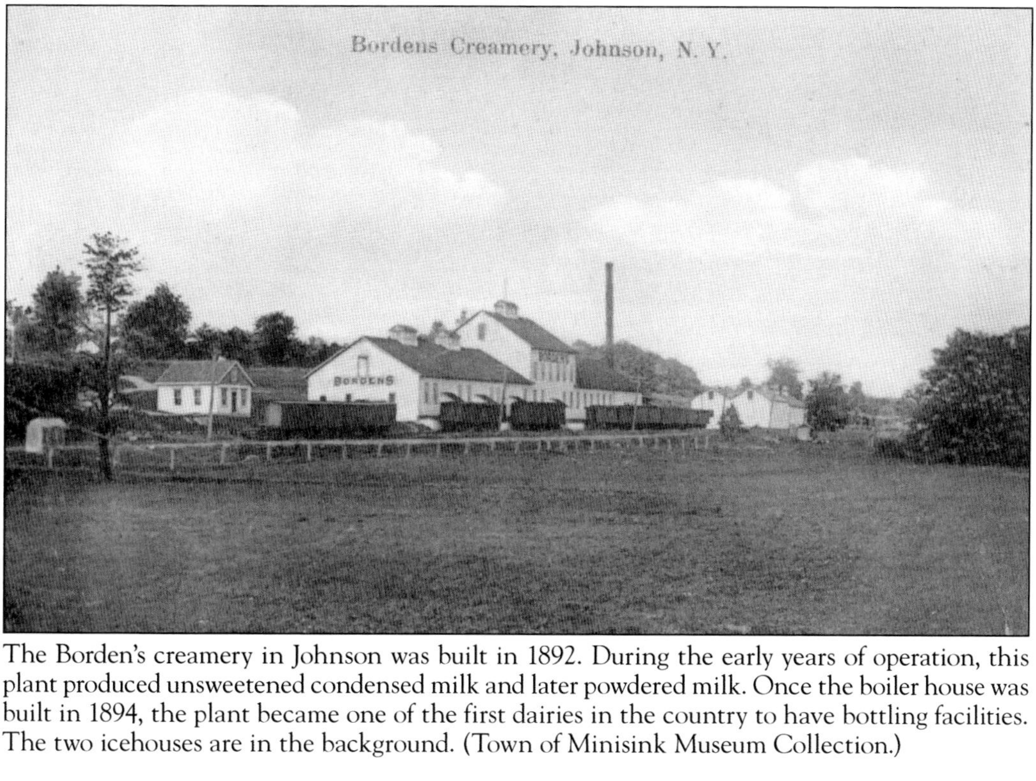

The Borden's creamery in Johnson was built in 1892. During the early years of operation, this plant produced unsweetened condensed milk and later powdered milk. Once the boiler house was built in 1894, the plant became one of the first dairies in the country to have bottling facilities. The two icehouses are in the background. (Town of Minisink Museum Collection.)

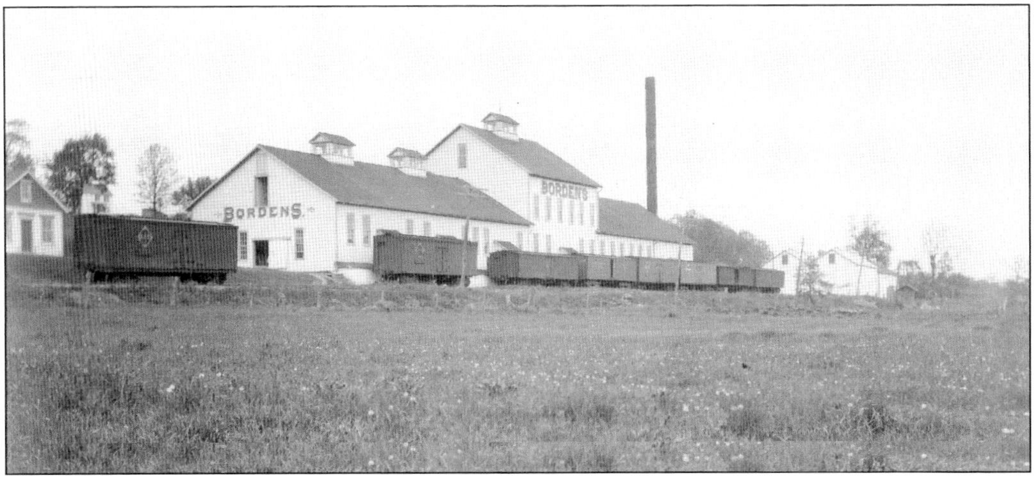

The Borden's Johnson plant received raw milk from local farms and by rail along the Erie Railroad from as far away as Deposit, New York. The M&U benefited financially from delivering inbound milk, milk bottles, and coal to Borden's as well as carrying the bottled milk to market via the NYS&W at Hanford Junction until September 29, 1936, when the milk traffic was rerouted to the Erie in Middletown. (George Shammas Collection.)

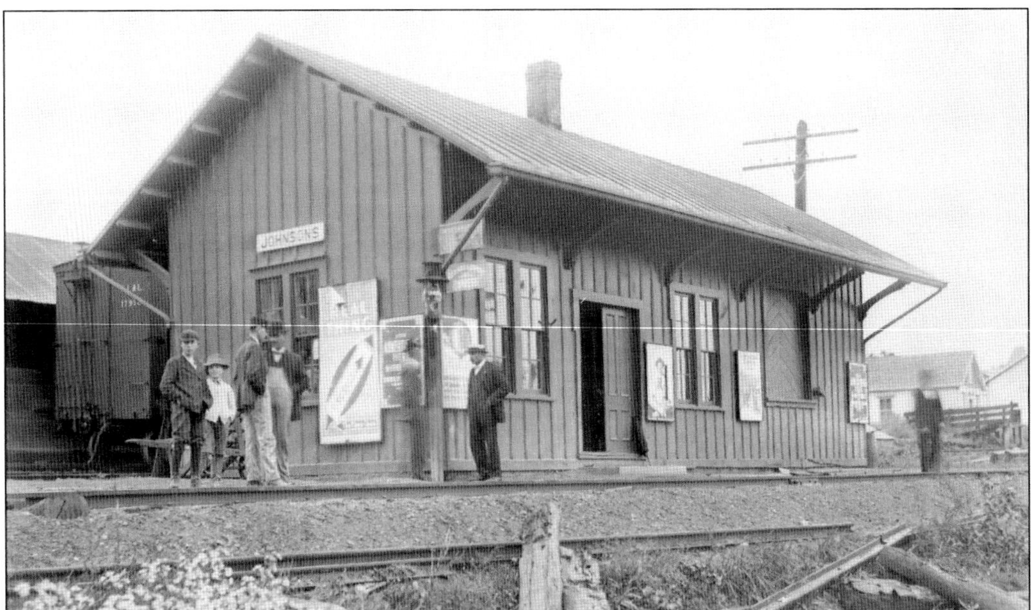

The Johnson depot was quite busy during the years of early passenger service prior to the automobile era. Here we see the depot around 1910 in the era of NYS&W operation of the railroad. The passengers are waiting for the NYS&W passenger train to Middletown. In the background to the right are the stock pen and the Borden's creamery. (New Jersey Midland Railroad Historical Society Collection.)

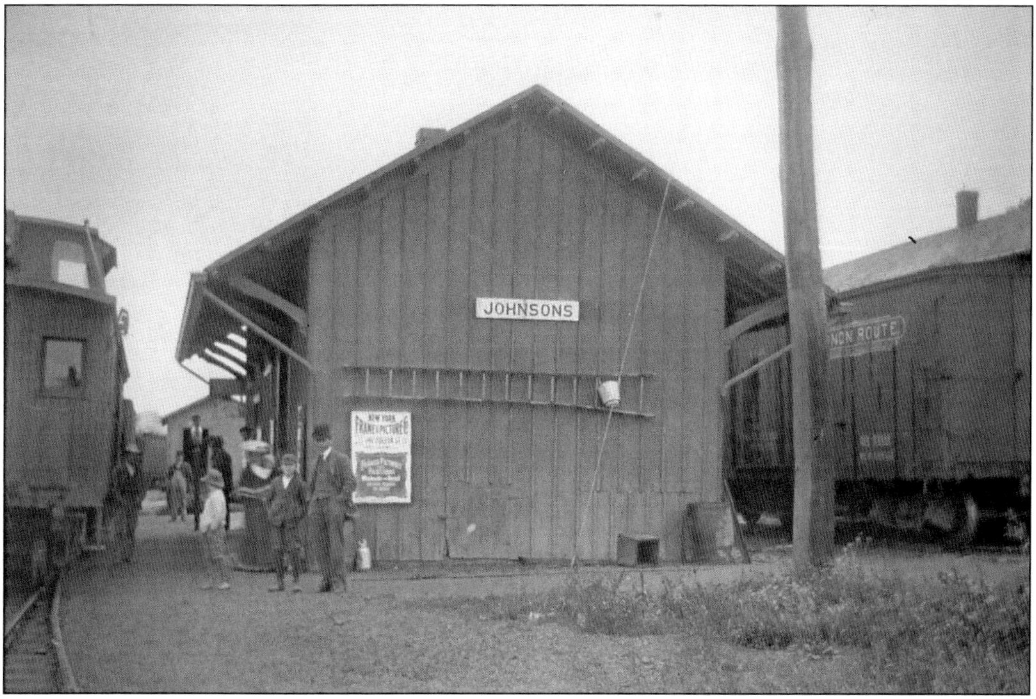

While passengers wait for the passenger train, a local freight has stopped at the depot. Note the cars to the right for the feed dealer and coal shed. The rural depot was the center of the hamlet's activities, until cars and trucks changed the pace of rural life. (Carl Detwyler Collection, M&NJRHS Archives.)

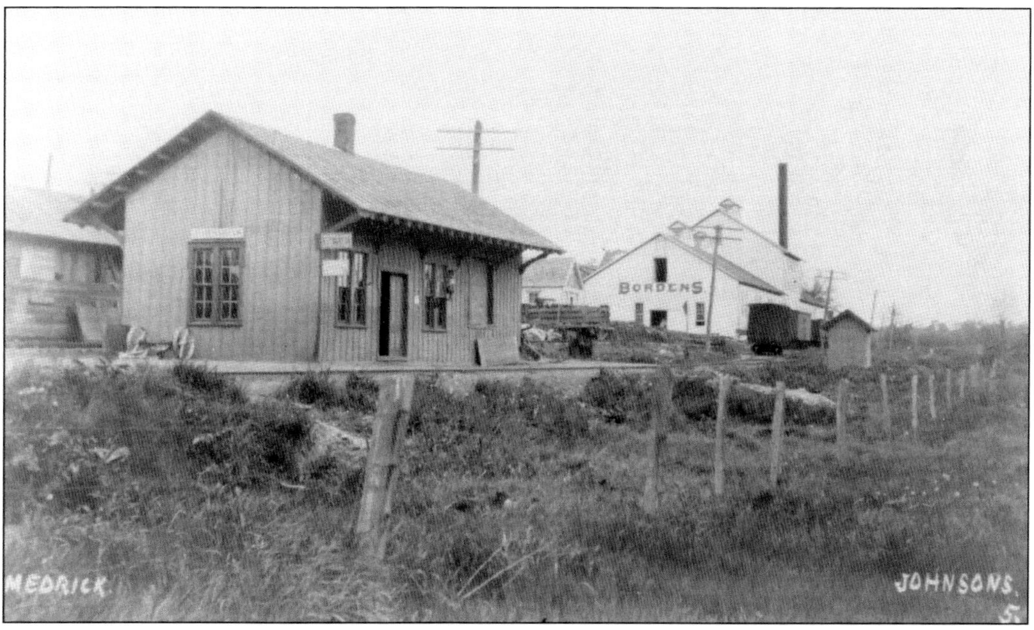

The Borden's creamery at Johnson was the largest creamery on the M&U and the last to ship milk by rail on August 18, 1941. The Johnson depot was east of the Borden's creamery. The building directly behind the depot is the feed dealer and coal shed. (Town of Minisink Museum Collection.)

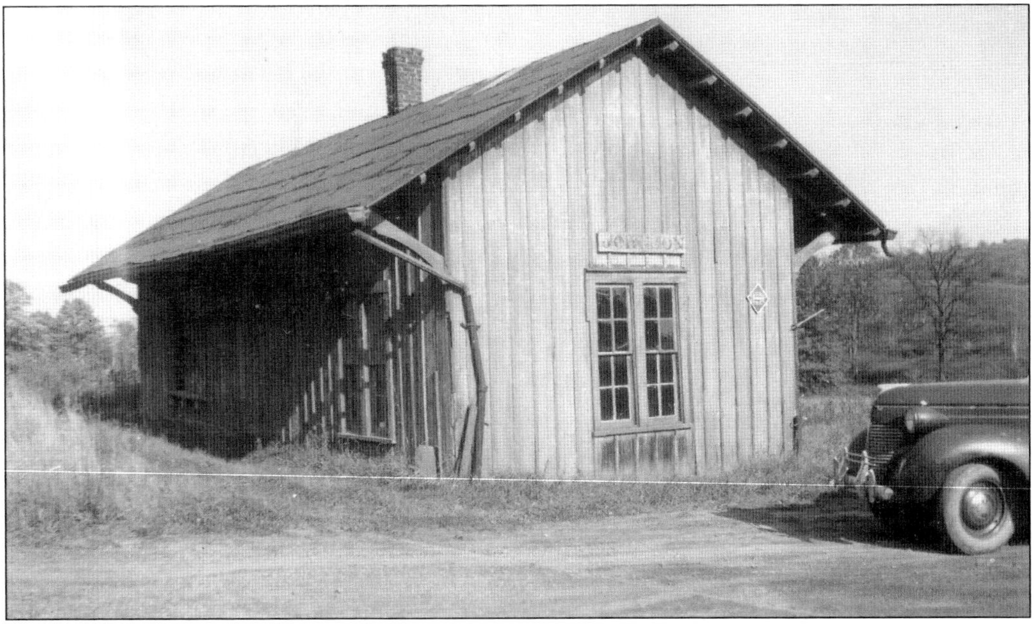

By late August 1941, the M&U's milk traffic was gone forever, as well as the passenger traffic. The Johnson depot's run down and worn out appearance reflects the tough times the M&U faced in its final years of existence. Note the "Johnson" sign on the depot, which replaced the earlier "Johnsons." (Ray Brown Photograph, M&NJRHS Archives.)

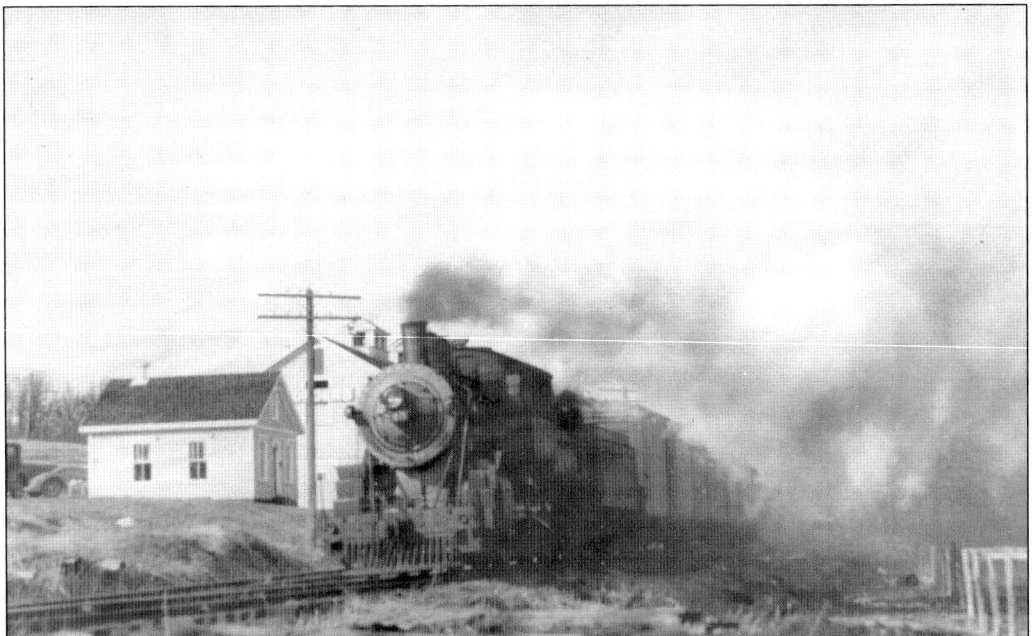

NYO&W U-1 245 is seen here at Johnson running eastbound to Hanford Junction. The M&U motive power is in the NYO&W shops, requiring rented NYO&W power until the M&U locomotive can be returned to the railroad. The large Borden's creamery is in the background with the Borden's office building to the left of the locomotive. (Ray Brown Collection, M&NJRHS Archives.)

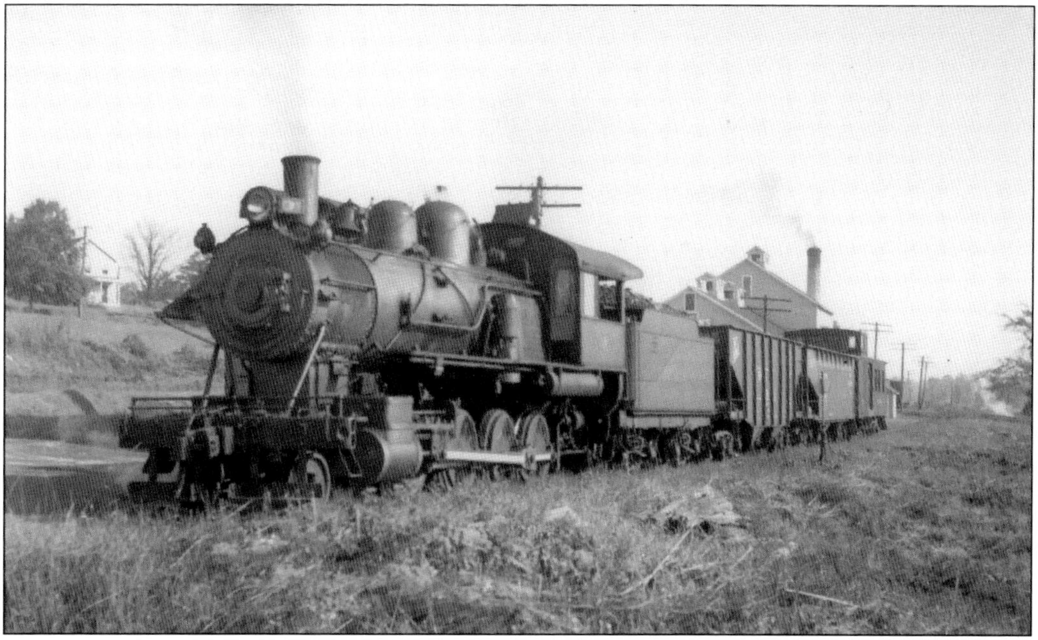

M&U No. 7 is at the Johnson depot on September 19, 1940. The No. 7's consist of two coal cars and caboose 51 is headed for the Hanford Junction interchange with the NYS&W. On the return trip to Middletown, No. 7 will pick up the loaded milk cars from Borden's and deliver them to the Erie. (Steven Maguire Photograph, M&NJRHS Archives.)

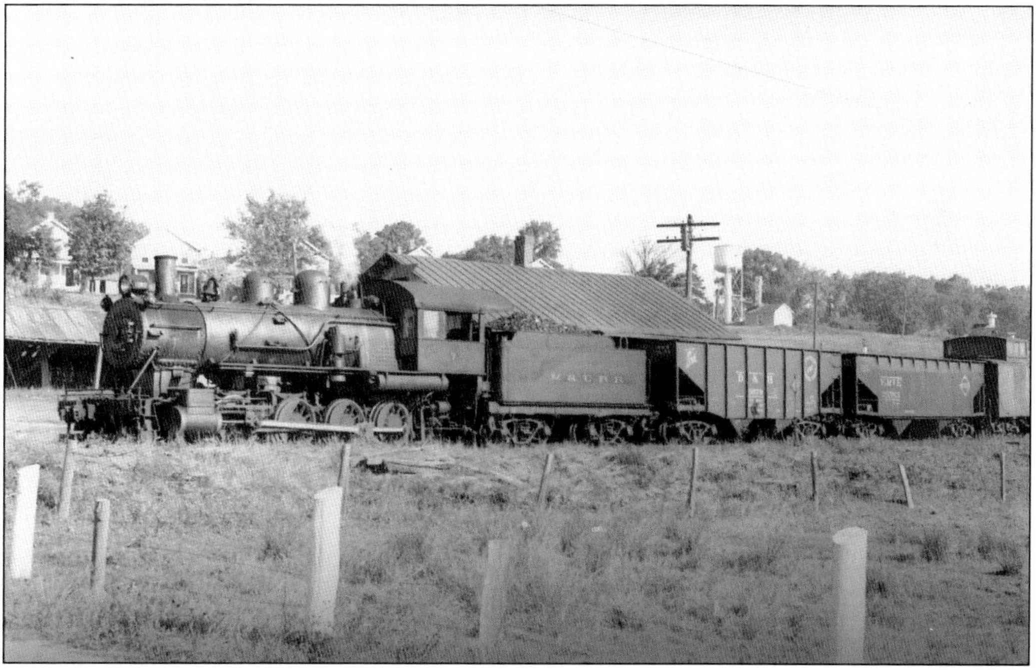

Another view of the train reveals the roof of the Johnson depot. M&U No. 7 has stopped at the depot to receive new train orders from the station agent. The Johnson depot's telegraph call symbol was "JO." The coal cars are lettered for the D&H (Delaware and Hudson) and Erie Railroads. (Steven Maguire Photograph, M&NJRHS Archives.)

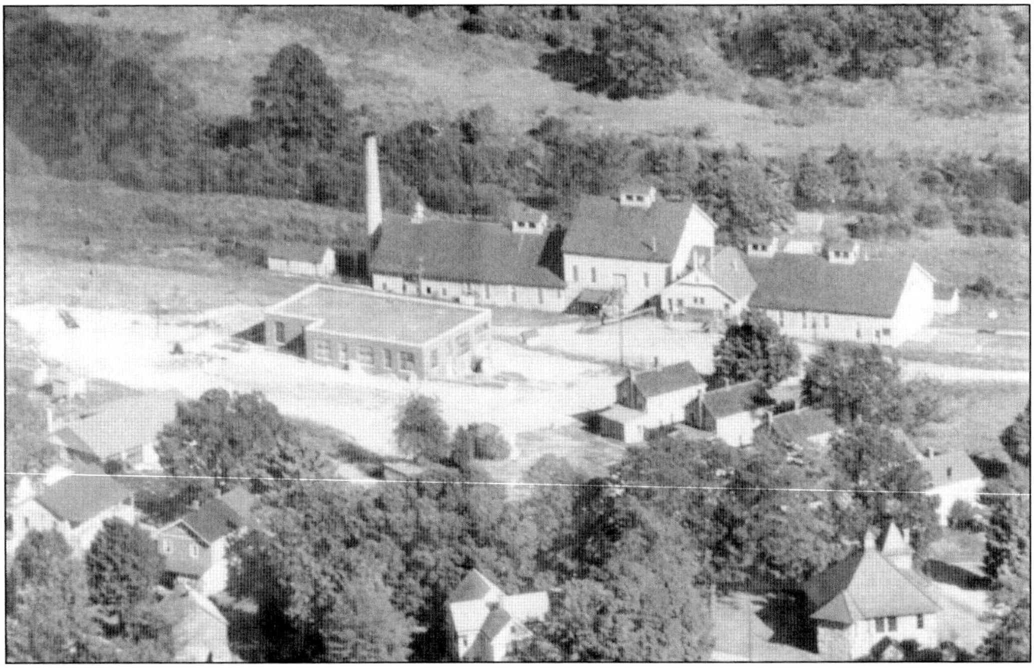

During the mid- to late 1940s, Borden's erected a new creamery and receiving milk station above the old creamery. The portion of the old creamery that has the roofline perpendicular to the rest of the plant was where the raw milk was delivered by local farmers. The boiler house was next to the tall chimney, and it received coal for heating and powering the creamery. (Town of Minisink Museum Collection.)

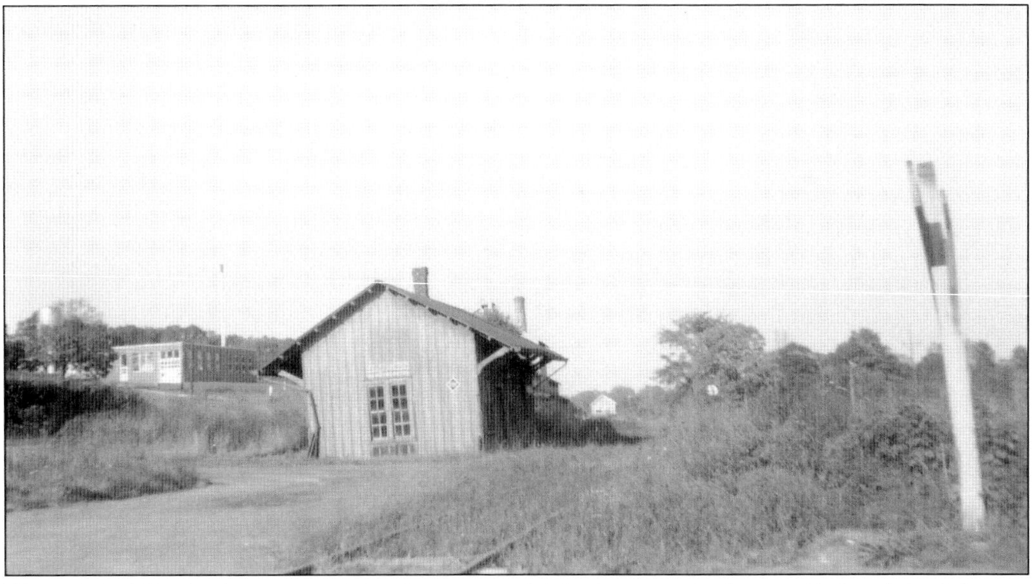

The original Borden's creamery is in the center of this photograph obscured behind the Johnson depot with one of the two remaining icehouses in the distance. The square modern building to the left of the original creamery was the last creamery built in Johnson. It was basically a receiving station for milk to be transported by truck to the Borden's milk plant in Yonkers, New York. (Ray Brown Photograph, M&NJRHS Archives.)

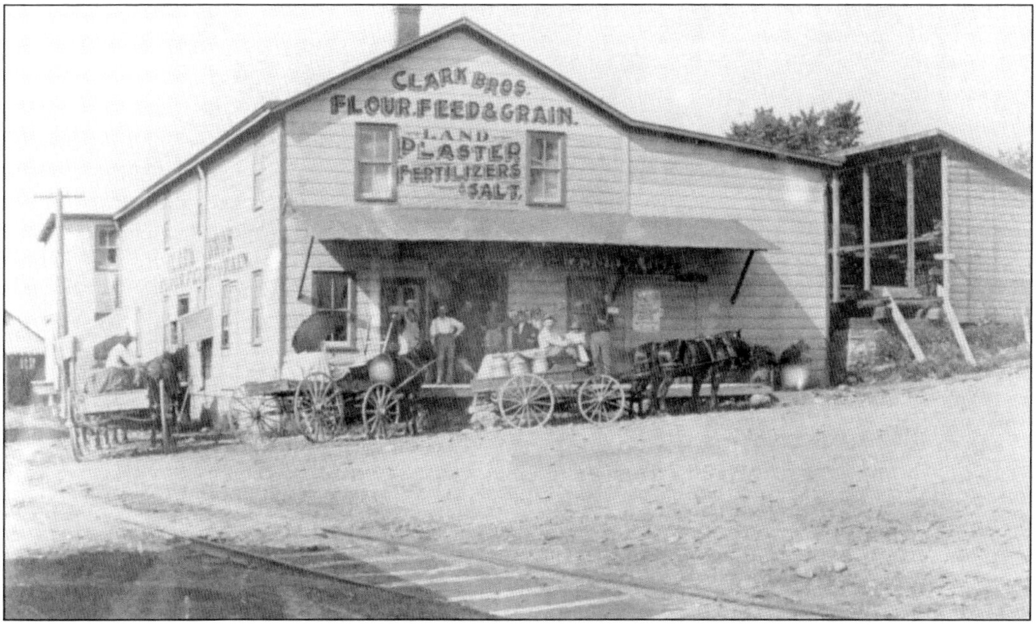

Hulet Clark opened his feed store in Johnson shortly after 1885. By 1898, his two sons, Clarence G. and Niven H., acquired the store and renamed it Clark Brothers. Later it became solely owned by Clarence who renamed the business Clark Feed. Finally grandson Hulet G. Clark ran the store as Clark Company until 1957 when the business was sold to Ford, Weld, and Cox. (Town of Minisink Museum Collection.)

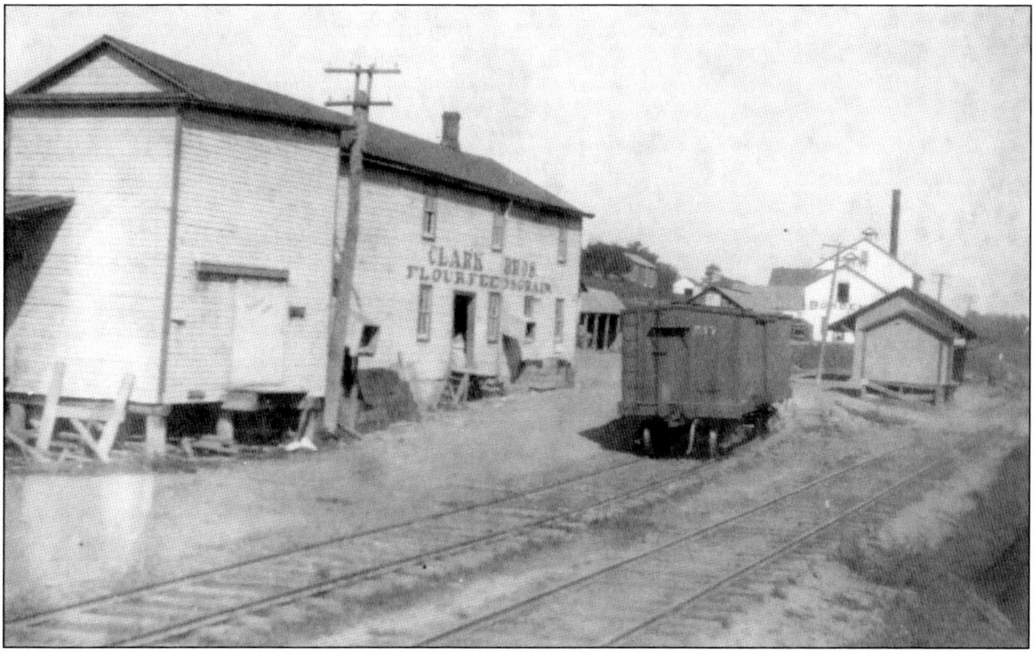

This view of Johnson around the early 1900s looks west on the MU&WG toward Middletown. Clark Brothers is to the left with the Johnson depot and Borden's in the background to the right. The switch for the Borden's creamery is visible to the right of the depot. The small building in front of the depot may be a former milk station. (Town of Minisink Museum Collection.)

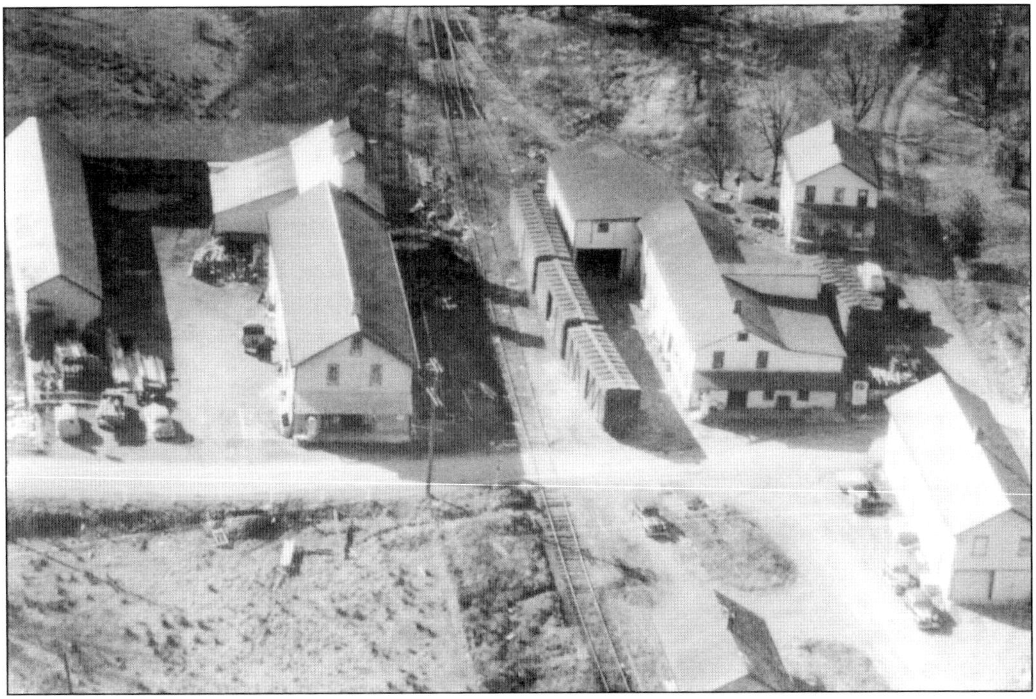

This view of Johnson shows the depot roof at the lower right; Manning Coal, Feed, and Lumber to the left; and Clarks feed store to the right. Clarks used two sidings: one visible with three boxcars is to the left while the other to the right was known as the "hill" track due to the severe grade required to place the boxcar shown at the second floor of the feed store. (Ray Brown Collection, M&NJRHS Archives.)

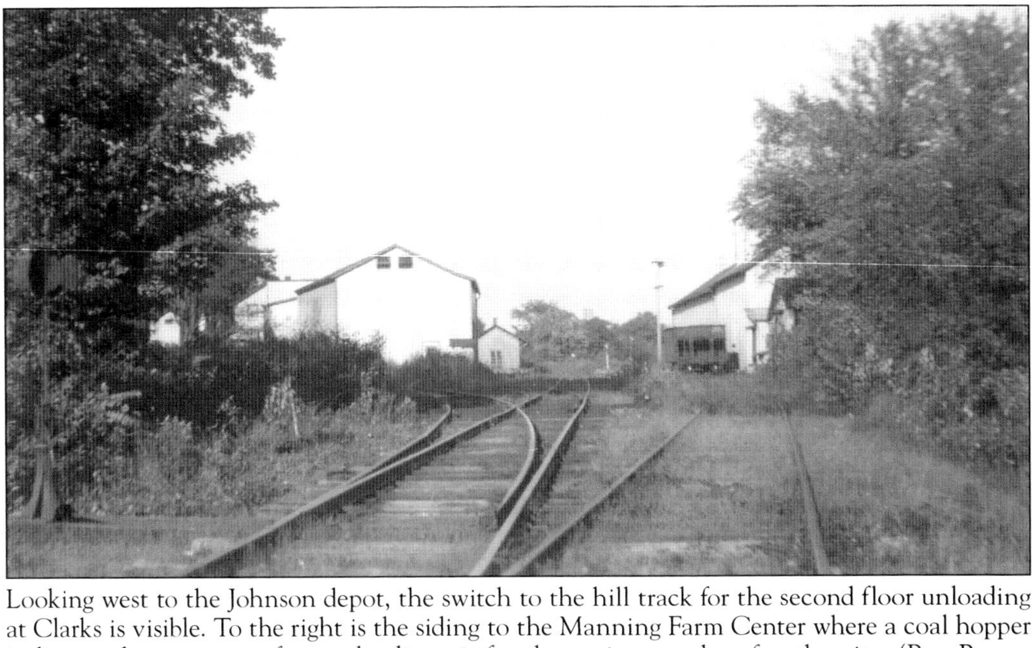

Looking west to the Johnson depot, the switch to the hill track for the second floor unloading at Clarks is visible. To the right is the siding to the Manning Farm Center where a coal hopper indicates the presence of an unloading pit for the various grades of anthracite. (Ray Brown Collection, M&NJRHS Archives.)

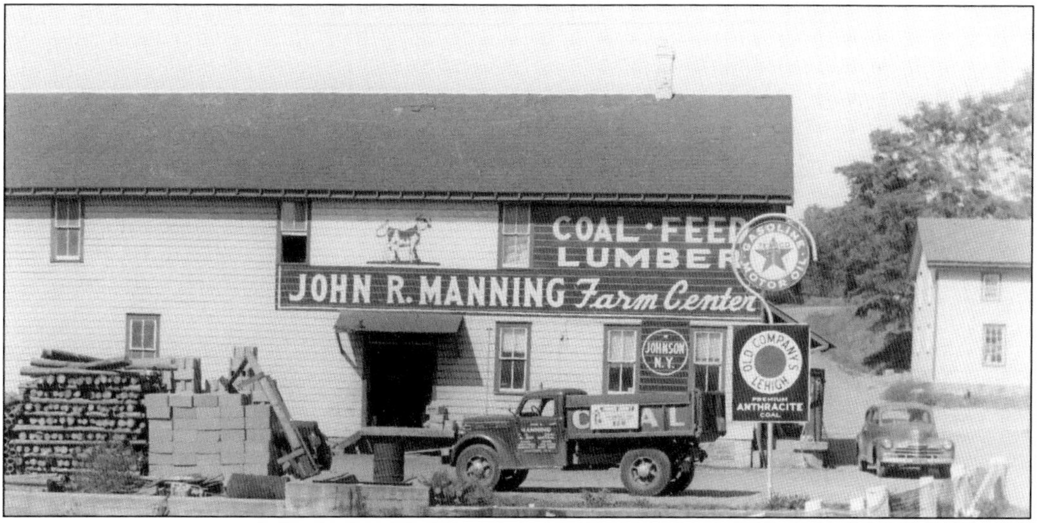

Hiram T. Manning moved his milling business from Gardnerville to Johnson in 1892 and served on the M&U board of directors. The business was conveyed to son John in 1946 when he returned from the army after the war. The Manning Farm Center sold feed and farm supplies along with coal, lumber, and building supplies. Note the signs indicating the sale of Texaco gasoline and Old Company's Lehigh anthracite coal. (Town of Minisink Museum Collection.)

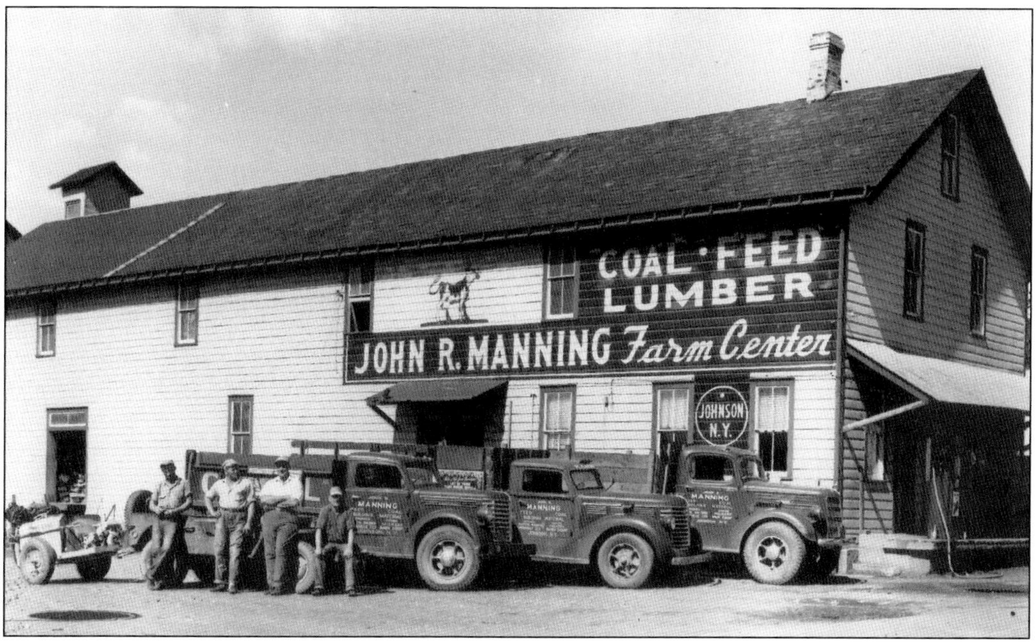

The employees of the Manning Farm Center pose with their trucks. The gas pump is visible under the awning. The focus of the business would change over time from coal, feed, and farm supplies to lumber and building materials. Manning Farm Center would remain a customer of the M&U into the M&NJ era until the late 1960s. (Town of Minisink Museum Collection.)

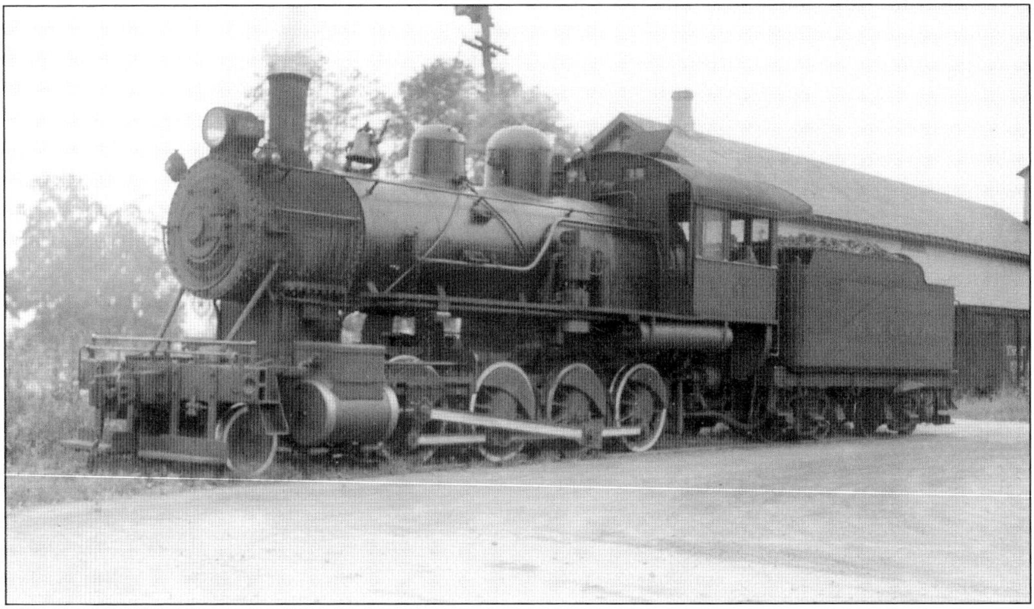

On August 4, 1940, M&U No. 7 is at Johnson switching Clark's Feed Store, Manning Farm Center, and Borden's creamery. After the last Borden's milk traffic was lost to trucks, the M&U still delivered coal and bottles until the new creamery began operation. The Manning Farm Center visible in the background has an Erie boxcar on their siding. (Harold Fagerberg Photograph, M&NJRHS Archives.)

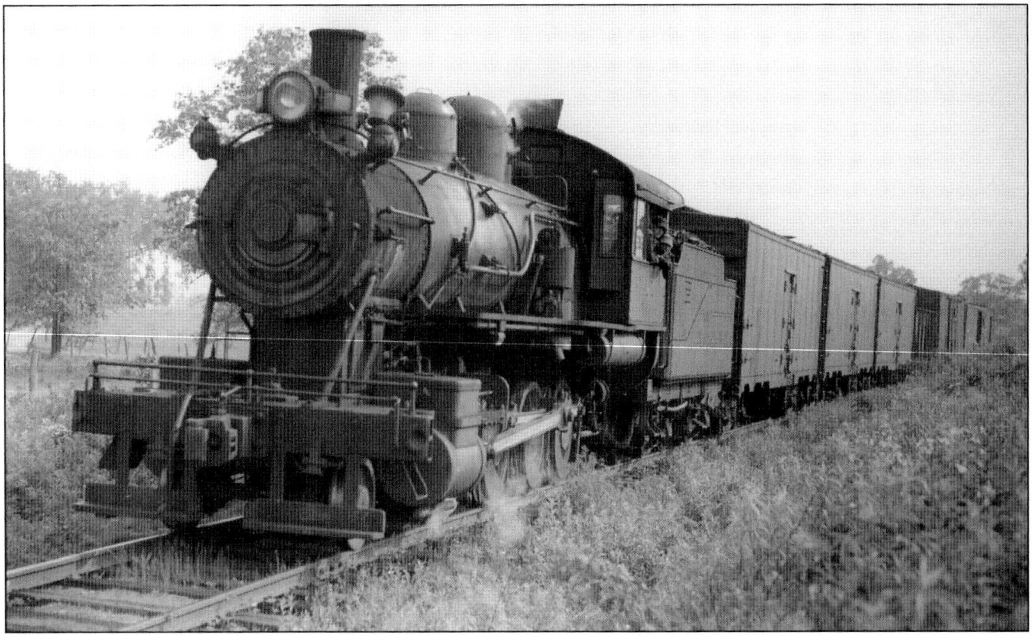

M&U No. 7 is eastbound near Johnson on June 7, 1941, with six cars including three Erie reefers for Borden's and perhaps a load of coal for the powerhouse. In three months, milk will no longer be shipped on the M&U, which will then rely on the overhead coal traffic between the NYO&W and the NYS&W to make up for the lost revenue until 1944. (Robert Collins Photograph, M&NJRHS Archives.)

Five

WESTTOWN

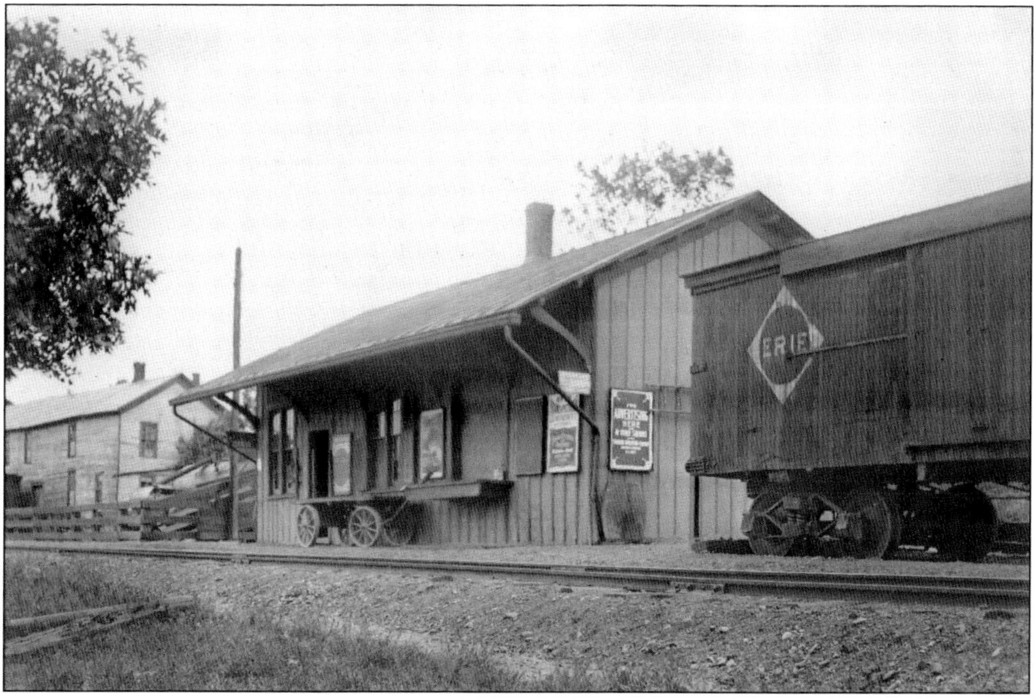

The Westtown depot is pictured around 1910 during the era of NYS&W control of the MU&WG. The M&U telegraph call letters for Westtown were "WT." In the left background is the stock pen used by the M&U to handle shipments of cows to and from farmers, and beyond the pen is the C. G. Clark feed Mill. The Erie boxcar on the station siding is being loaded with less-than-carload freight. (New Jersey Midland Railroad Historical Society Collection.)

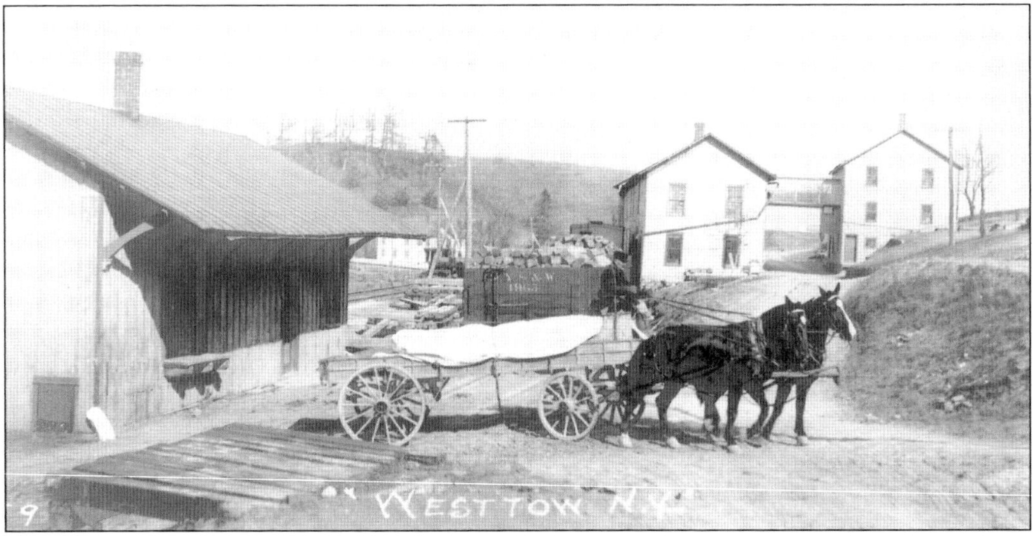

This photograph shows the rear of the Westtown depot around 1900 during the period the NYS&W leased the M&UWG. The runaround siding is visible with an NYS&W gondola behind the team of horses. Of particular interest are the two buildings in the right background. This is the C. G. Clark feed mill, which burned in 1929 and was rebuilt as a large elevator in 1931. (Ray Brown Collection, M&NJRHS Archives.)

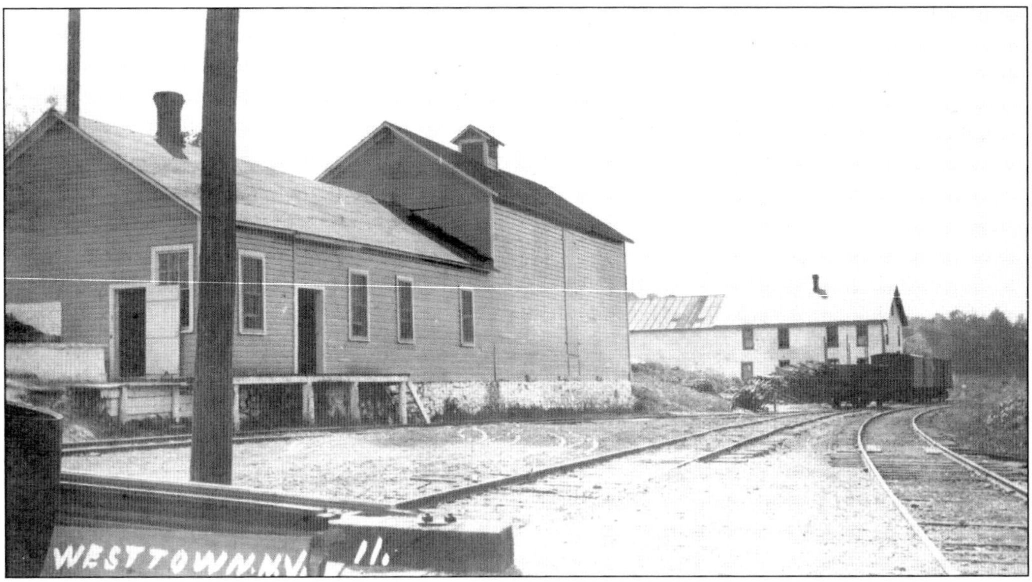

This view was taken from the Westtown depot looking east toward Unionville during the early 1900s. The Borden's creamery is to the left, while the former Sheffield creamery is in the background. The Borden's building would eventually become a Grange League Federation (GLF) feed store. In the early 1940s, GLF built a large feed mill along the M&U at Dolson Avenue in Middletown. (Ray Brown Collection, M&NJRHS Archives.)

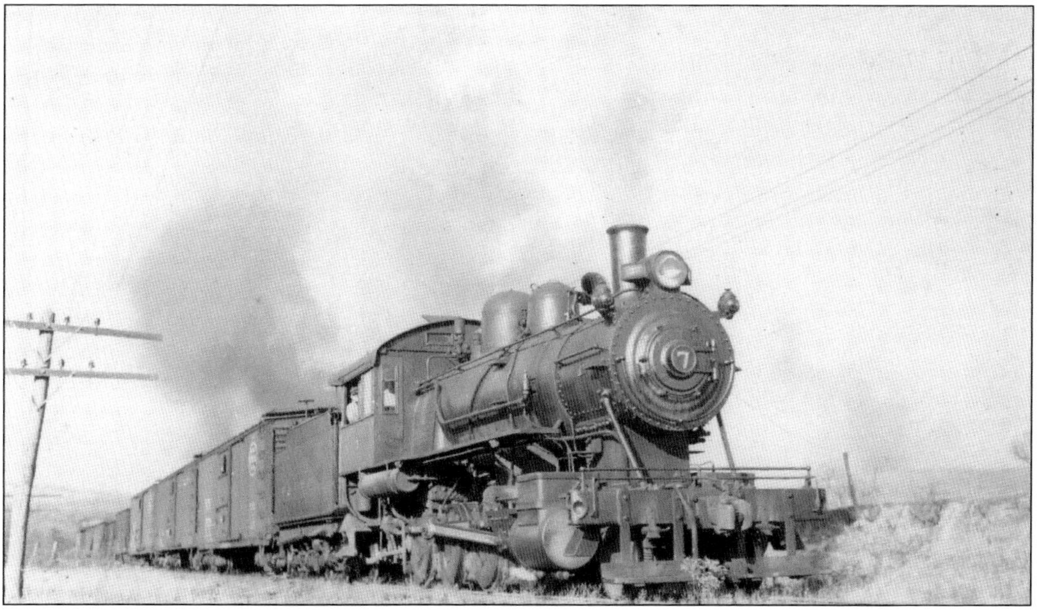

Nearing Westtown around 1940 to 1944, M&U No. 7 leads an eastbound to Hanford Junction with a consist of three boxcars and five hopper cars. The coal cars most likely came from the NYO&W at Middletown and are filled with hard coal from the northern anthracite field around Scranton, Pennsylvania. (Ray Brown Collection, M&NJRHS Archives.)

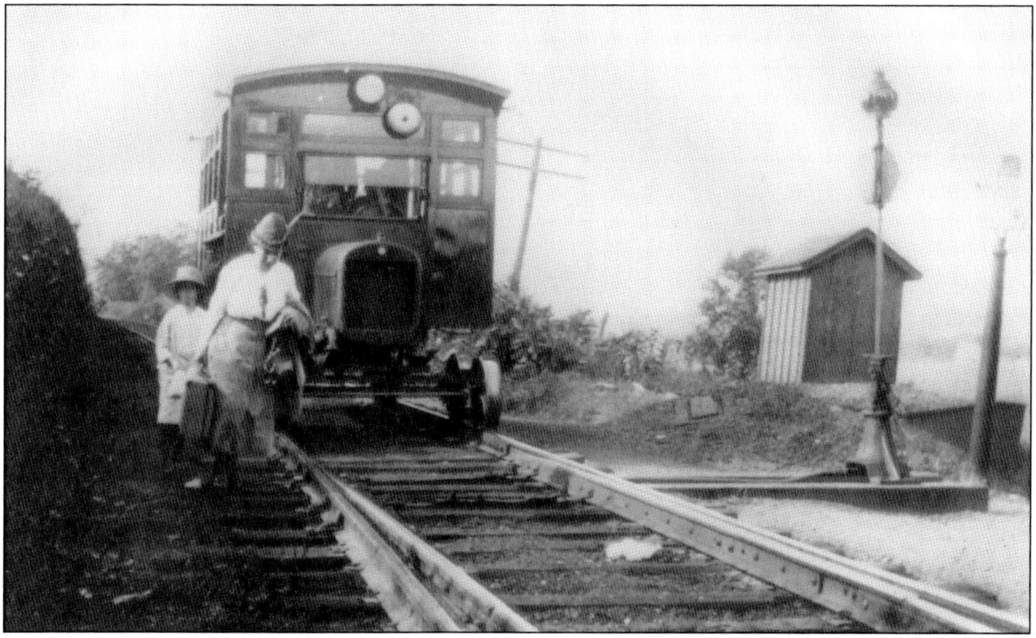

This photograph, around 1922 to 1926, shows M&U Reo rail bus No. 11 westbound to Middletown having just dropped off a mother and daughter at Westtown. The switch stand at the right is for the runaround track that ran east to west for the Clark feed mill and the two former creameries. During 1926, Reo's No. 11 and No. 10 will be traded in for the Brill M-55 railcar. (O&WRHS Collection.)

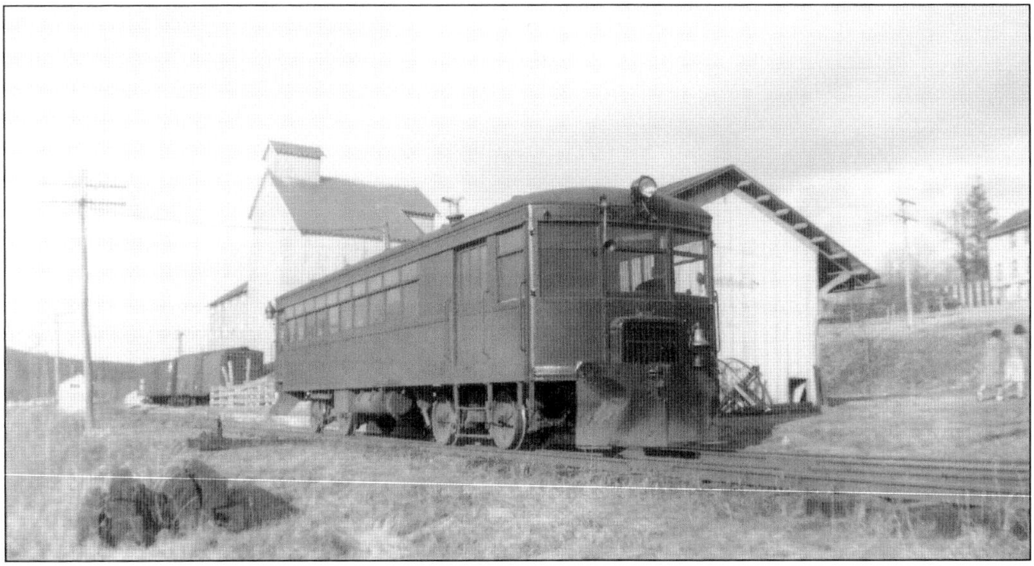

The M&U's M-55 Brill car has just dropped off two high school girls returning from Middletown High School. The former Clark feed mill burned during late 1929 and was rebuilt during 1931 into the large feed mill seen in the background. This facility would receive feed along with other farm supplies including bagged cement, lumber, and coal. The plant would be sold in 1954 to Ford, Weld, and Cox. (Edgar Mead Photograph, M&NJRHS Archives.)

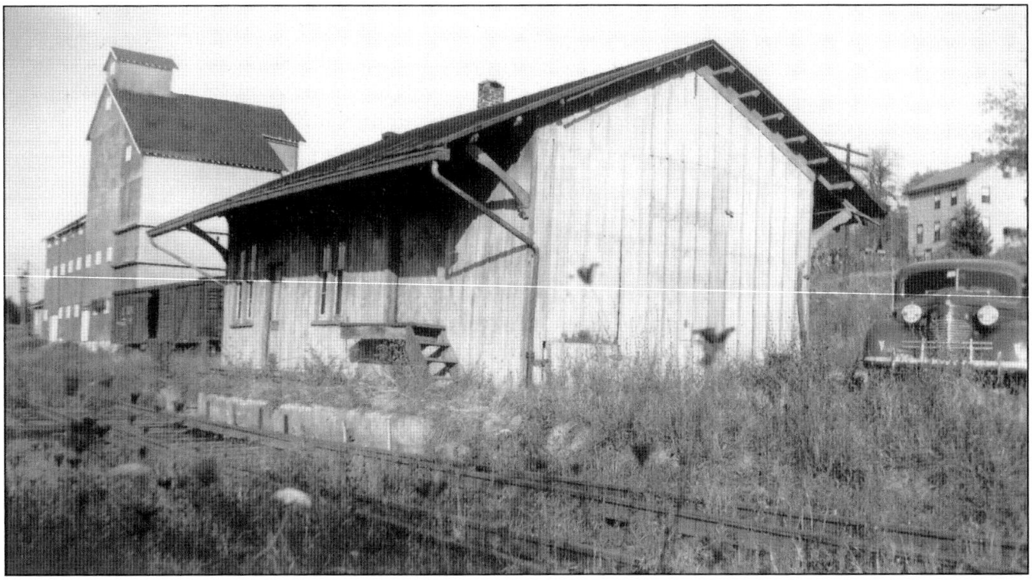

The Westtown depot looks a bit worse for wear during the 1940s. Towering over the Westtown depot is Clarks feed mill and farm store, which was one of the largest feed mills in all of Orange County. The boxcars were filled with grain and were manually shoveled out into an unloading pit from which a conveyor would take the grain into various bins within the elevator. (Ray Brown Photograph, M&NJRHS Archives.)

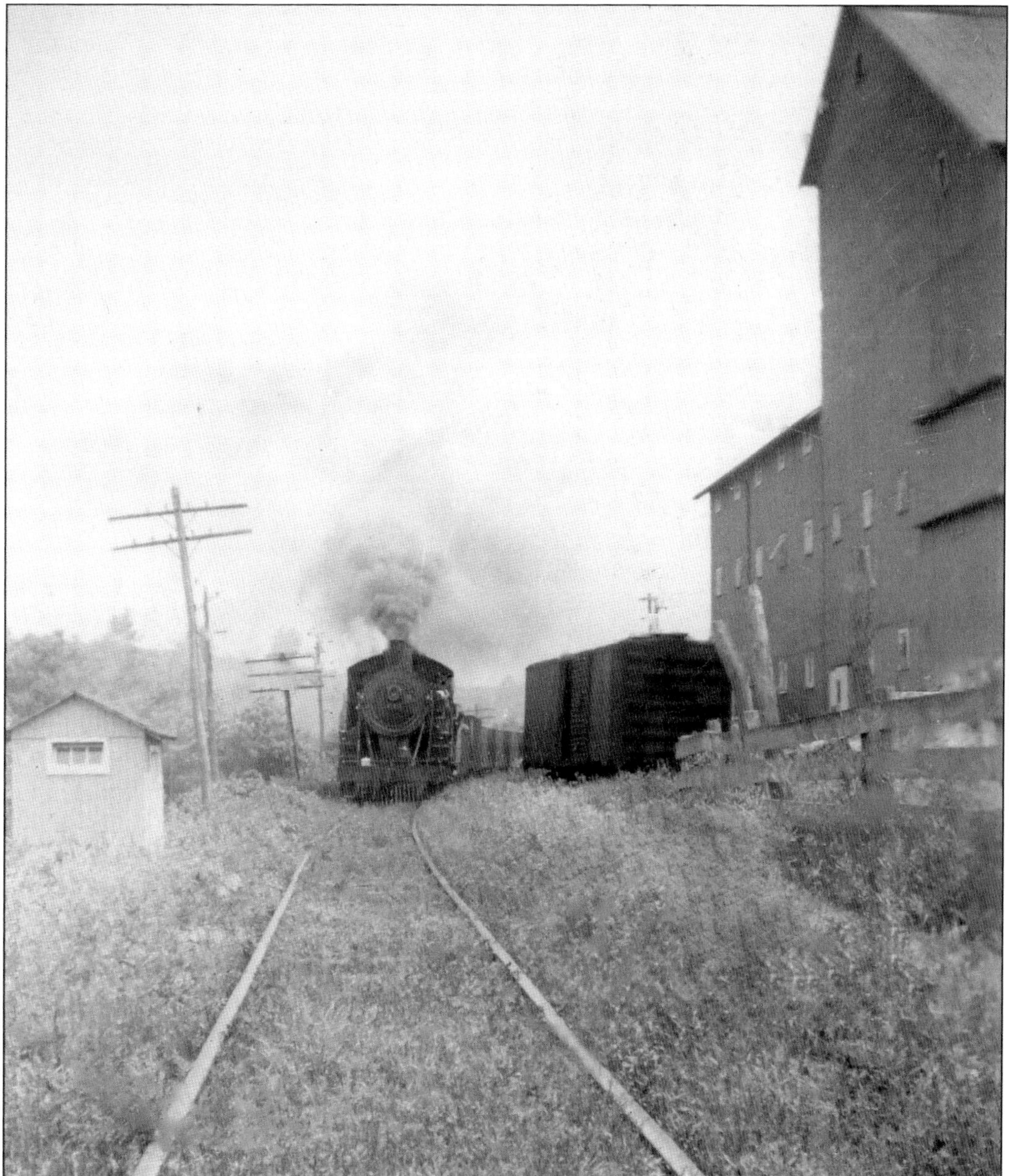

NYO&W U-1 class 4-6-0 244 is eastbound from 1940 to 1943 passing Clark's feed mill in Westtown. The 244 has a solid train of coal cars from the NYO&W destined for the NYS&W at Hanford Junction approximately 3.5 miles east of the Westtown depot. During this era, two to three round trips a day from Middletown to Hanford Junction and return were being operated. One or more of these trains would deliver and pick up cars at the various M&U stations running in either direction between Middletown and Unionville/Hanford Junction There is a small portion of the cattle pen visible to the right of the photograph with a tool shed on the left of the main line. Directly behind the photographer, Westtown station agent Herb Hockenberry, is the Westtown depot. This photograph does put into perspective just how massive the Clark feed mill and farm store was compared to railroad equipment. (Herb Hockenberry Photograph, Town of Minisink Museum Collection.)

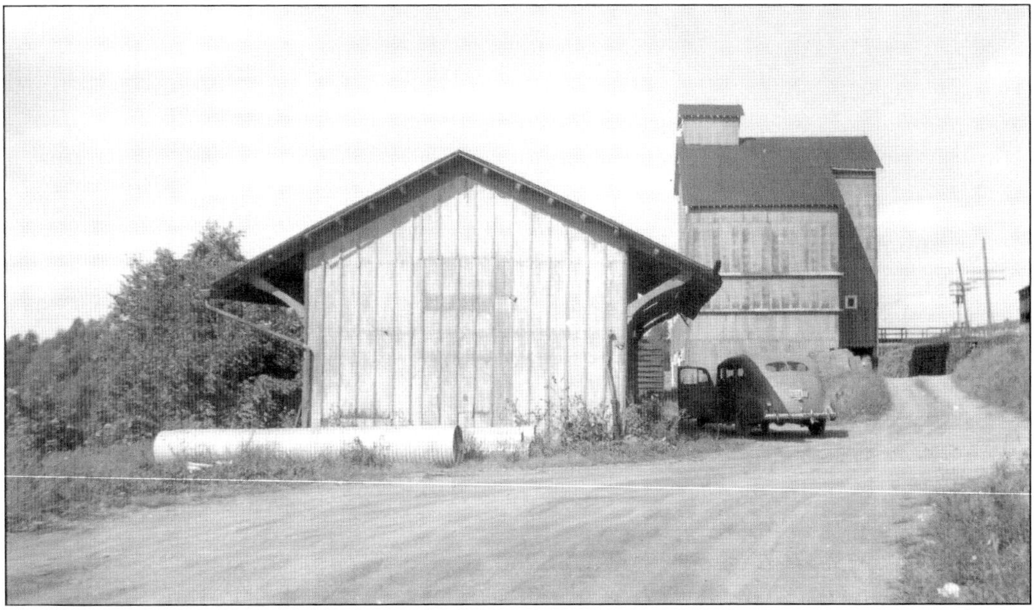

In this 1940s view of the Westtown depot, pictured is the side of Clark's feed mill. Note the bridge over Depot Street in the distance. In addition to feed, Clark's received lumber, farm supplies, and coal. The lumber shed still stands but is out of sight to the right. (Ray Brown Photograph, M&NJRHS Archives.)

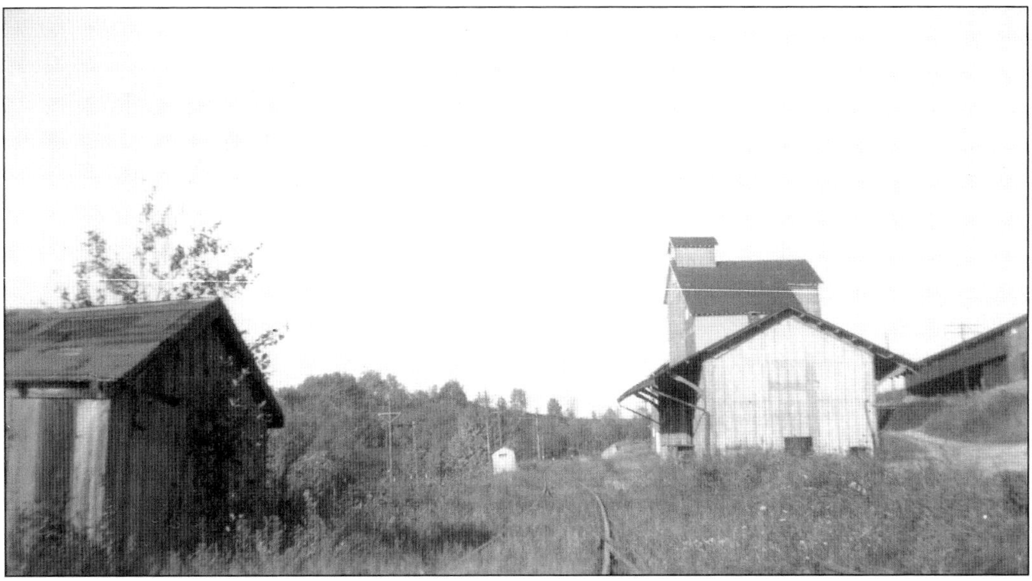

In this view around the 1940s looking west from the Westtown depot, the motorcar shed for the maintenance of way crew is to the left. In the background is Clark's feed mill with the associated lumber shed visible to the right above Depot Street. Note that the track is obscured by weeds now that the volume of traffic has dropped on the M&U, allowing Mother Nature to begin to reclaim the right-of-way. (Ray Brown Photograph, M&NJRHS Archives.)

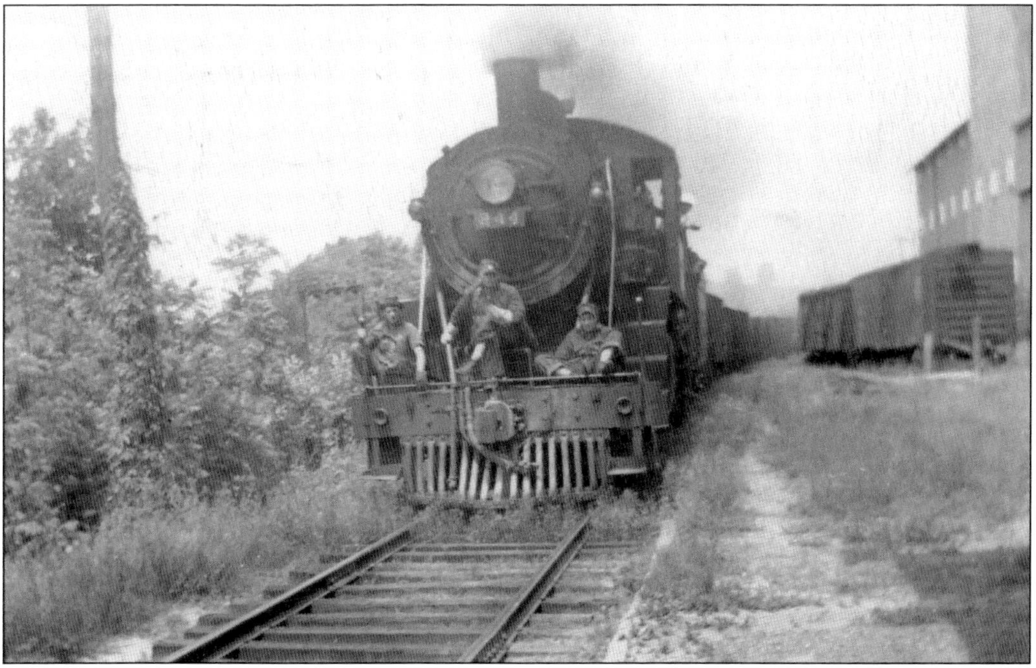

On May 31, 1944, Westtown station agent Herbert Hockenberry photographed O&W 244 with a long eastbound coal train headed to Hanford Junction during the last surge in overhead traffic between the NYO&W and the NYS&W. The last period of this coal traffic occurred from late 1943 to December 1944 requiring only one train to Hanford each day. To the right of the locomotive is the shadow of the Westtown depot. (Herb Hockenberry Photograph, M&NJRHS Archives.)

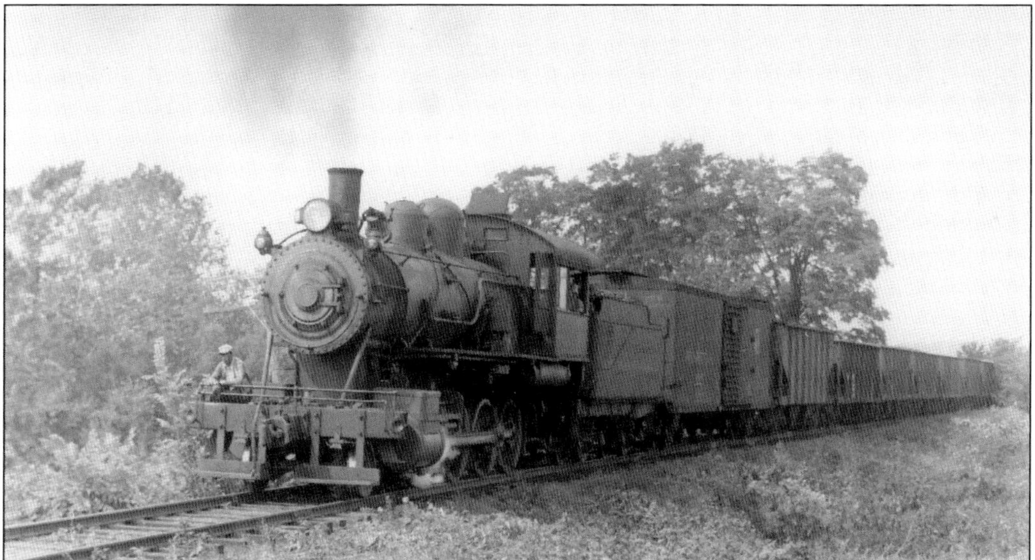

On July 17, 1940, an M&U crewman is riding on the front of engine No. 7 in an attempt to stay cool on a summer day. The train is eastbound near Westtown with a boxcar and a long string of loaded hopper cars filled with anthracite coal during the first surge in overhead traffic with all of these cars bound for the NYS&W interchange at Hanford Junction. (Jack Farrell Photograph, M&NJRHS Archives.)

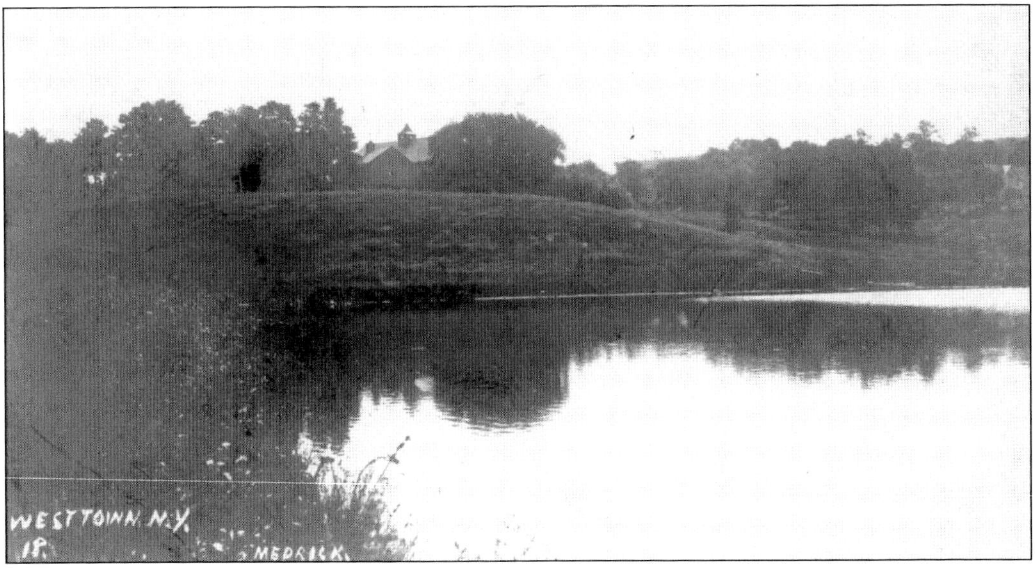

Just east of Westtown was Lockenhurst Pond, shown here during the warmer months of the year. Like many local ponds, it was used for ice harvesting by local creameries and icehouses during the winter. On occasion, ice was shipped via the M&U to other creameries in the northeast, which required large quantities of ice to fill their icehouses. (Ray Brown Collection, M&NJRHS Archives.)

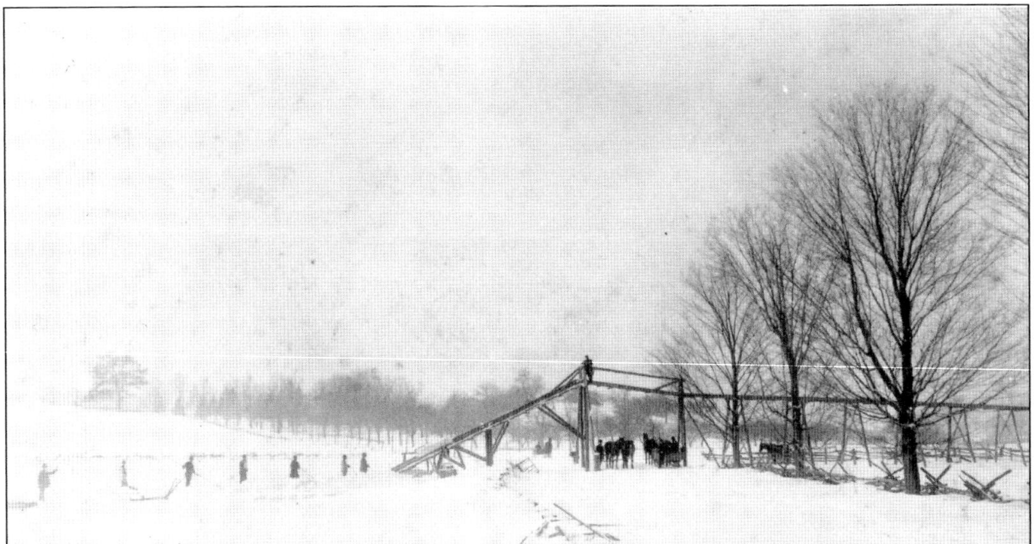

During the winter, Lockenhurst Pond's ice would be cut and loaded onto refrigerator cars stored on a special siding. The wood scaffolding allowed the ice to slide to the siding on the other side of the highway. During the winter ice-harvesting seasons, prior to the time Borden's built its own ice manufacturing plant in Johnson; ice occasionally was shipped to Borden's via the M&U. (Ray Brown Collection, M&NJRHS Archives.)

Six

Unionville and Hanford Junction

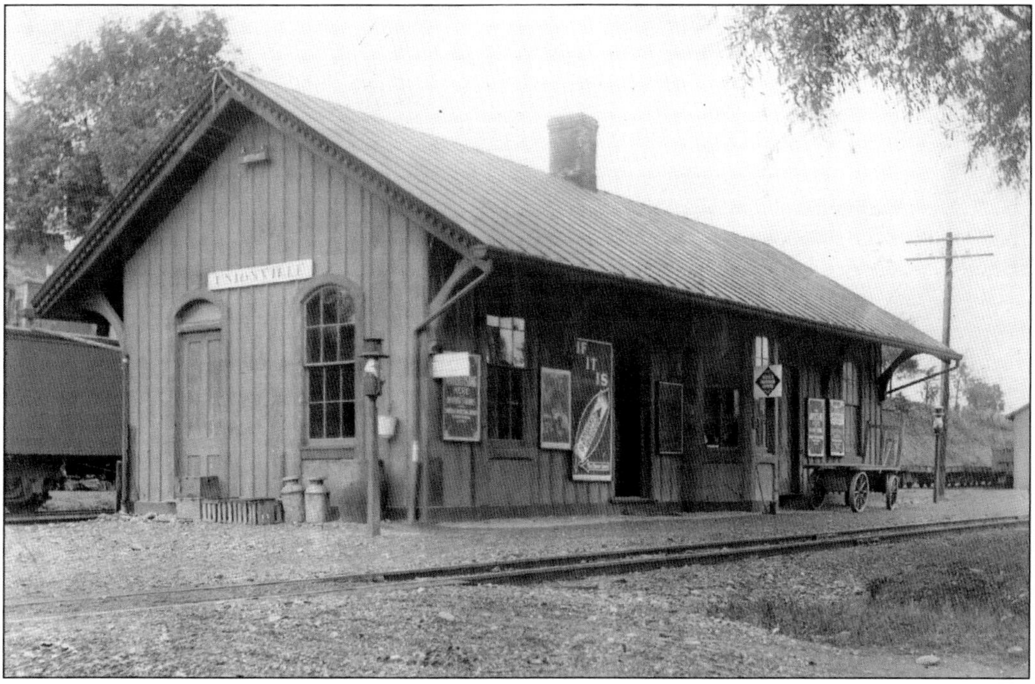

The second largest depot on the M&U was located at Unionville and is shown here around 1910. The NYS&W built an engine terminal with a one-stall engine house and a 50-foot turntable just west of the depot. A two-track yard was used for team track service just west of the depot as seen here in the left and right background. (New Jersey Midland Railroad Historical Society Collection.)

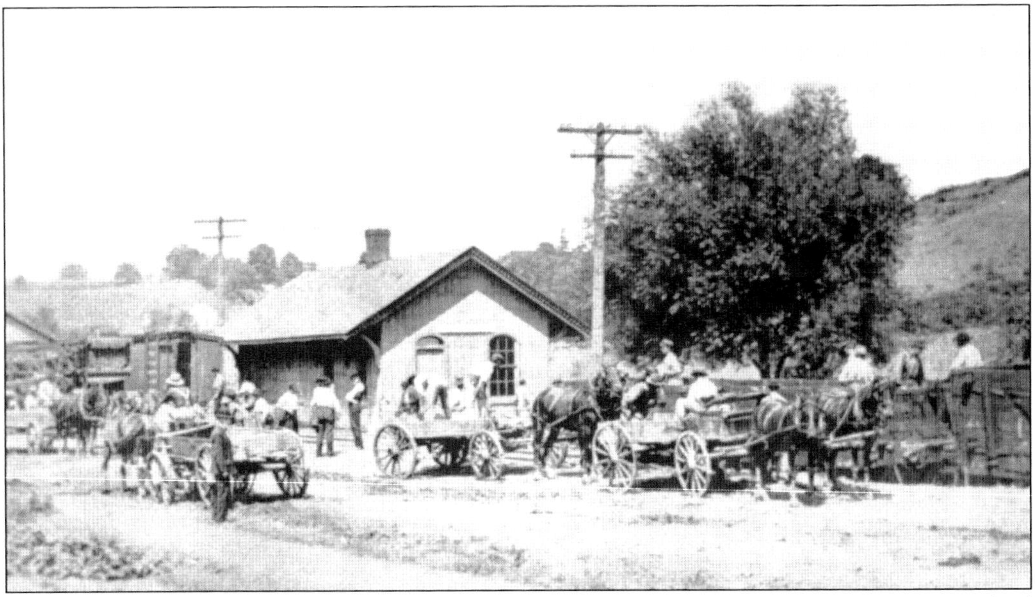

These two images, above and below, were taken during the 1906 construction of the Standard Oil pipeline from upstate New York through Oil City, south of Unionville. A large oil tank and pumping station were located at Oil City to send the oil down the pipeline into New Jersey. The railroad cars are in the two-track yard that was used for team track service and carry construction materials and pipes for this large project. The M&U Unionville depot is in the center above and to the right in the picture below. The Unionville freight house is in the left background in both photographs. The mode of transportation to move the materials to the construction sites was a wagon with a team of horses. That is where the name "team" track comes from. The receiver or shipper was not located along the railroad and thus required transportation, a team of horses, to or from the railroad siding to receive or ship freight. (Both photographs, Town of Minisink Museum Collection.)

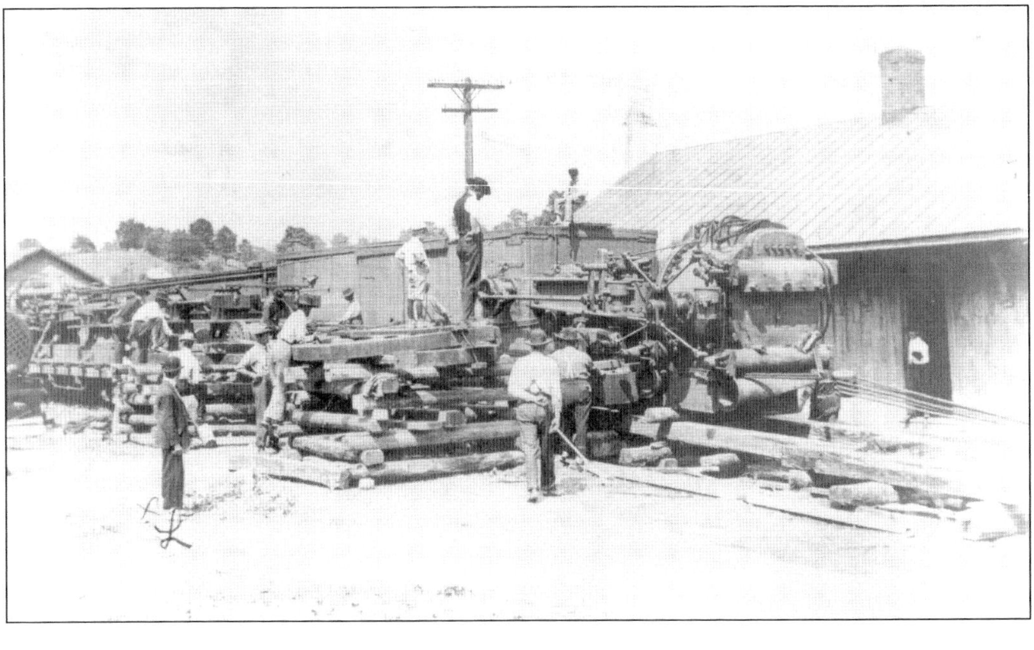

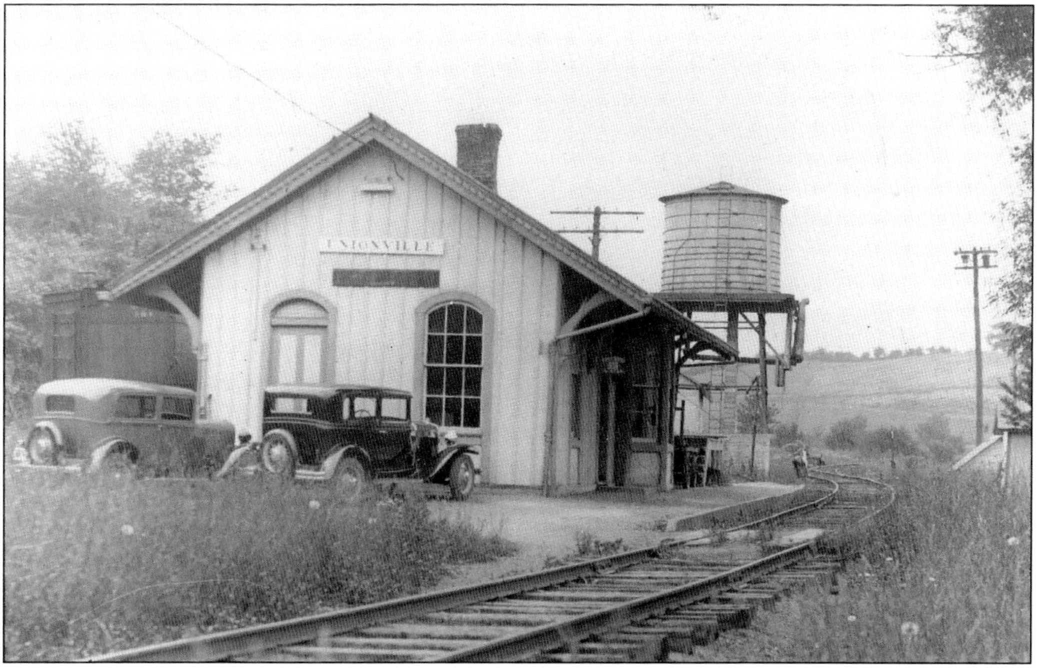

Looking west along the M&U in June 1932, there is a boxcar in the two-track yard next to the Unionville depot. The automobiles are quite a change from the teams of horses in the previous images around 1906. The M&U water tank is behind the depot along with the freight house. In the 1937 view below, the automobile has changed in style and horsepower, and the depot has lost the sign bearing its name. The water tank and freight house are more clearly seen as the M&U main line curves west out of the village toward Westtown. The telegraph call letters for the Unionville depot under M&U management and later the M&NJ were "UN." (Both photographs, Ray Brown Collection, M&NJRHS Archives.)

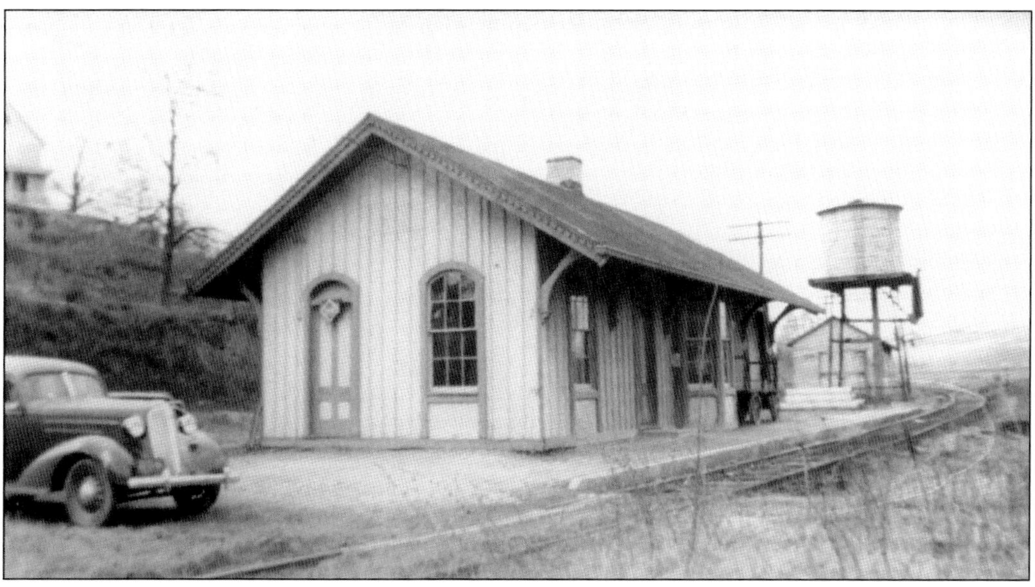

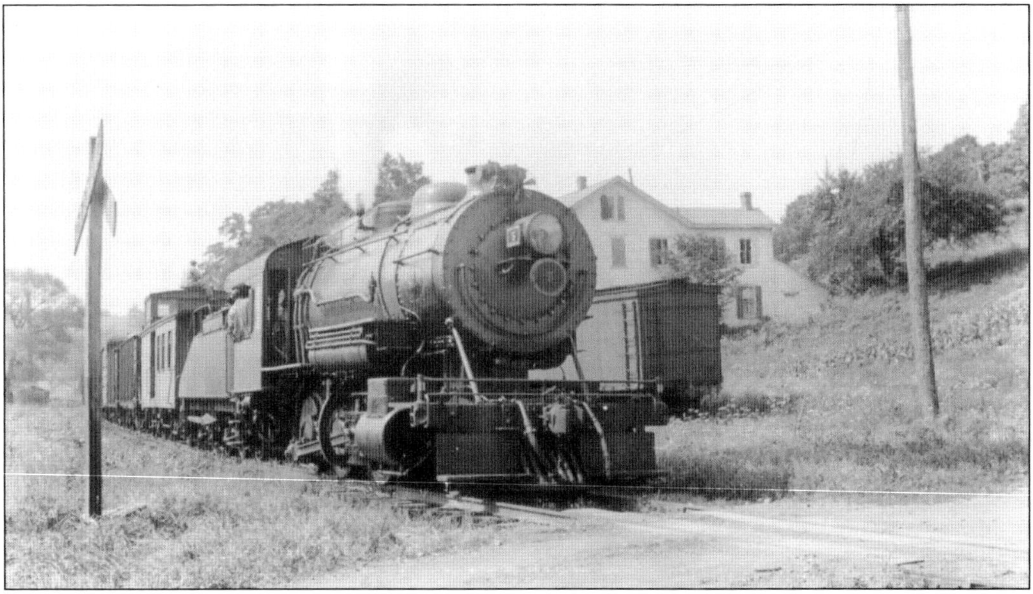

M&U No. 5 is switching in Unionville next to Railroad Avenue and the Unionville yard on August 17, 1931. Upon closer inspection of this photograph, the engineer can be seen leaning out of the locomotive cab while running the engine in reverse and looking up to the crewman on top of the caboose for hand signals from the members of the crew farther down along the train. (James Speer Photograph, M&NJRHS Archives.)

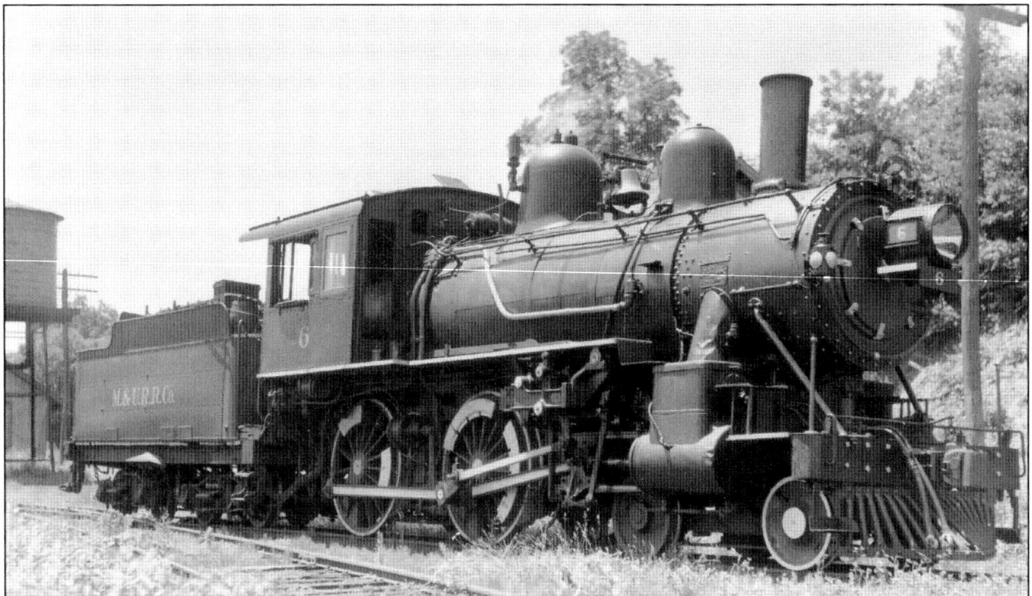

On June 26, 1937, M&U No. 6 is next to the east leg of the Unionville wye having been turned for the return trip west to Middletown. The water tank and freight house are in the left background along with the Unionville depot out of sight to the far left. (Ray Brown Collection, M&NJRHS Archives.)

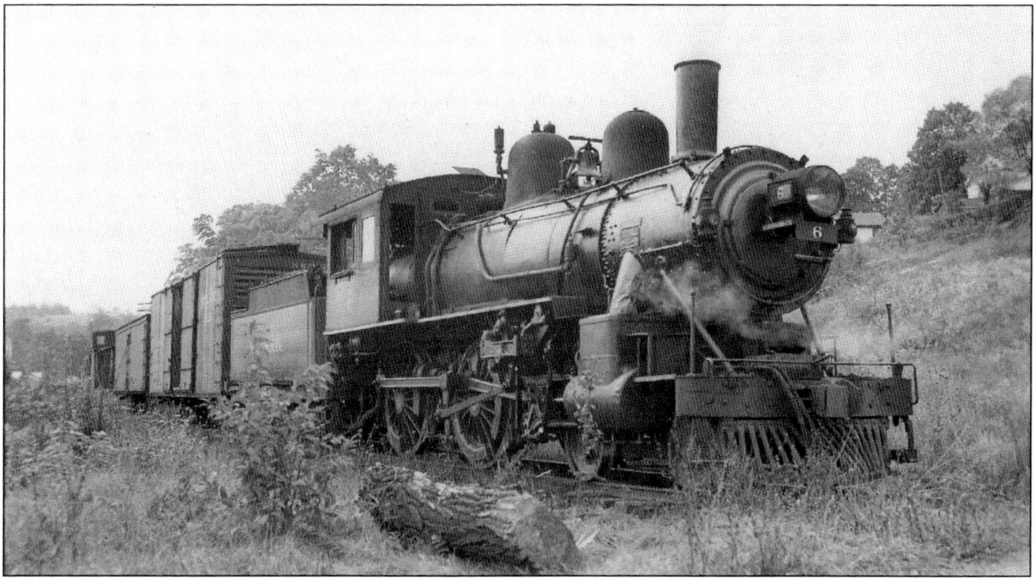

Just east of the Unionville depot, M&U No. 6 waits for her crew who are getting their train orders during an October day in 1936. The train has a boxcar, a refrigerator car, and a coal hopper along with caboose 51. The Unionville depot is to the right behind the photographer. (Ray Brown Collection, M&NJRHS Archives.)

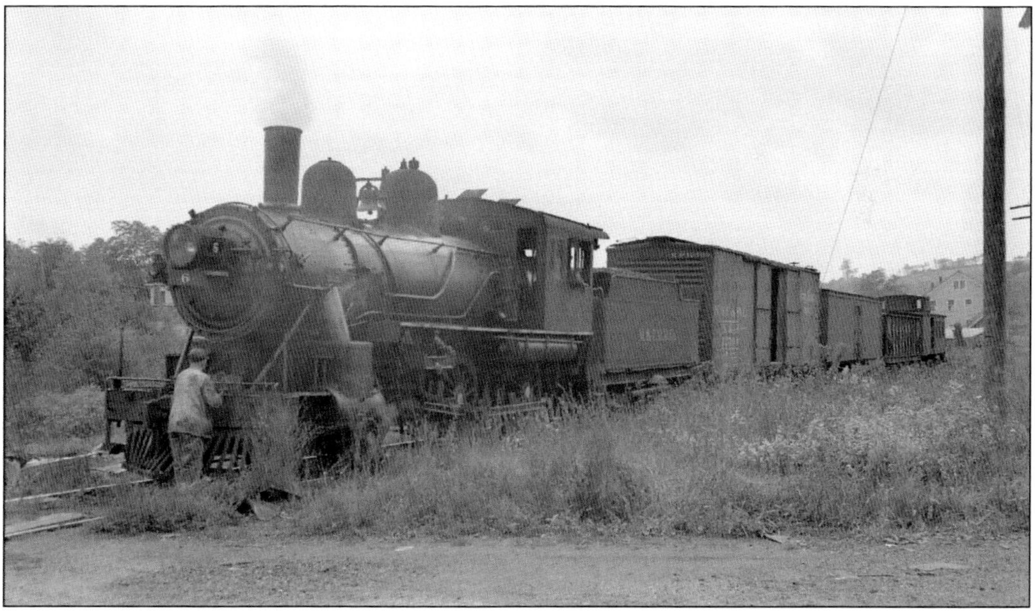

In another view of the train, Railroad Avenue is in the foreground with the depot directly behind the photographer. A crewman is in front of No. 6's pilot with the fireman in the cab window of the engine. In the background to the right of caboose 51 is the creamery in Unionville. No. 6 has returned from Hanford Junction and performed all switching in the village. (Ray Brown Collection, M&NJRHS Archives.)

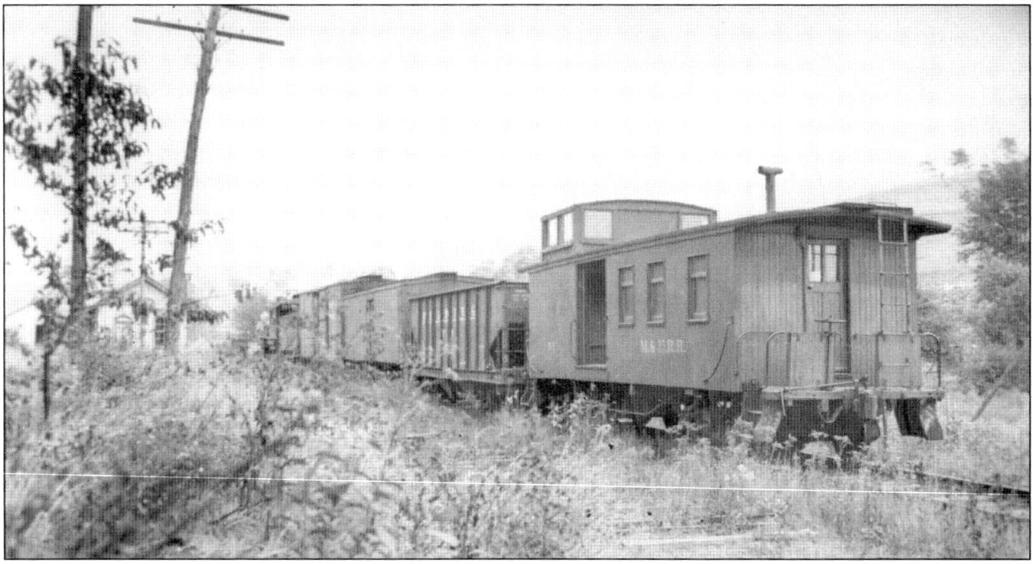

Looking at caboose 51 from the rear of the train clearly shows the location of the depot, freight house, and water tank relative to the westbound freight. Obscured in the weeds to the left of the caboose is the lead track to the two-track yard next to the depot. The M&U's daily freight train schedule at this time was simply one train east to Hanford Junction and the return trip west to Middletown. (Ray Brown Collection, M&NJRHS Archives.)

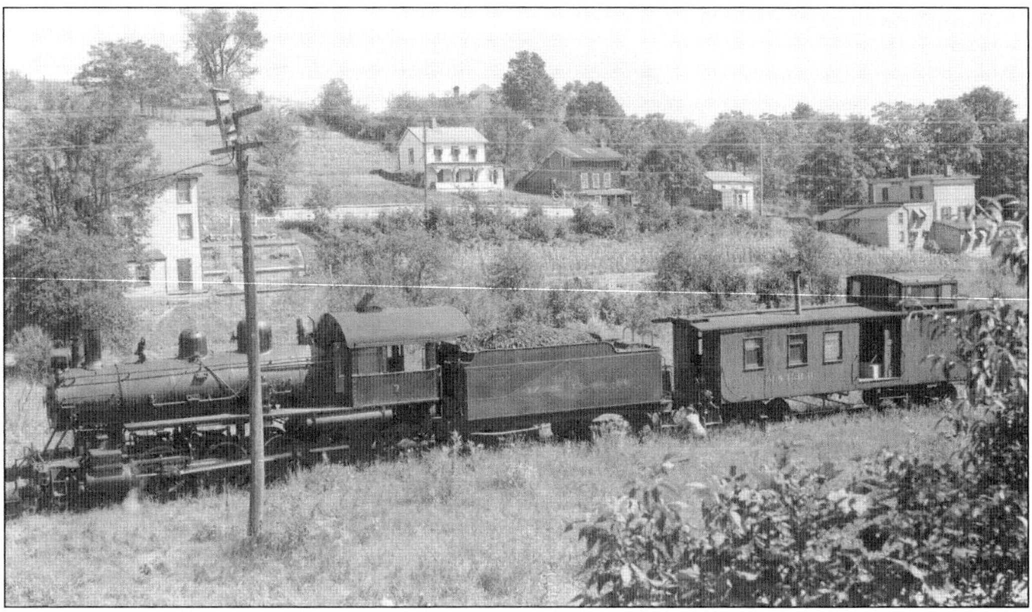

On September 3, 1941, No. 7 and caboose 51 are on the M&U main westbound just east of the Unionville depot and Railroad Avenue as two crewmen converse while passing the time. Visible inside the door of the caboose are various packages known as less-than-carload freight, LCL, for local residents to pick up at various M&U depots. (Howard Sell Photograph, M&NJRHS Archives.)

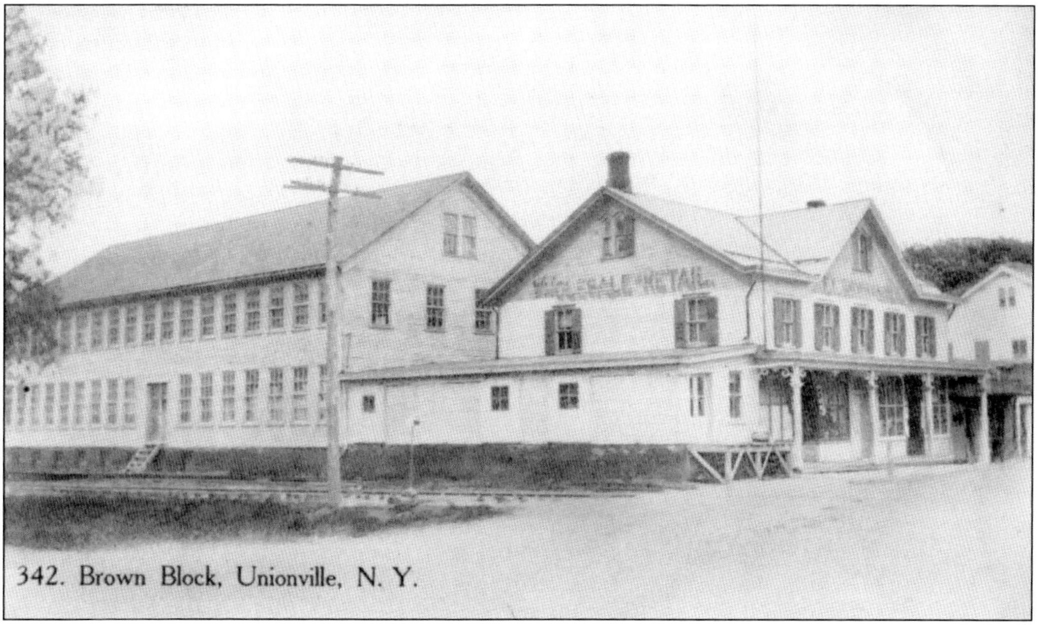

The two-story building to the left was the Chardovoyne Creamery located just off Main Street and Railroad Avenue. The store on Main Street would become E. L. Brown's store as seen below. In later years, Charles Hanford would purchase the store and allow his daughter to run the business, which included a soda and ice cream fountain as shown below with the arched sign "Ice Cream Parlor." Mr. Hanford was the owner of the property along the railroad right of way that became Hanford Junction. (Both photographs, Town of Minisink Museum Collection.)

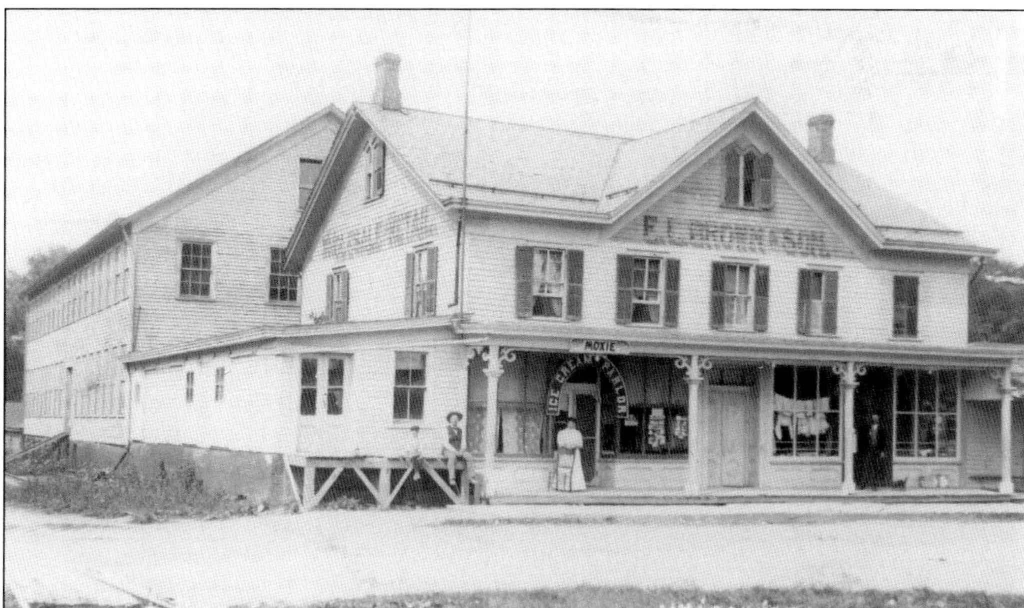

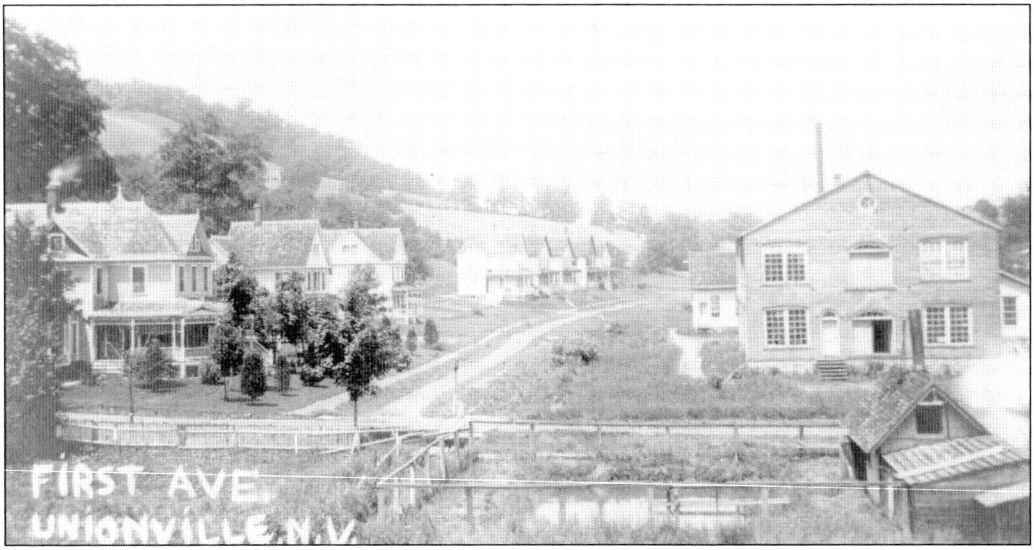

One of the major industries in Unionville was the silk mills. The building to the right was originally the Toner and Prescott Silk Mill, which manufactured silk ribbons. It was purchased in 1919 by the American Silk Label Manufacturing Company, which remained in business until 1986. The Unionville Silk Manufacturing Company also received work for their company from Toner and Prescott. (Town of Minisink Museum Collection.)

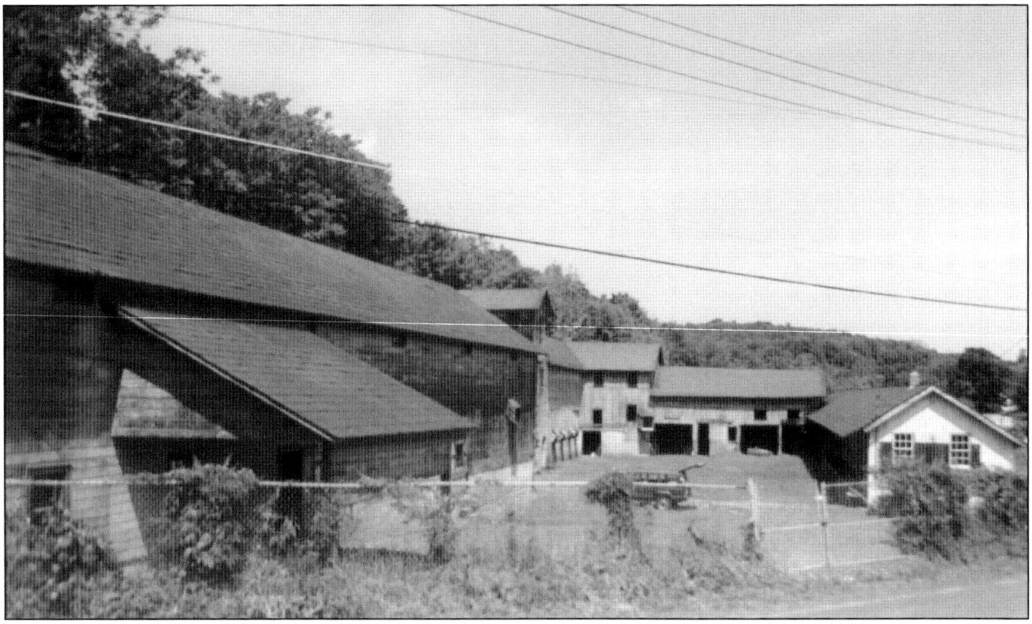
In 1991, the author took this photograph of the former Manning and Clark Feed, Coal, and Lumber facility in Unionville that is located off Jersey Avenue just below the M&U main line. The business was serviced by one sidetrack directly off the M&U main. The large building on the left carried the company name and received feed along with various grades of anthracite coal. (Author's photograph.)

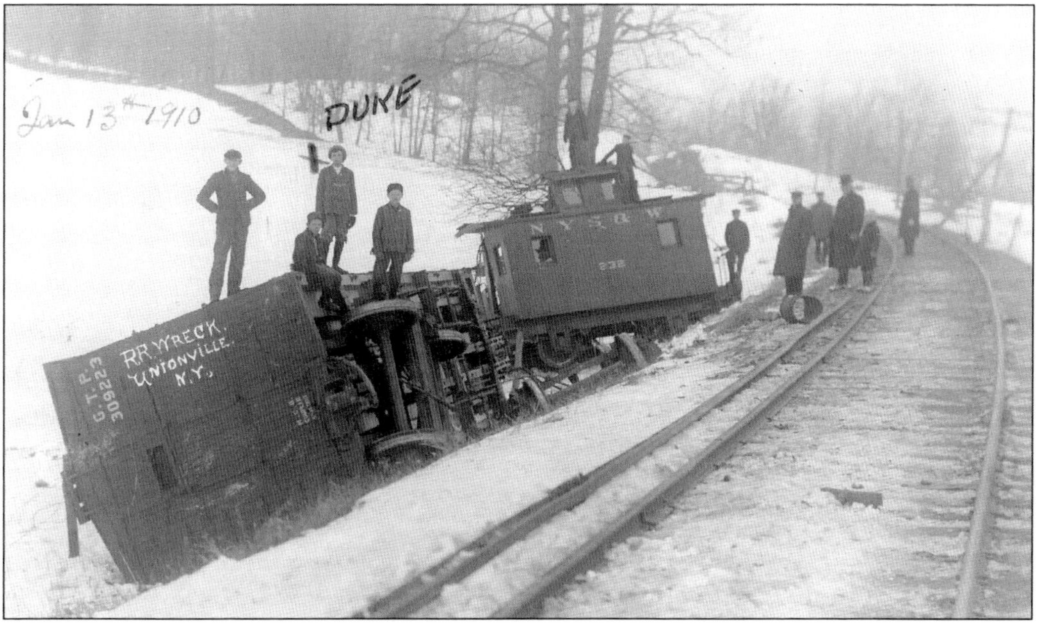

On January 13, 1910, a NYS&W freight train derailed while entering the village of Unionville. One boxcar and the caboose derailed. There was no security in those days and local residents walked freely among the wreckage. Duke and friends are on top of the boxcar. Note the bobber caboose does not appear to be damaged badly. Closer inspection of the photograph below reveals the caboose sustained far more damage as it is split almost in two by the tree. If any crew member in the caboose escaped injury, it would have been a miracle. Duke and his friends did climb the caboose as well as indicated by the arrow to his name. (Both photographs, Town of Minisink Museum Collection.)

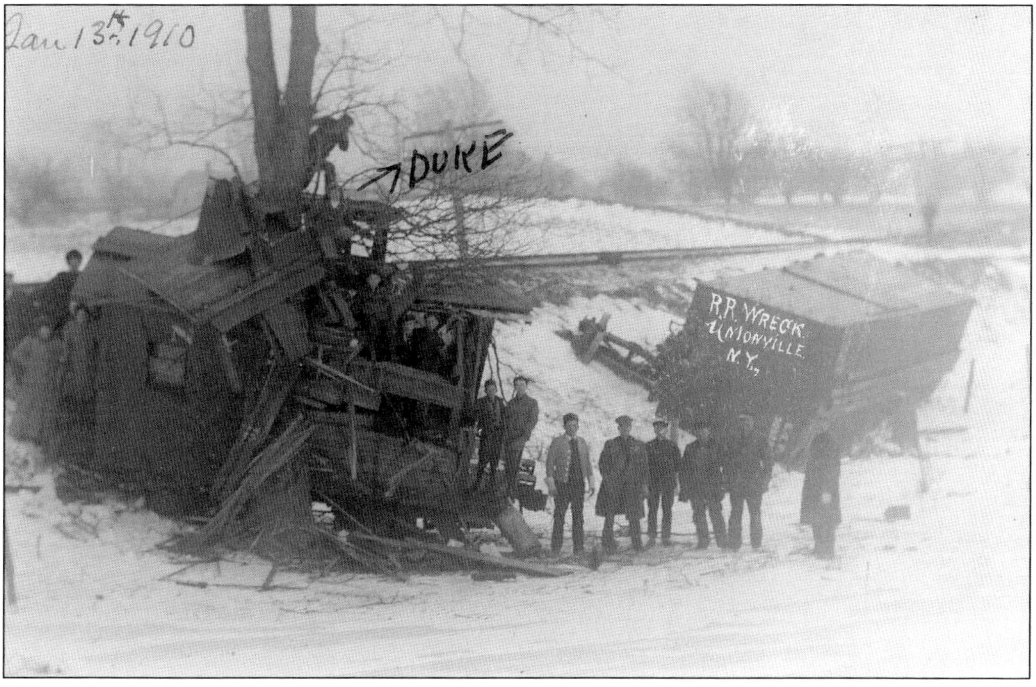

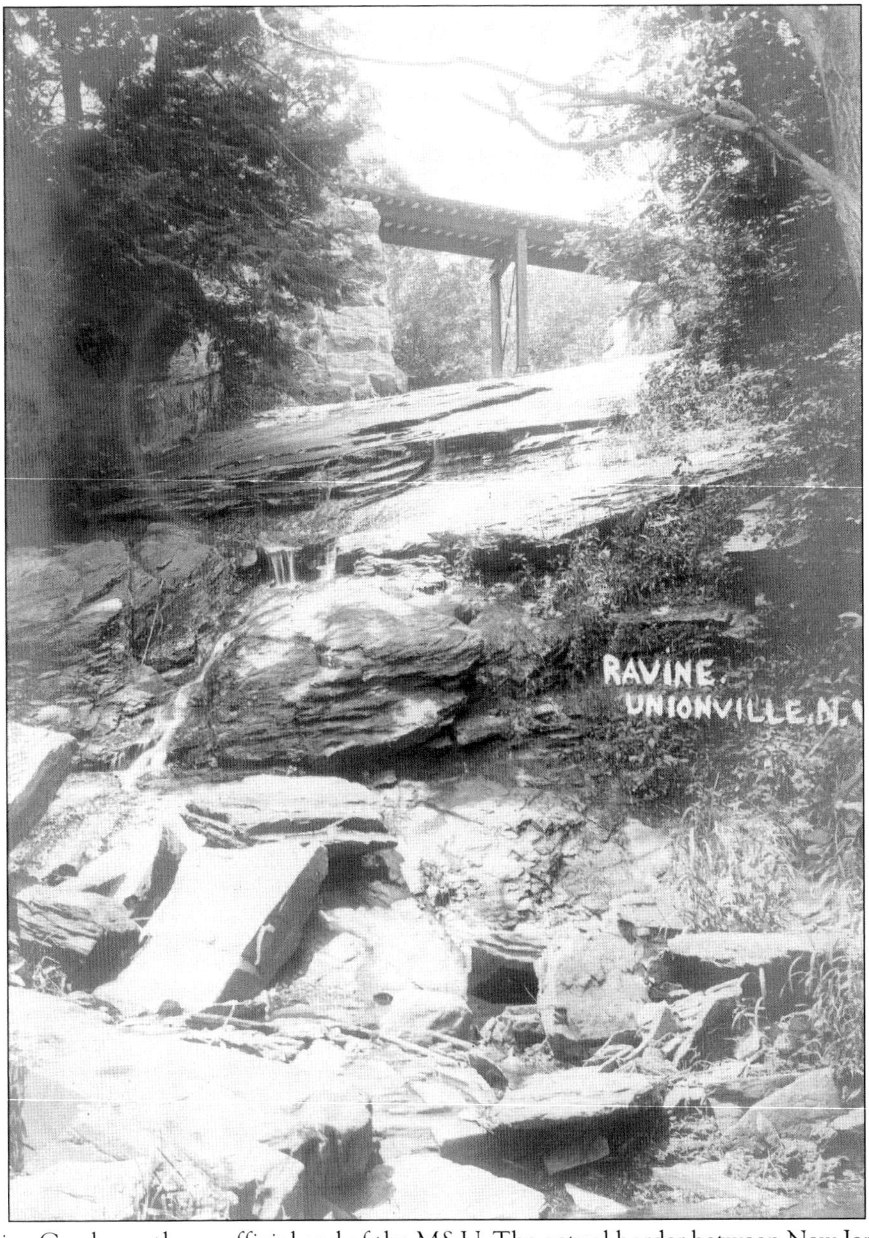

State Line Creek was the unofficial end of the M&U. The actual border between New Jersey and New York was approximately a hundred yards east of the bridge shown in the upper portion of this image. Hires Condensery is just to the right of this bridge. The bridge would be replaced to support heavier locomotives and traffic. During periods of heavy rain this dry creek bed would become a raging river with the white water of a waterfall replacing the serene trickle of water shown in this image. This was a favorite spot for many people visiting and living in Unionville during the warm months of the year. Lucky individuals could take a photograph of an M&U locomotive pushing the cars upgrade to Hanford Junction to be interchanged with the NYS&W, which would have been quite a sight indeed. There would be an abundance of smoke as the M&U steamer was struggling to ascend the grade, which extended from Main Street in Unionville to the State Line. (Author's collection.)

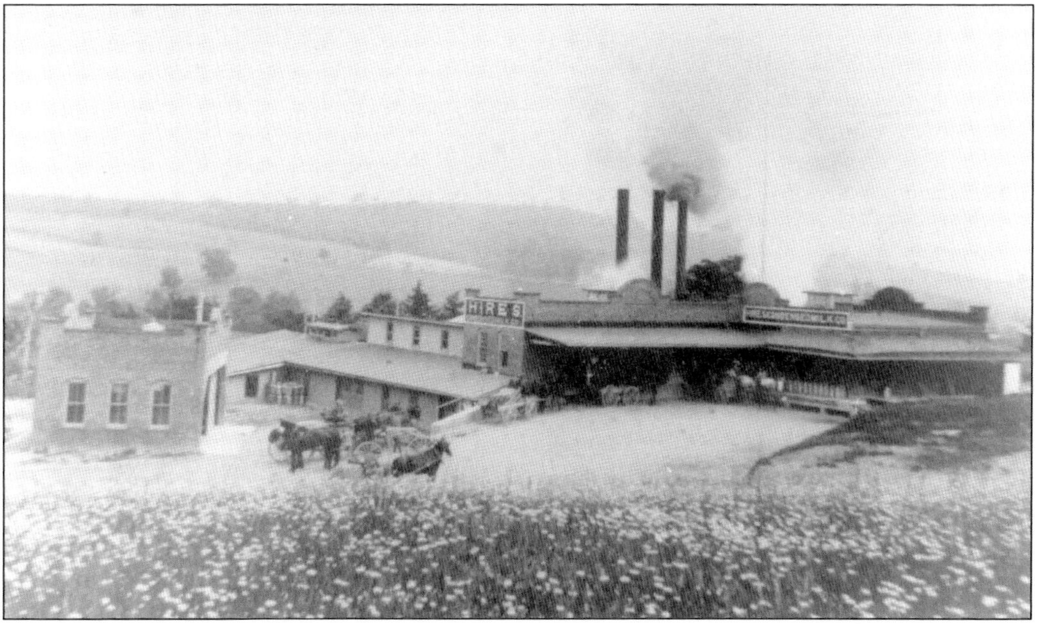

The Hires Condensed Milk Company served by the M&U was adjacent to State Line Creek. Hires received coal and cans while shipping out the condensed milk by rail. Later this facility was sold to R. F. Stevens but was not in operation in 1928. It eventually would house a rubber mill. (Larry Hansen Collection, M&NJRHS Archives.)

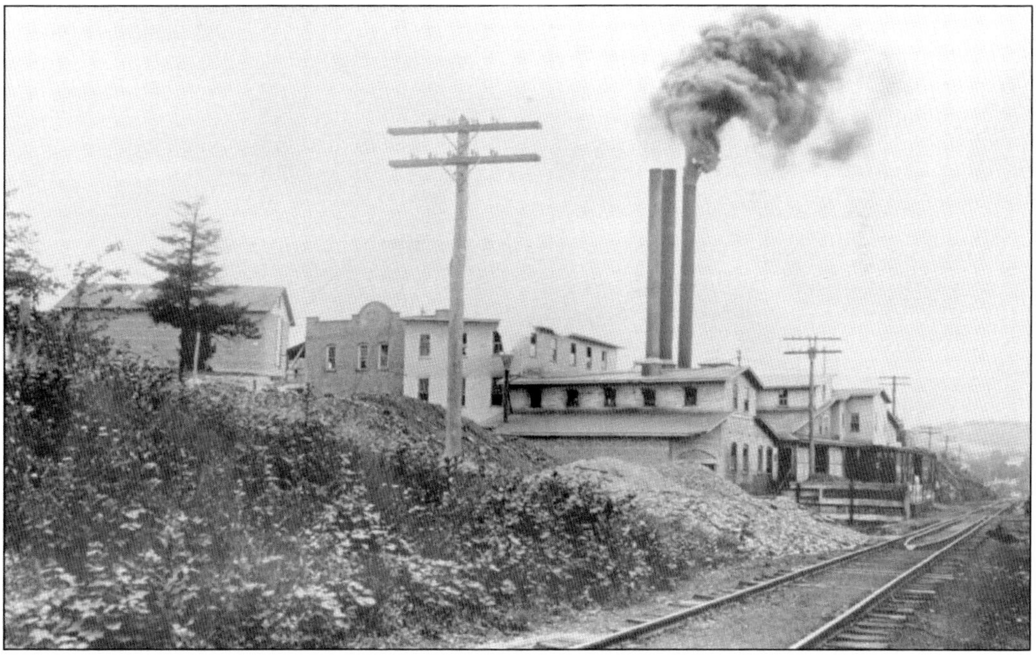
This view looking west toward the village of Unionville along the M&U is across the railroad's State Line Creek bridge. The Hires Condensed Milk Company is to the left with a boxcar on its siding. There were plans to extend this sidetrack by building a bridge over the State Line Creek. The foundations were constructed out of concrete, but the bridge and siding were not completed. (Town of Minisink Museum Collection.)

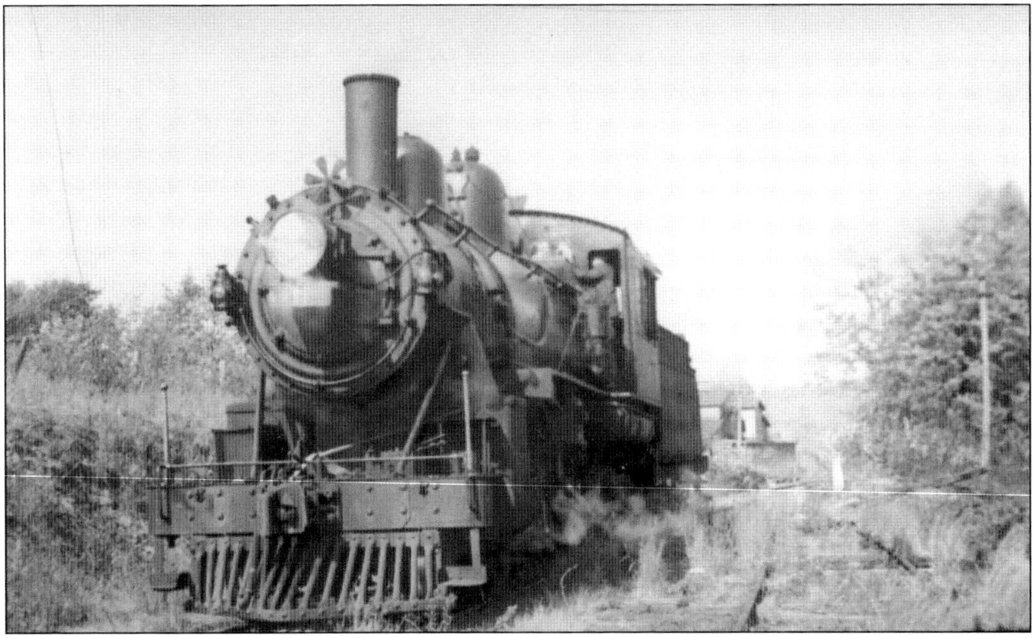

M&U No. 6 has just crossed the State Line Creek Bridge. The former Hires Condensery is in the background. The track to the right of the locomotive is the M&U interchange track used in conjunction with the tracks at Hanford Junction some 400 feet east of this location. (Ray Brown Collection, M&NJRHS Archives.)

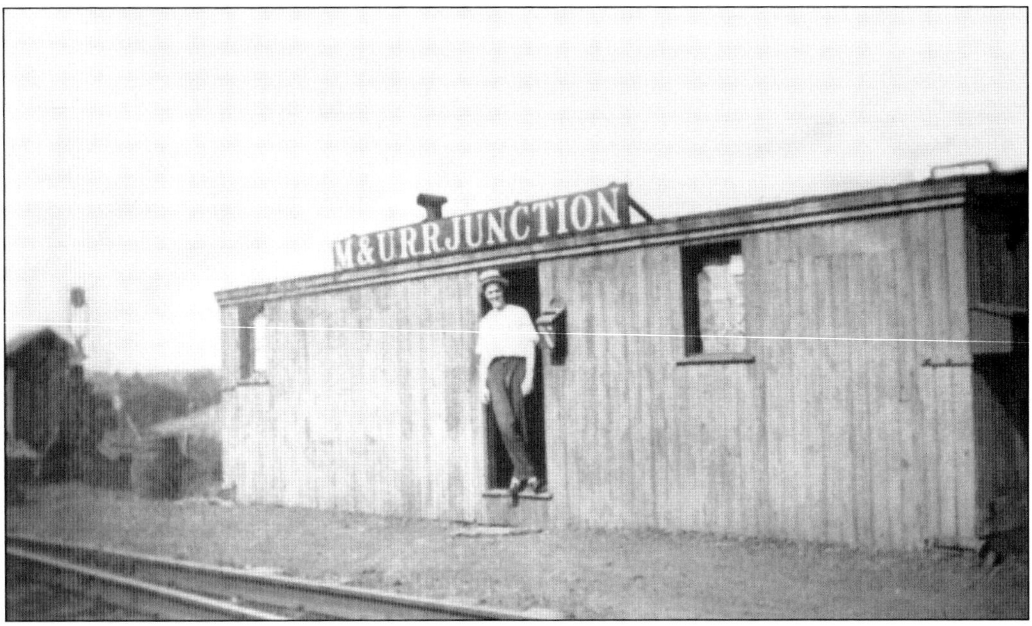

The NYS&W did not run any trains into Unionville after the M&U became an independent railroad. Instead, the NYS&W built this depot from a boxcar during 1914 at M&U Junction, Hanford Junction on the M&U. After the 1946 M&U reorganization into the M&NJ, the Hanford Branch train on the NYS&W was still referred to as the M&U job. (Town of Minisink Museum Collection.)

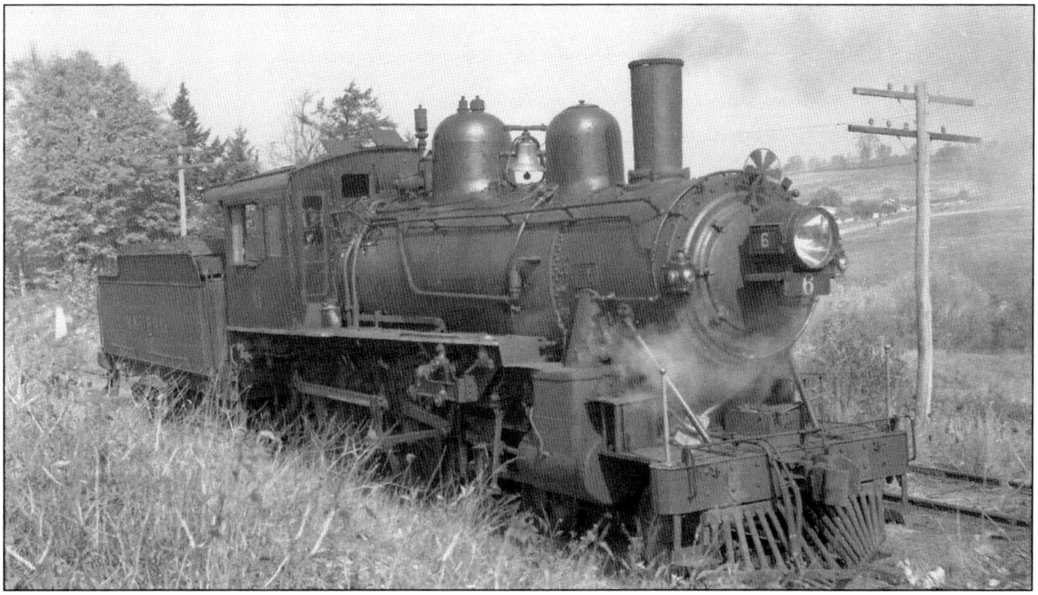

M&U No. 6 is at Hanford Junction on October 19, 1939. The valley below carries the state highway that connected Unionville to Sussex County, New Jersey. In less than six months, No. 6 would finally wear out and be replaced by No. 7. The NYS&W tracks head southeast through Sussex County to their mainline at Beaver Lake, New Jersey. The background depicts the rich agricultural region served by the M&U. (Ray Brown Collection, M&NJRHS Archives.)

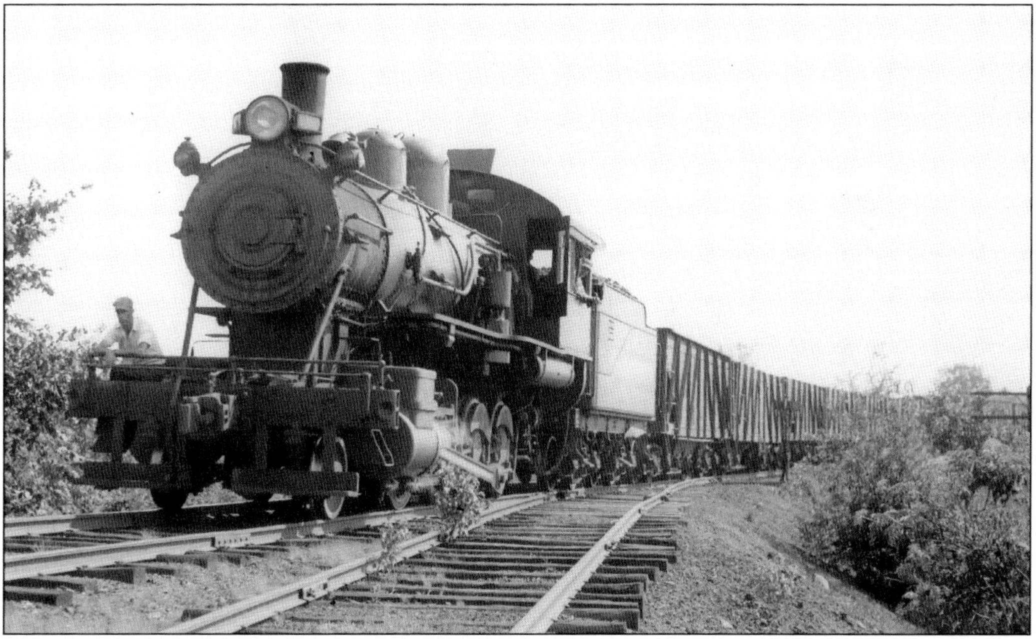

Robert Collins captured M&U No. 7 on August 11, 1940, with an eastbound train entering Hanford Junction. This train consisted of 28 cars with many of them being loaded coal-hopper cars delivered to the M&U by the O&W at DG yard in Middletown. The NYS&W would deliver some of the coal to industries along its line with the balance going to the NYS&W coal dumper at Edgewater, New Jersey. (Robert Collins Photograph, M&NJRHS Archives.)

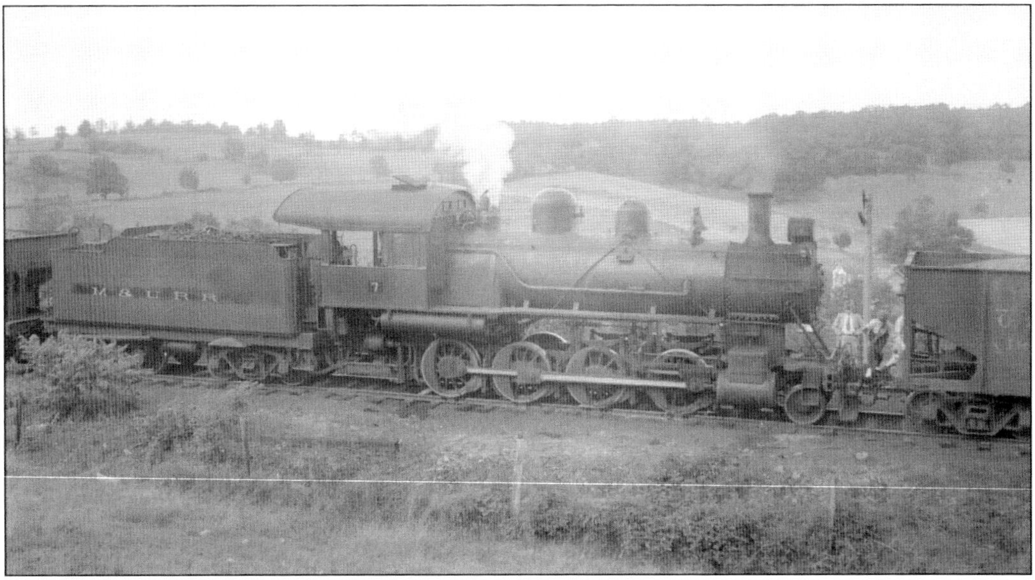

On June 23, 1940, M&U No. 7 demonstrated one of her major shortcomings at Hanford Junction. Besides not having the power required for larger trains, the drive rods were not quartered properly. This meant that both driver rods could be stopped parallel to the rails. If one or both of the drive rods are stopped and they are not parallel to the rails, the engine can create motion with its pistons and begin to move. However, on this day the No. 7's flaw was exposed to all. An NYS&W fan trip in a streamlined passenger motorcar arrived, and the fans took a number of pictures. Some of the railroad fans can be seem between the front of the engine and the coal car. The railroad fans on this trip recorded this bit of M&U history for all time. (Both photographs, Ray Brown Collection, M&NJRHS Archives.)

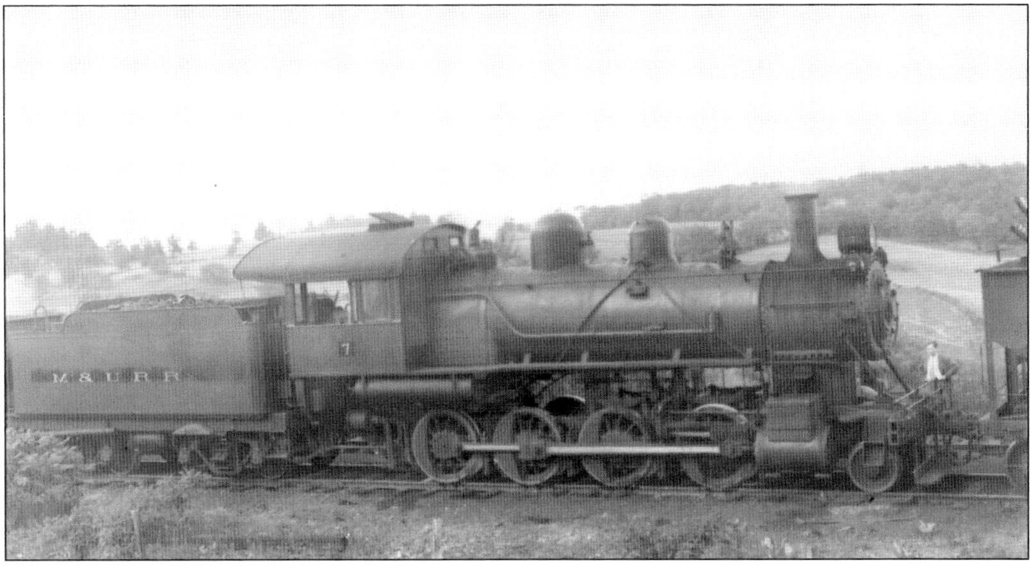

Seven

The Middletown and New Jersey Railway

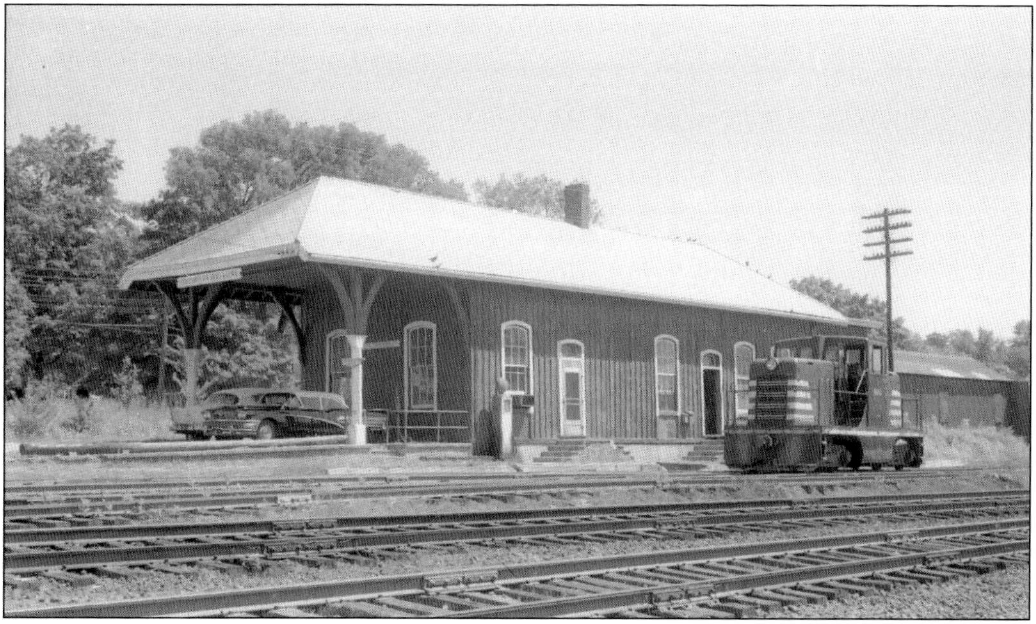

M&NJ No. 1 idles outside the East Main Street depot waiting for the crew to begin the assignment on the day's train. An old-style fuel pump with a ball on top stands to the left of the engine. It was once used to fuel the buses and trucks owned by the M&U's subsidiary, the Middletown and Sussex Transit Company. In addition, two classic cars are parked under the remaining roof overhang. (John Stellwagen Collection, M&NJRHS Archives.)

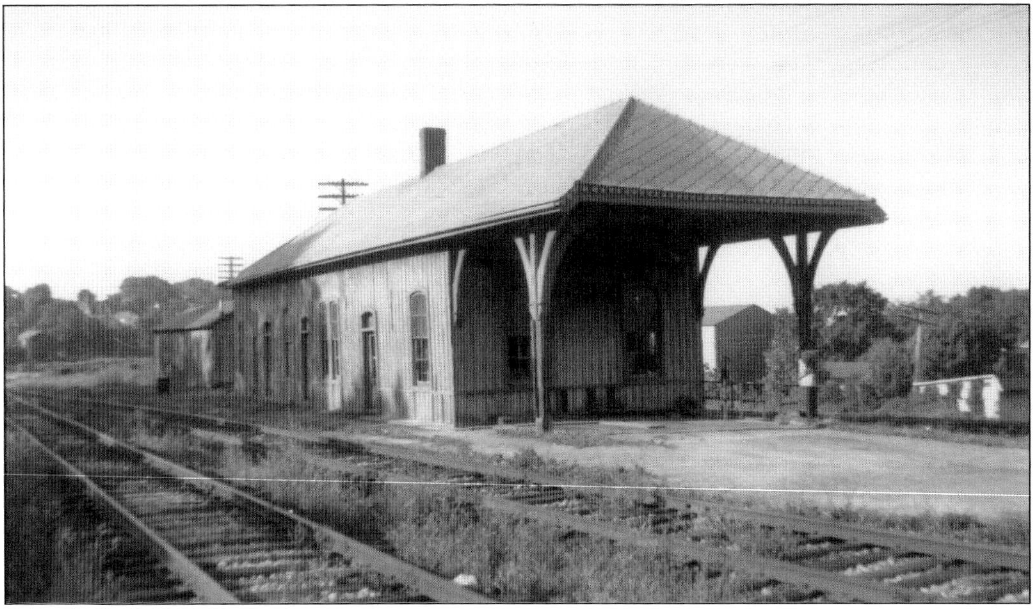

This photograph of the M&NJ's Middletown depot was taken in 1954 from East Main Street along the NYO&W main line. The depot is now quite plain, lacking even a station sign. This was yet another indication of the railroad's decline. During 1946, the NYO&W single tracked their main line leaving a segment of double track intact in Middletown beginning just east of the M&NJ depot. (John Stellwagen Collection, M&NJRHS Archives.)

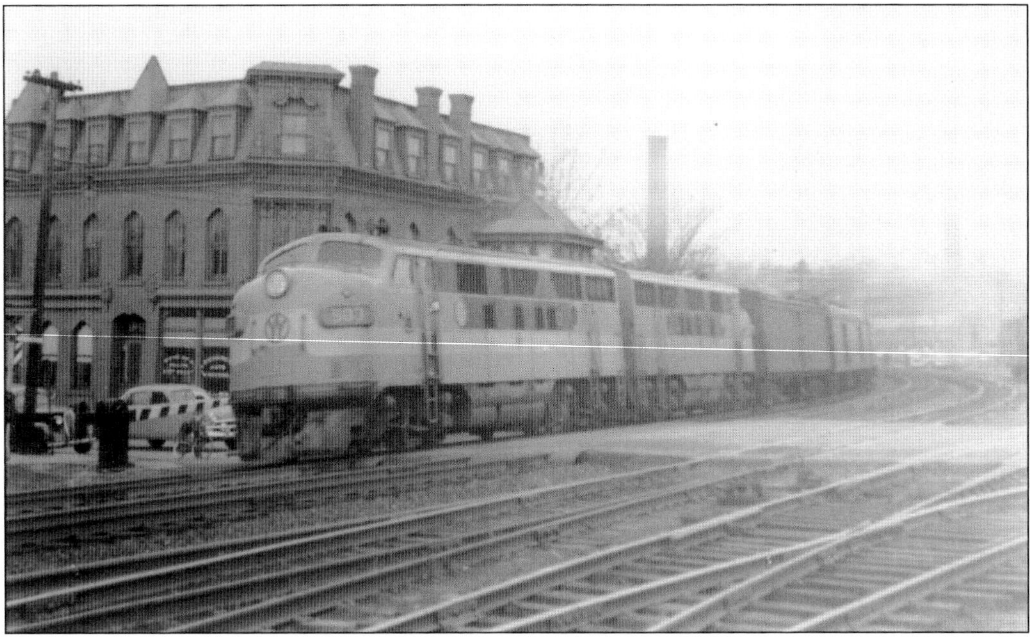

On April 6, 1951, the Erie had a derailment on the main line requiring NYO&W F3 diesels led by the 503, seen here at East Main Street passing EM tower, to pick up the Erie's passenger train in the Erie's Middletown yard. The train, with Erie pilots, traveled via the Erie to Goshen and onto their Montgomery branch to reach the NYO&W rails at Campbell Hall for the journey to Jersey City. (Marvin Cohen Photograph.)

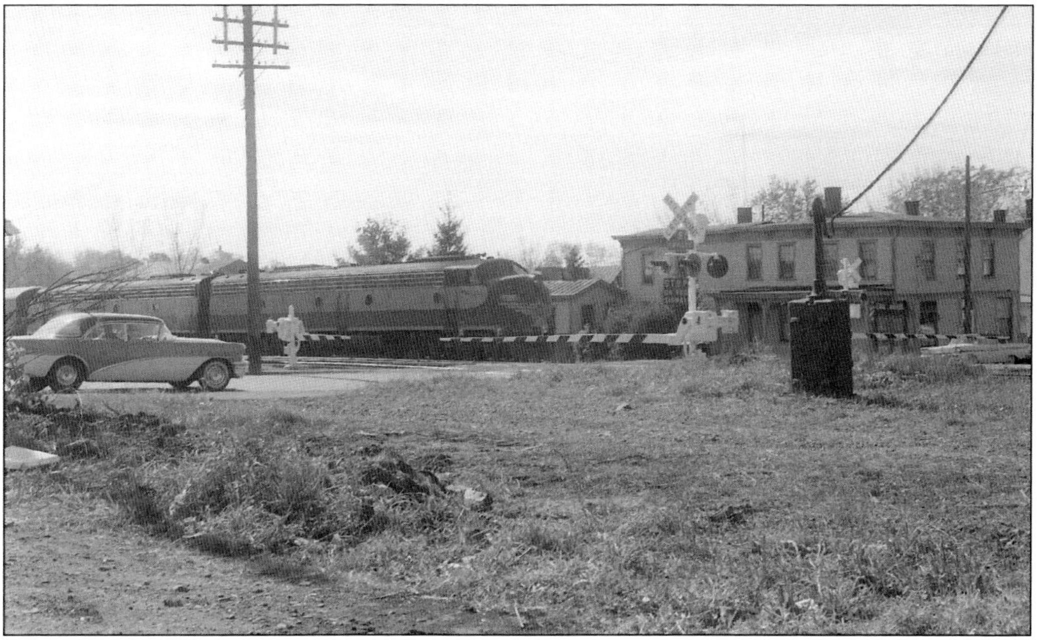

It is 1954 as a pair of Erie E8 passenger locomotives led by 825 is crossing East Main Street heading westbound to the Erie's Middletown depot. The car on the left is between the M&NJ and Erie tracks to the right and the O&W main line out of sight to the left. The building behind the lead diesel is the Switch Inn, which still stands today. (John Stellwagen Collection, M&NJRHS Archives.)

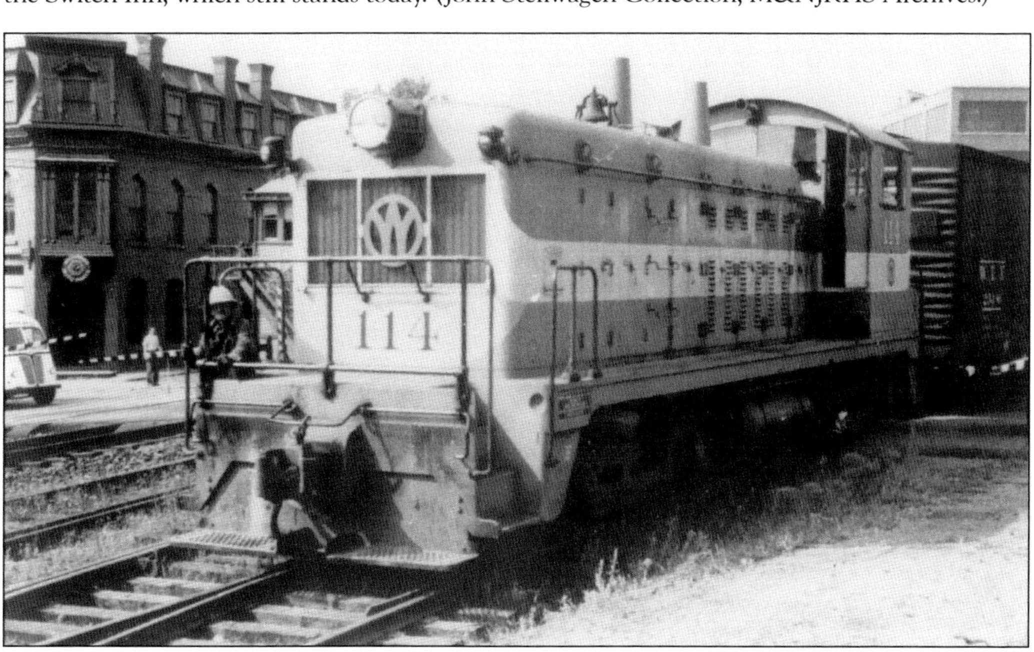

It is post-1951 as the NYO&W has received delivery of their NW-2 diesel switchers from the Electro Motive Division of General Motors and the Clemson Lawn Mower factory can be seen over the train. NYO&W 114 is on the long crossover track having just crossed East Main Street to interchange cars with the M&NJ and Erie. Note EM tower to the left of the 114. (John Treen Photograph, O&WRHS Collection.)

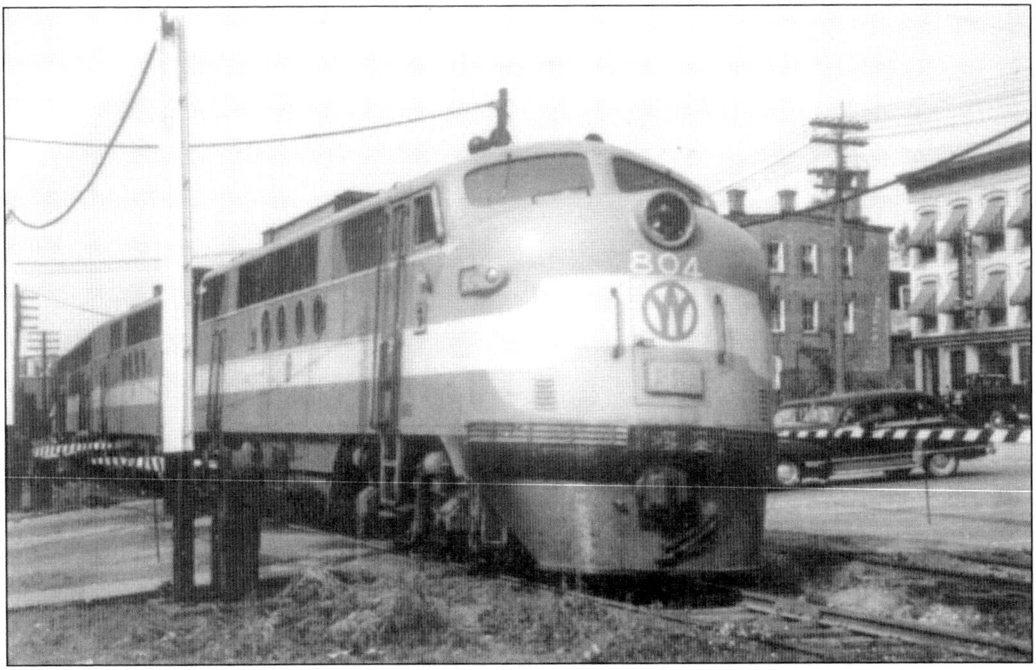

John Treen also captured a four-unit set of NYO&W FT diesels led by 804 crossing East Main Street with a symbol freight from Mayfield Yard, on the NYO&W's Scranton Division, headed for Maybrook Yard and a connection with the New Haven Railroad. (John Treen Photograph, O&WRHS Collection.)

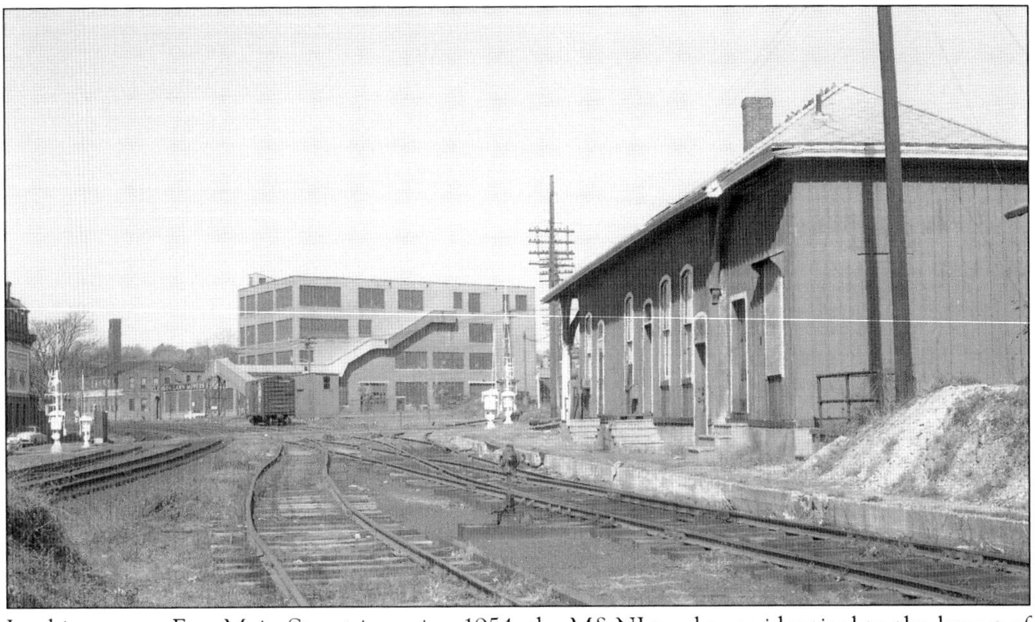

Looking across East Main Street in spring 1954, the M&NJ tracks are identical to the layout of the old M&U. The Erie main line is to the left but EM tower is now a distant memory. Across East Main Street behind the boxcar is a new industry, a large box-like building constructed by the Clemson family in 1951 to manufacture lawn mowers, which were shipped out in boxcars. (John Stellwagen Collection, M&NJRHS Archives.)

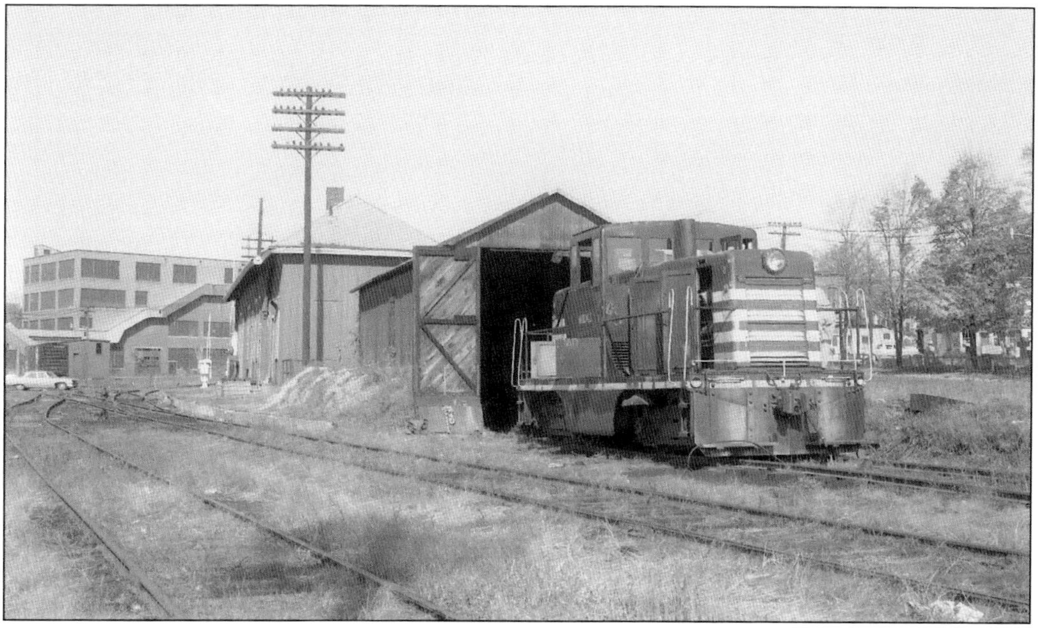

The former M&U rail bus shed has its doors opened wide as its new resident, M&NJ No. 1 is idling outside. The doors are open on the front hood of the diesel indicating some minor repairs or maintenance is being performed. A close inspection of the shed's doors clearly shows that the building was raised to accommodate the new engine. (John Stellwagen Collection, M&NJRHS Archives.)

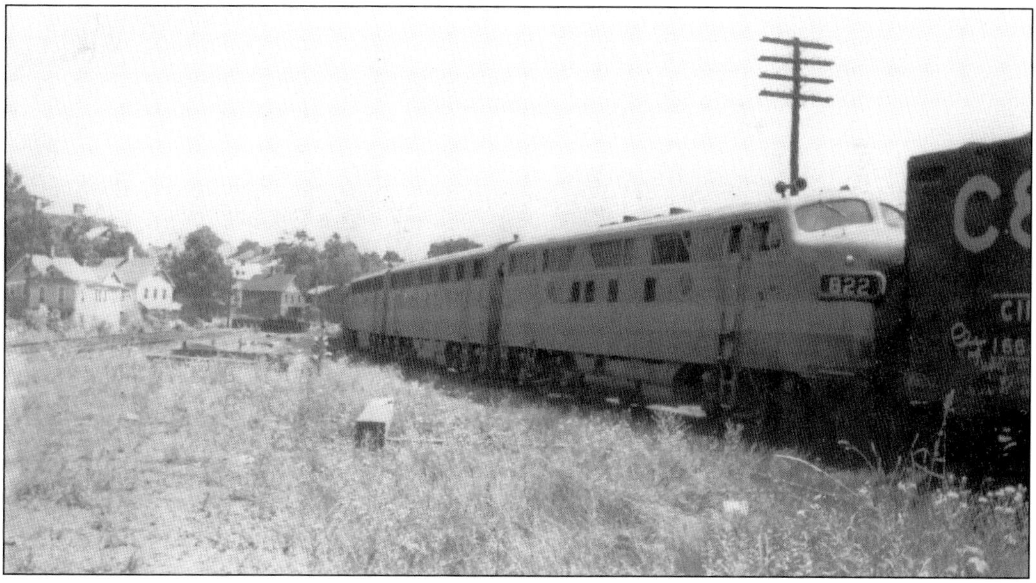

After March 29, 1957, the NYO&W Railway was abandoned. The NYO&W main line can be seen in the left of this picture. During the late summer, the Erie purchased F3 diesels 821 and 822, which actually were two engines per number. Pictured above are the 822 A and B unit along with the 821 on the M&NJ's main track as they are being delivered to the Erie Railroad in Middletown. (Ray Brown Collection, M&NJRHS Archives.)

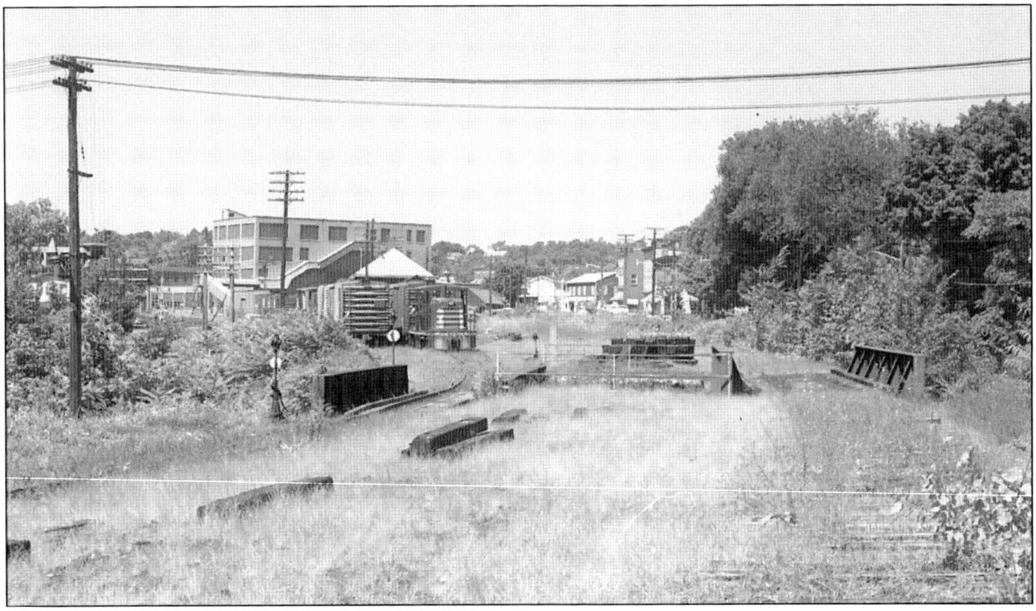

During 1959, M&NJ No. 1 is bringing cars from the Erie interchange toward DG yard. The Middletown depot and the Clemson lawn mower factory can be seen above the M&NJ's diesel. The former NYO&W right of way is being reclaimed by nature. The M&NJ Sprague Avenue bridge to the left will be replaced by the higher capacity, abandoned NYO&W bridge seen to the right in the late 1970s. (John Stellwagen Collection, M&NJRHS Archives.)

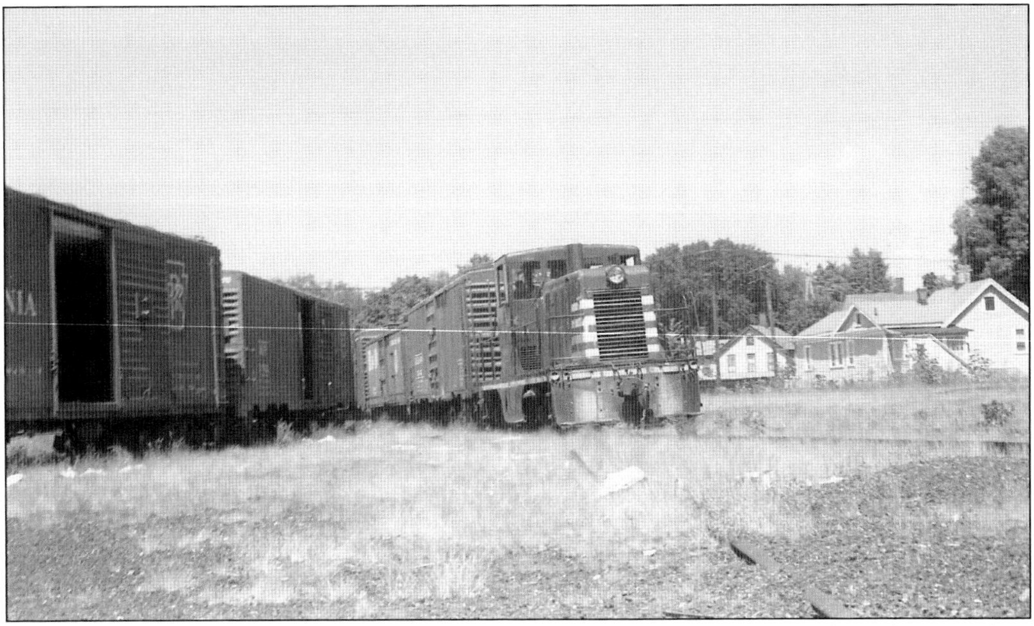

M&NJ No. 1 has just crossed the Sprague Avenue bridge entering DG yard on the main line heading south to Unionville. The boxcars to the left are on the remaining yard track that today is still known as the "coach track" from the days of Erie passenger service. The slightly raised land to the right of No. 1 is the former NYO&W right of way. (John Stellwagen Collection, M&NJRHS Archives.)

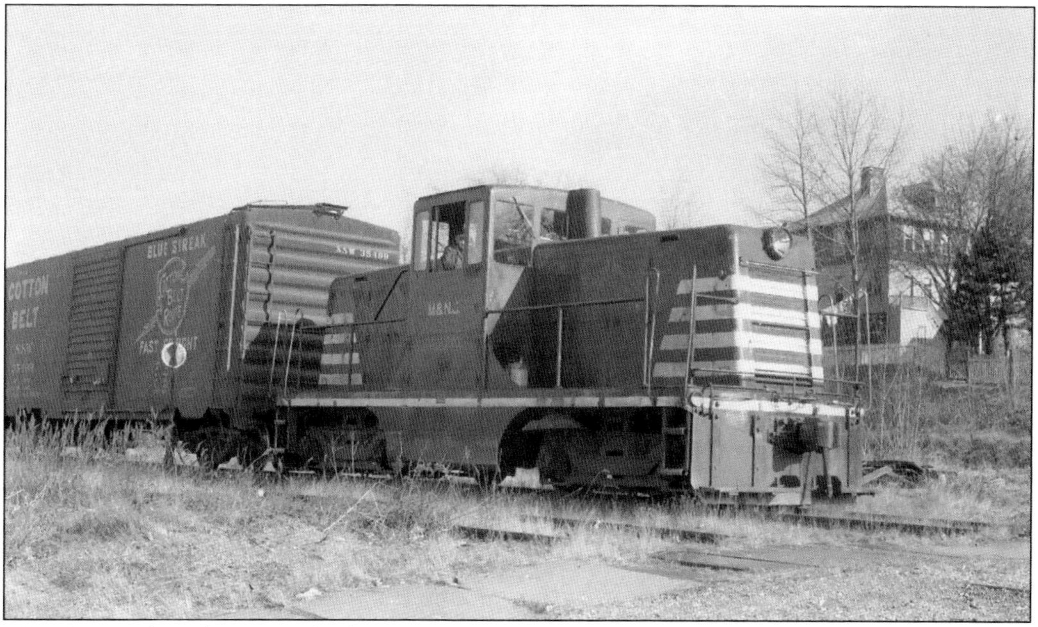

M&NJ No. 1 has almost reached Houston Avenue as the southbound train travels to Unionville during April 1959. The M&NJ at this time connected only to the Erie in Middletown as the NYO&W had been abandoned for two years, and the NYS&W had abandoned the Hanford branch from Franklin, New Jersey, to Hanford Junction in 1958. (John Stellwagen Collection, M&NJRHS Archives.)

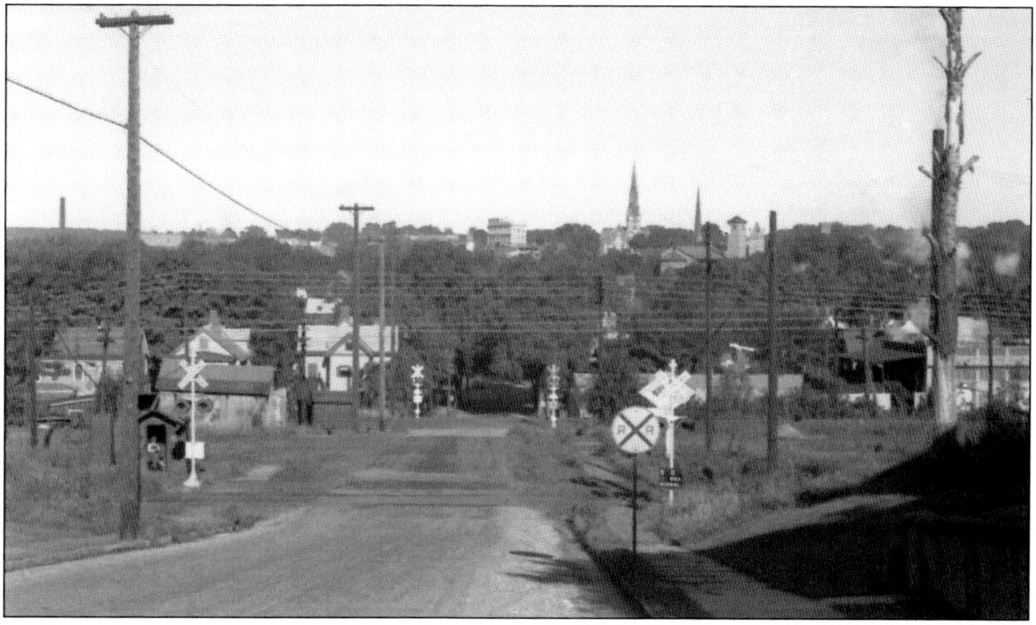

In this view looking west on Houston Avenue, the NYO&W main line, the M&NJ, and farther down the road, the two-track Erie main line are evident as is the center of the City of Middletown with a number of churches. All three railroads ran on this shelf eastward for about three-fourths of a mile from East Main Street. Note the presence of the NYO&W crossing guard in his shed despite the automatic signals. (Marvin Cohen Photograph.)

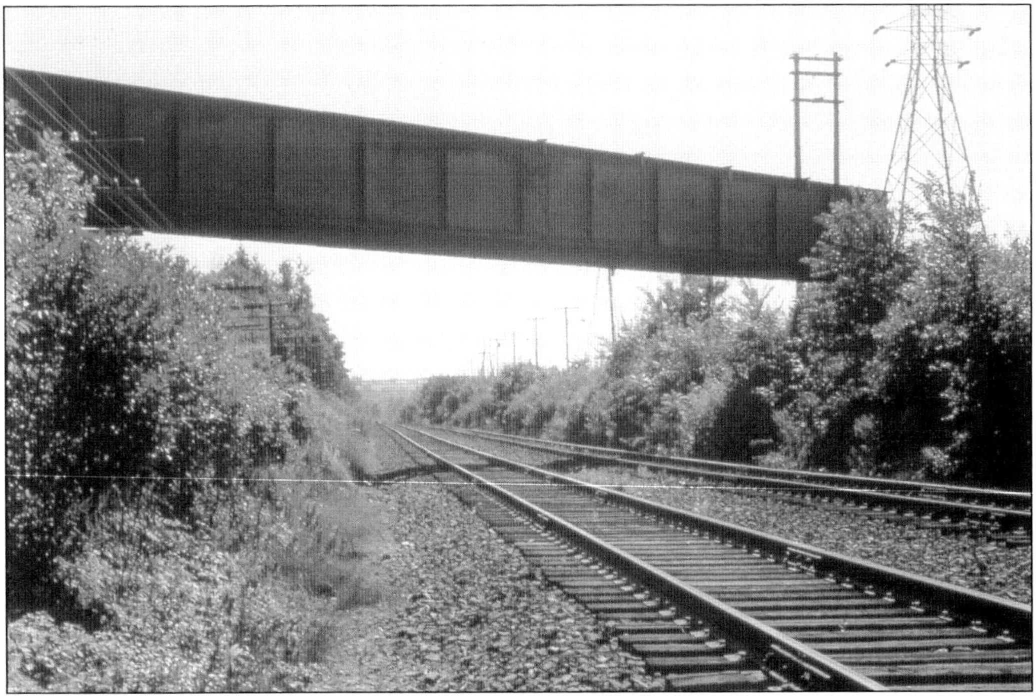

The Erie main line ducks under the M&NJ about a mile from East Main Street. The close clearance of this bridge was one of the major factors in the Erie's decision to build the 42-mile Graham line cutoff around the villages of Orange County. Former M&NJ superintendent Carl Detwyler remarked that in the 1960s automobile rack cars on the Erie and Erie Lackawanna would clear this bridge by less than a foot. (Carl Detwyler Collection, M&NJRHS Archives.)

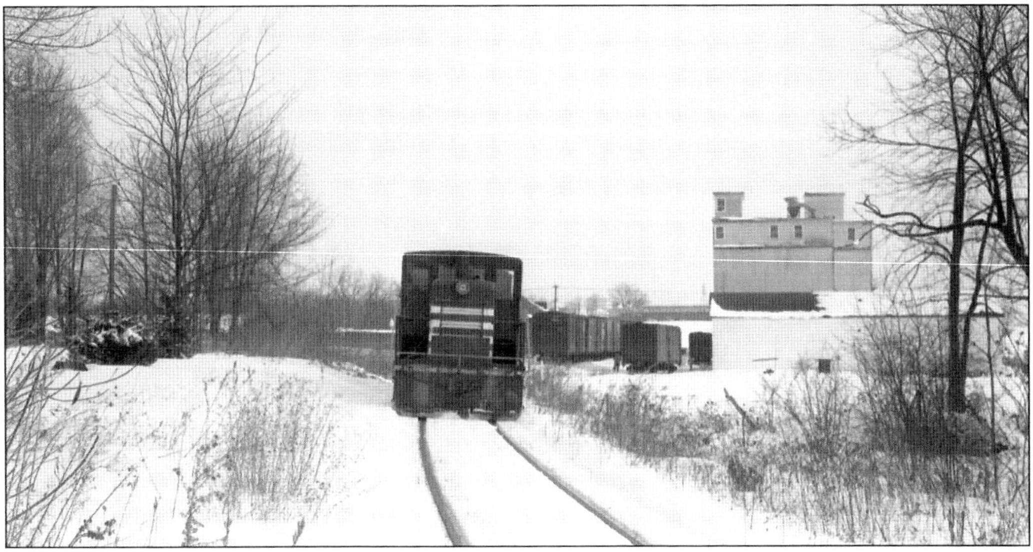

M&NJ No. 1 is switching the Grange League Federation feed mill that was built in the early 1940s. The GLF plant was attached to a feed store on the opposite side of the complex. This was a major customer of the M&U and M&NJ until a fire destroyed the facility on March 30, 1962. The new GLF plant was modernized, and a bulk depot was added as well. (John Stellwagen Collection, M&NJRHS Archives.)

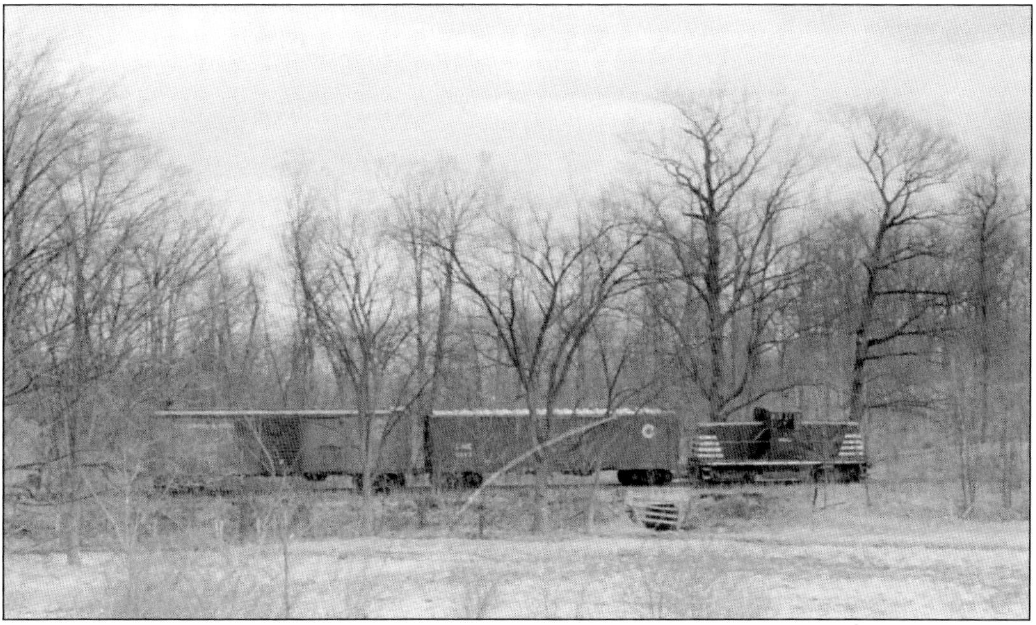

Heading east toward Slate Hill, M&NJ No. 1 is moving upgrade to Creeden's Hill with a two-car freight. The traffic pattern had changed in this late 1950s picture since the Lehigh and New England boxcar would formerly have been delivered by the NYS&W at Hanford Junction. However, with the NYS&W abandonment of the branch to the interchange all traffic to and from the M&NJ came from the Erie after 1958. (John Stellwagen Collection, M&NJRHS Archives.)

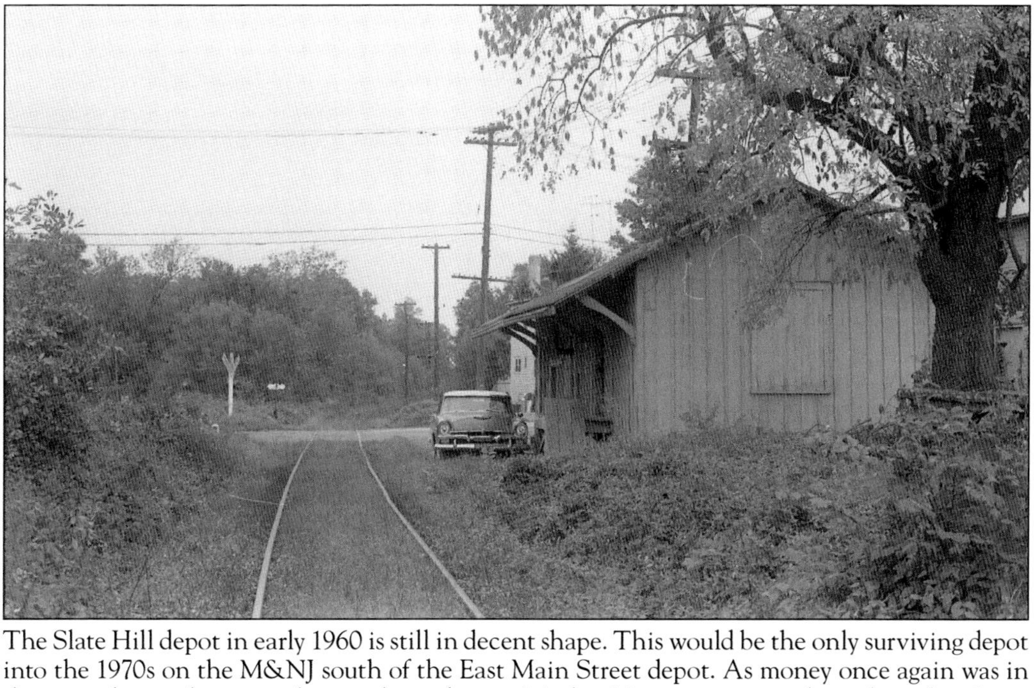

The Slate Hill depot in early 1960 is still in decent shape. This would be the only surviving depot into the 1970s on the M&NJ south of the East Main Street depot. As money once again was in short supply, weed spraying has not been done as Mother Nature tries to reclaim the right of way. That is a battle the M&U and the M&NJ would fight throughout the railroad's existence. (John Stellwagen Collection, M&NJRHS Archives.)

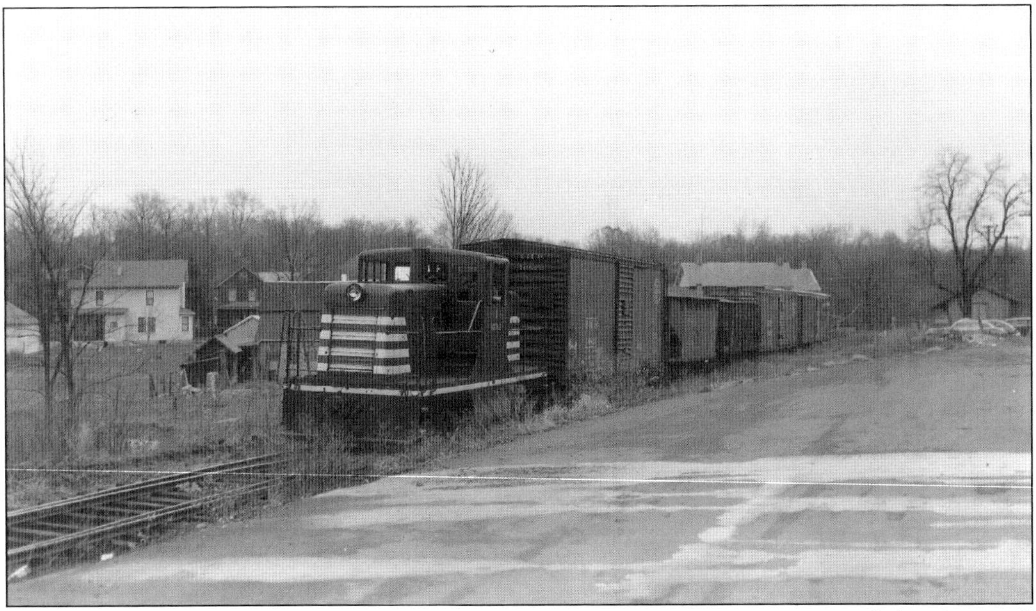

John Krause captured M&NJ No. 1 with an eastbound freight having just passed the Slate Hill depot. The engine has almost crossed over the switch to Martins Feed, out of sight to the right of the picture. In a moment, the crew of M&NJ No. 1 will be switching out the feed mill track before heading east to Johnson. (John Krause Photograph, M&NJRHS Archives.)

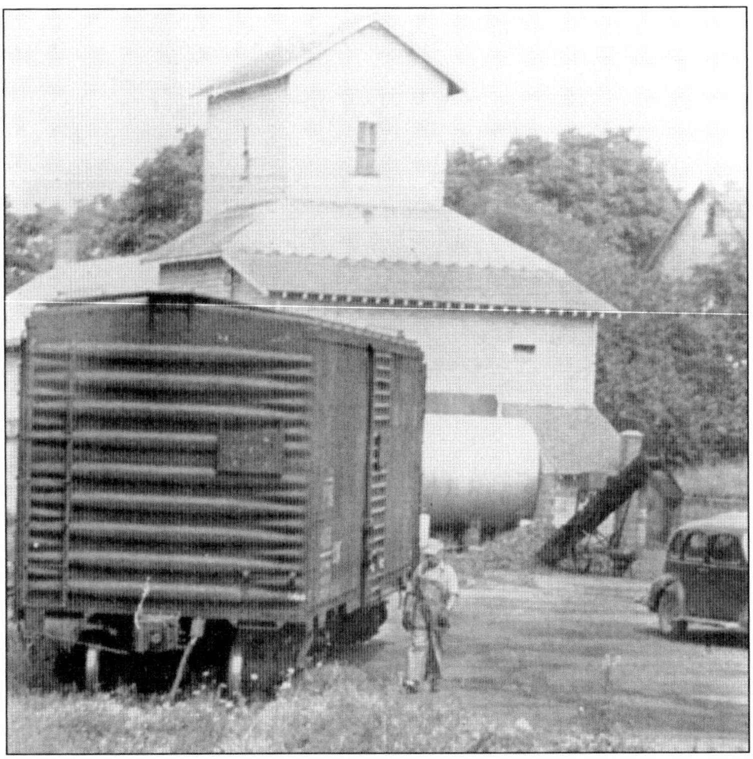

Martins Feed is being switched by the M&NJ crew during spring 1947. This mill received feed, coal and fuel oil as evidenced by the oil tank and coal pile in the background. Martins Feed had the distinction of being the only feed mill on the railroad that never suffered a major fire. (Ray Brown Collection, M&NJRHS Archives.)

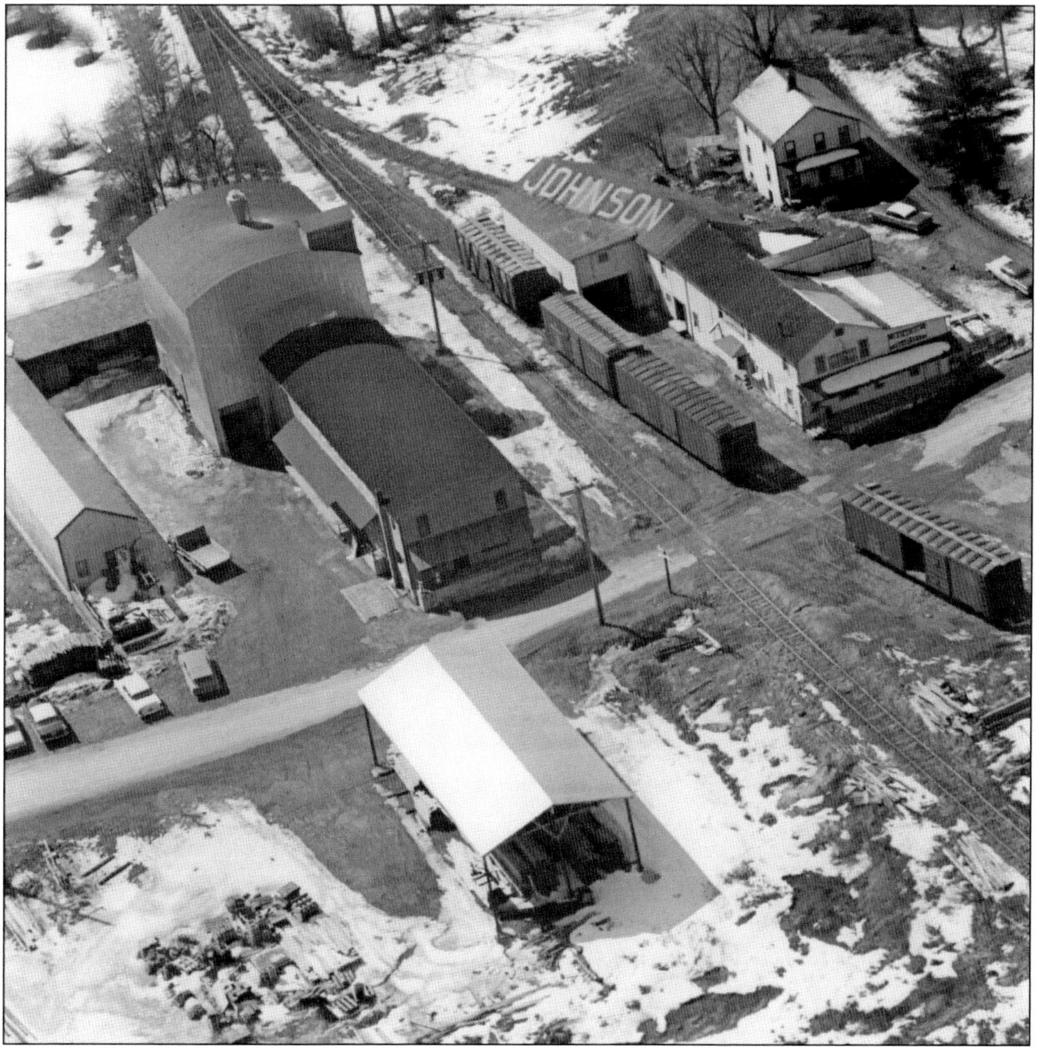

During 1952, the Manning Coal, Feed, and Lumber facility at Johnson caught fire. The late Edna Raymond told the author that she was working at Manning's the day of the fire and was the last person to see Terry Manning, brother of John Manning, alive. Edna told Terry not to go into the fire but he insisted in an effort to try to save the building telling Edna that if he died, she could put flowers on his grave. Unfortunately Terry did die and the entire complex along the railroad burned to the ground. John Manning, despite the loss of his brother, rebuilt the facility including a larger feed mill at the rear as shown in this 1963 aerial view. An additional lumber shed was built across from the facility. The former Johnson depot foundation is visible just below the boxcar on the team track across from Clark's Feed. The M&NJ would service both Manning's and Clark's until the early 1970s. Note that on the rear building of Clark's facility, the hamlet's name adorns the roof. (Town of Minisink Museum Collection.)

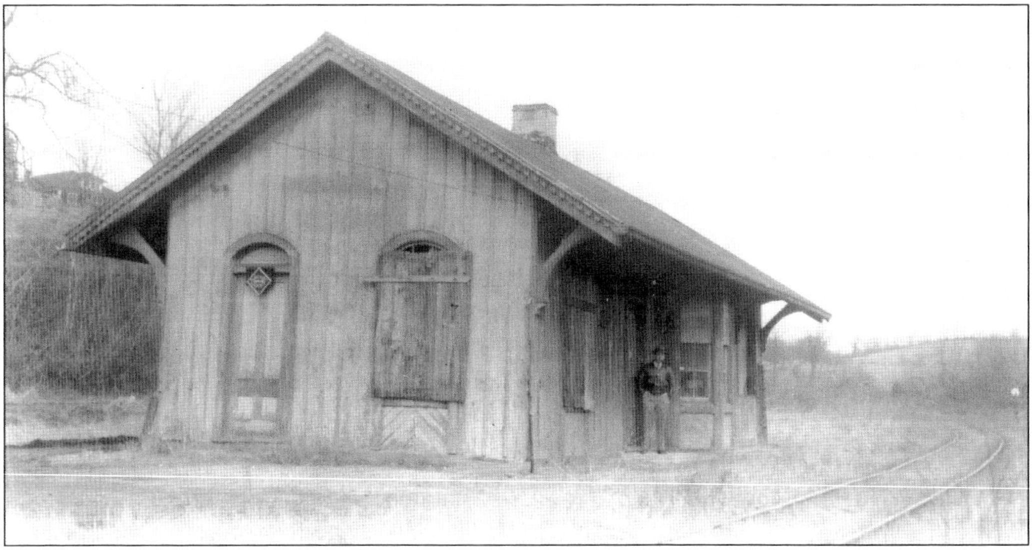

The Unionville depot, on February 22, 1957, looks battered and abused over 16 years after the end of passenger service. The freight house, water tank, and wye are gone along with the sounds of steam. U.S. Route 284 is visible in the background as the M&NJ main line heads west to parallel it for about a half mile. An M&NJ employee stands under the station eves next to the bay window. (Ray Brown Collection, M&NJRHS Archives.)

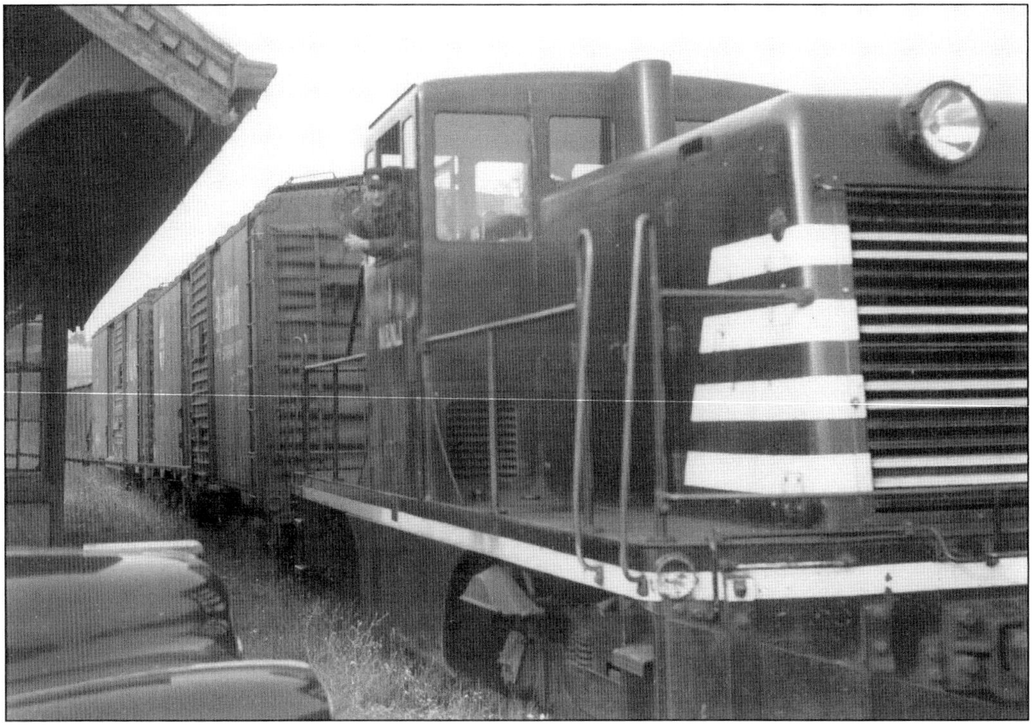

During the late 1940s, the engineer peers out of M&NJ No. 1 as a three-car freight passes the Unionville depot. The engineer will take his train and crew through the village and make a run for the hill to get to Hanford Junction, the interchange with the NYS&W. (John Treen Photograph, M&NJRHS Collection.)

Eight

The NYS&W Hanford Branch

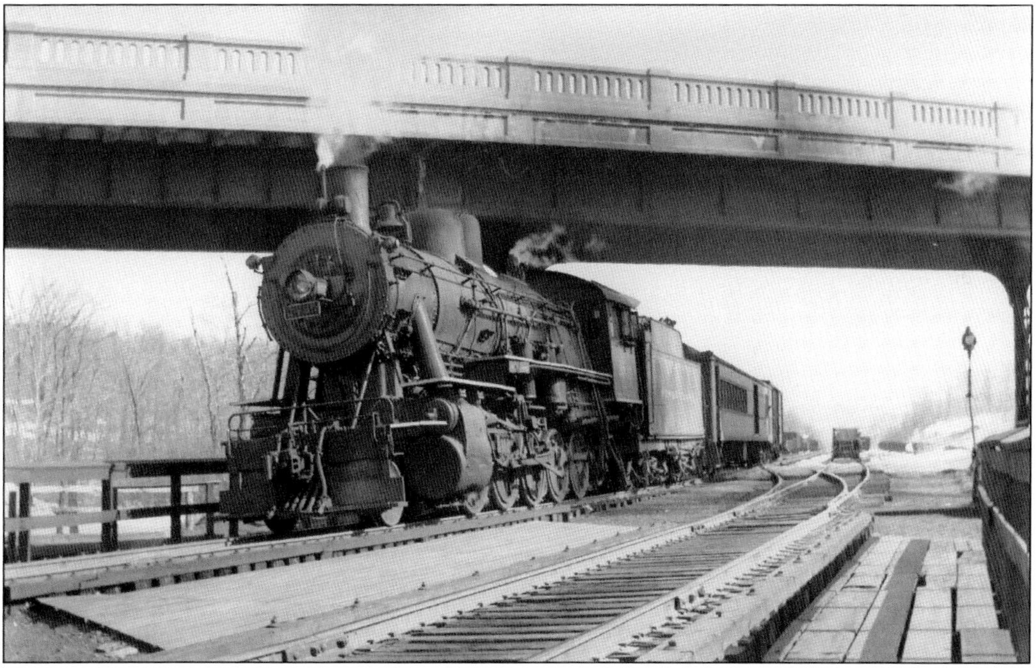

NYS&W J2 decapod 2435 is at Beaver Lake, New Jersey, on March 22, 1941, under U.S. Route 23 picking up cars in the yard for the M&U and points along the Hanford Branch. The 2435 will be leading the last westbound mixed train to Sussex. The train carries a combination car for passengers and also freight for the M&U and thus functions as a local train all the way to M&U Junction. (Railroad Avenue Enterprises Collection.)

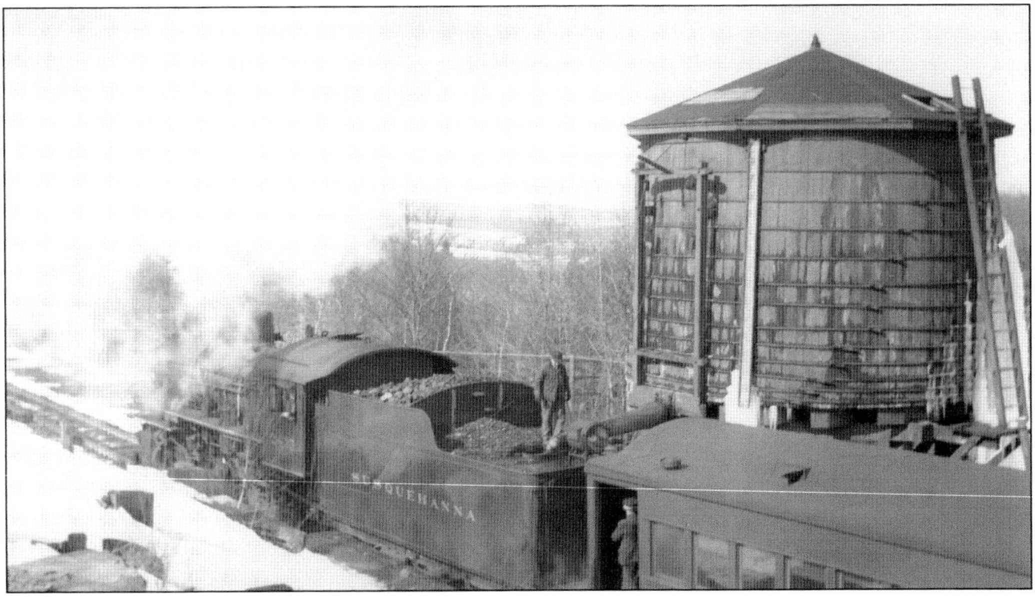

Before leaving Beaver Lake, the 2435 takes water on March 22, 1941. The coal bunker is already filled with coal as the fireman is filling the water tank for the hill and dale ride to the village of Sussex and M&U Junction. After the 2435 returns with the eastbound mixed train, an era will end, and only local freights will run between Beaver Lake and M&U Junction. (Railroad Avenue Enterprises Collection.)

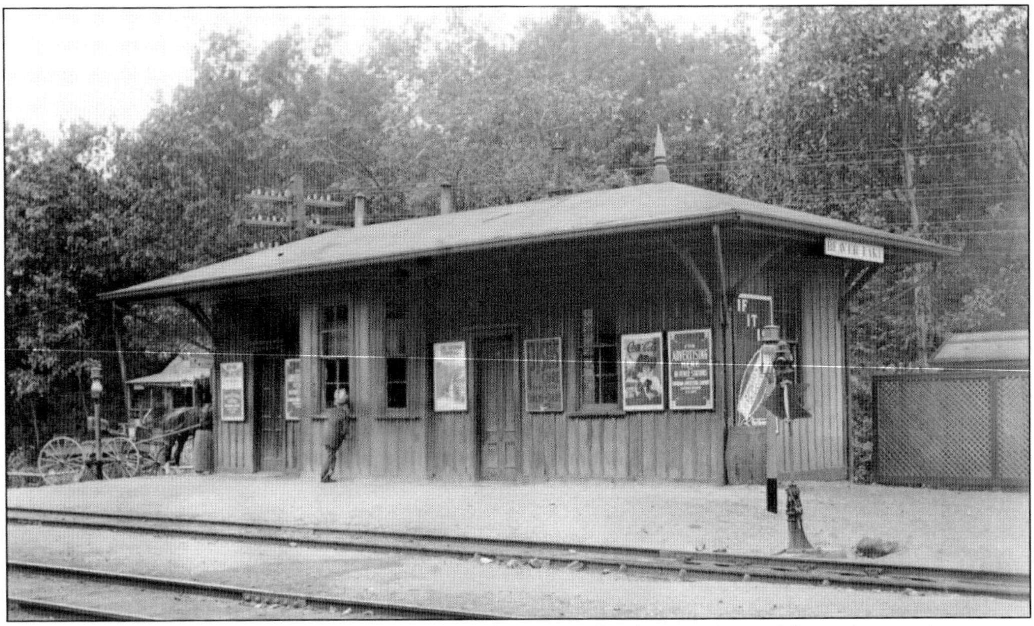

When the NYS&W completed, its extension from Two Bridges to Stroudsburg, Pennsylvania, in 1882 the former main line to Middletown became the NYS&W's Middletown branch. The name "Two Bridges" was eventually changed to "Beaver Lake" as is depicted in this image of the depot around 1910. After the M&U became an independent railroad, the NYS&W line from Beaver Lake to M&U Junction was referred to as the Hanford branch. (New Jersey Midland Railroad Historical Society Collection.)

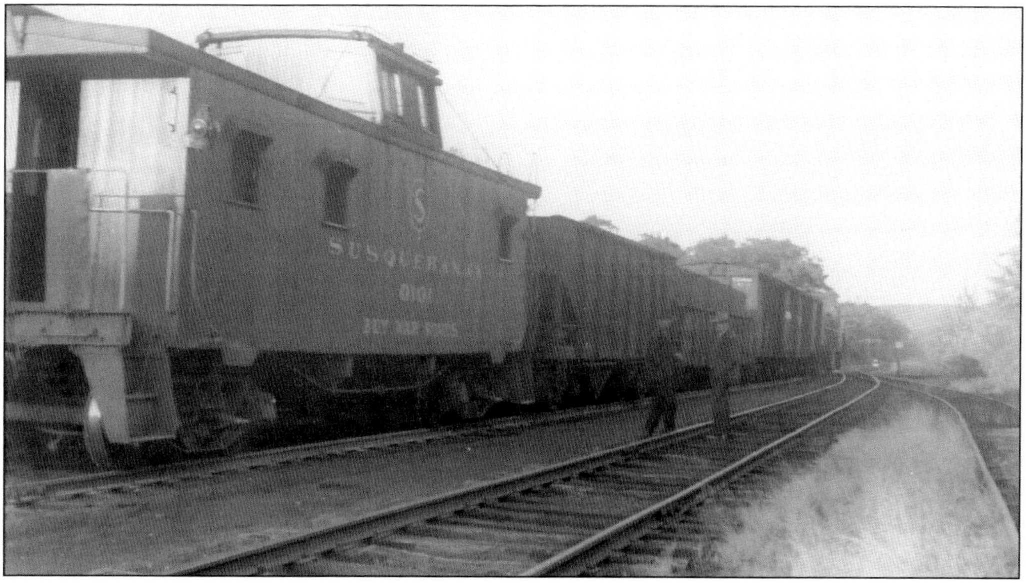

On October 11, 1944, RS1 231 and caboose 0101 are on the eastbound M&U job with four cars at Beaver Lake. The once large yard is now only three tracks used primarily for interchanging cars between the Hanford branch job and east and westbound main line trains to and from Little Ferry yard and the western connections; Jersey Central, Lehigh, and Hudson River and Lehigh and New England railroads. (John Treen Photograph, Robert Mohowski Collection.)

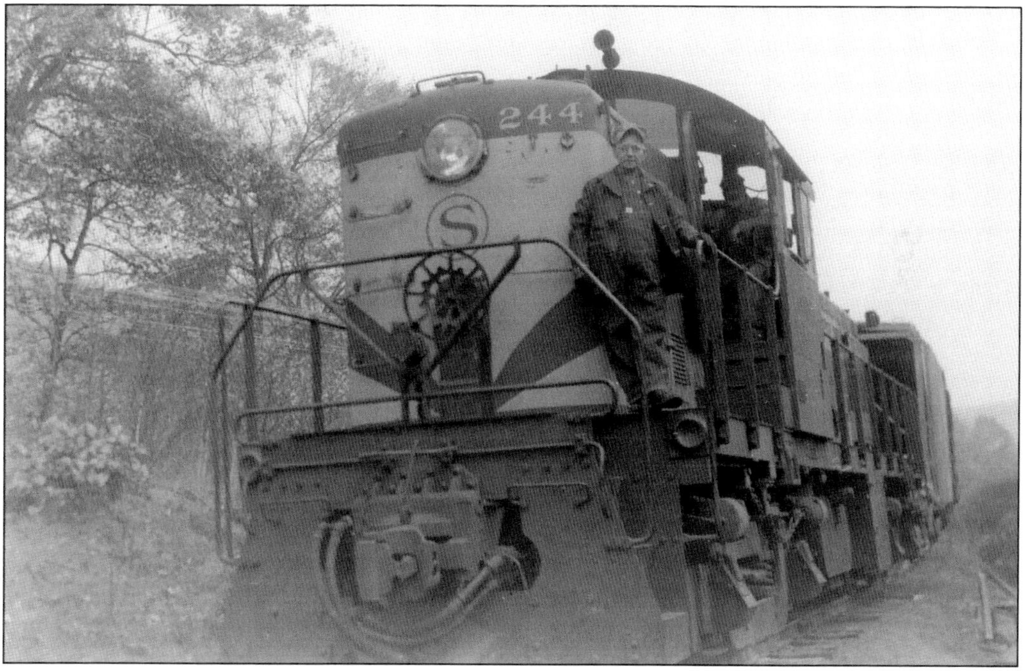

On November 3, 1948, the M&U job is west of Beaver Lake on the Hanford branch. Brakeman Clark Day and engineer E. Dorman, in the cab, are seen on RS1 244. The number "244" was significant on the NYS&W as only even-numbered diesel locomotives could be used with a multiple unit connection allowing one engineer to run several diesels from one set of controls. (John Treen Photograph, Robert Mohowski Collection.)

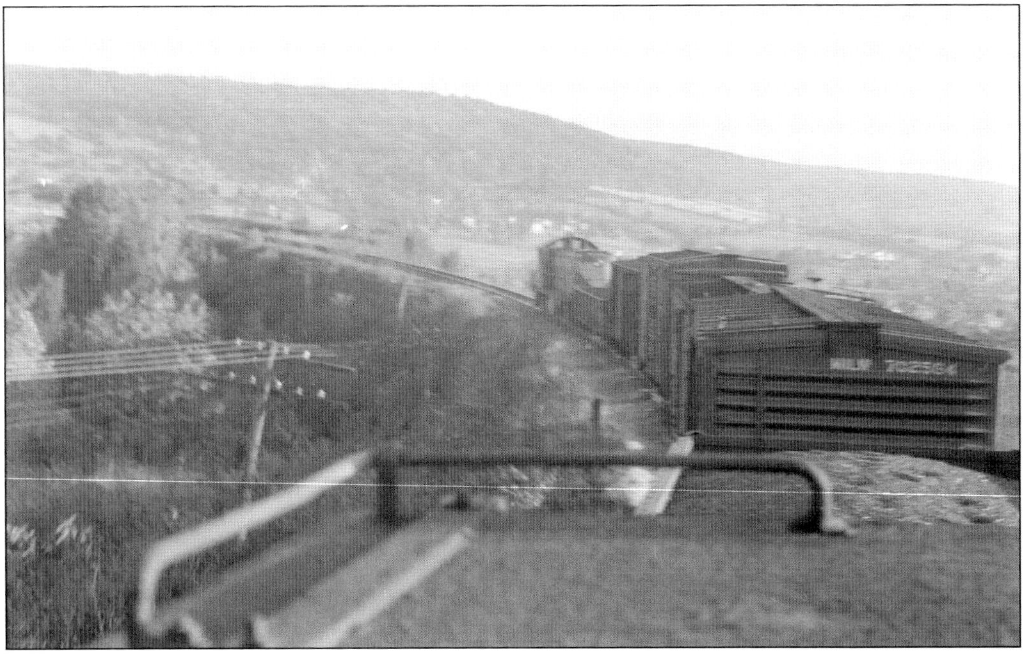

On October 4, 1945, RS1 231 is eastbound on the Hanford branch on the Ogdensburg fill. The train is heading to the Ogdensburg depot as it passes by the New Jersey Zinc switch. Zinc was transported from the Ogdensburg mine to the New Jersey Zinc facility at Franklin, New Jersey, west of this location. (John Treen Photograph, Robert Mohowski Collection.)

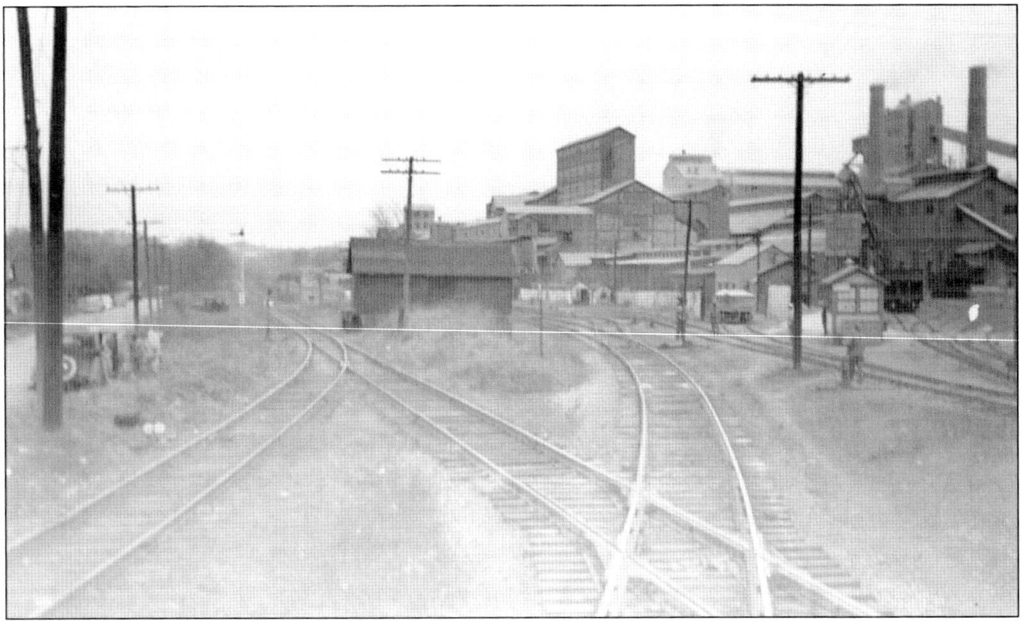

The NYS&W crossed the Lehigh and Hudson River Railroad just east of New Jersey Zinc's Franklin mine seen along the L&HR tracks. When the NYS&W filed to abandon the Hanford branch west of Franklin in 1958, M&NJ No. 1 ran from Hanford Junction to Franklin on April 29 inspecting the line. The NYS&W rejected the M&NJ's purchase bid, abandoning the line on June 30, 1958. (John Treen Photograph, Robert Mohowski Collection.)

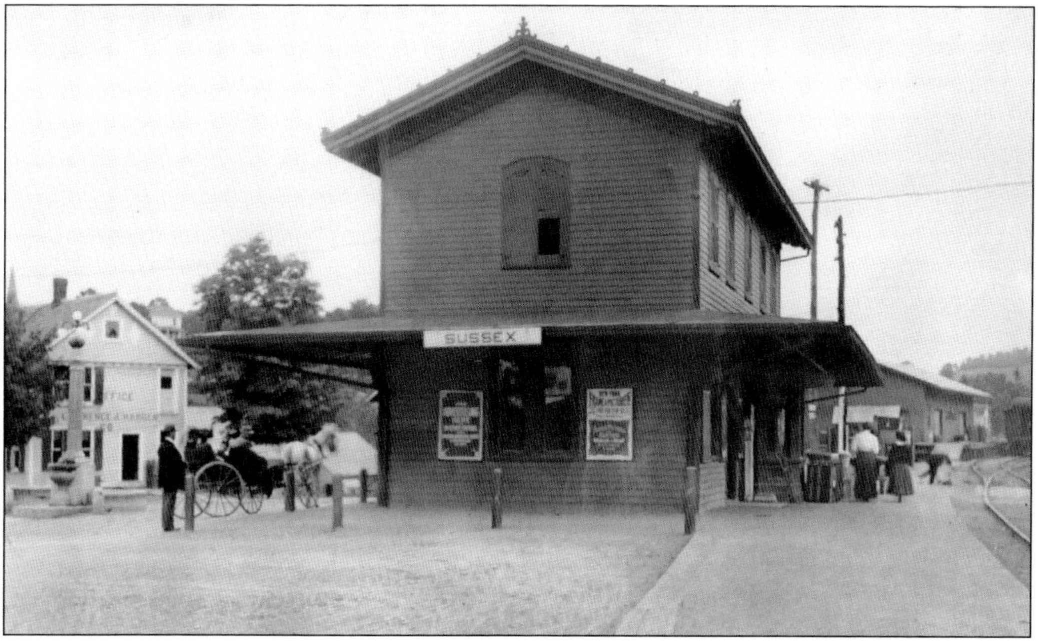

The Sussex depot in 1910 was the largest depot on the Hanford branch. Sussex station boasted a coal pocket, freight house, and team track. In later years, Agway would operate a feed and farm store west of the freight depot. Passenger service ended to the village when the mixed train ceased operation on March 21, 1941. Sussex also boasted the Lehigh and New England Railroad, which served the village on a branch off their main line. Below is a view of the Sussex depot taken from across the tracks showing the baggage cart with crates along with several freight parcels and passengers in front of the station agent's bay window. (Both photographs, New Jersey Midland Railroad Historical Society Collection.)

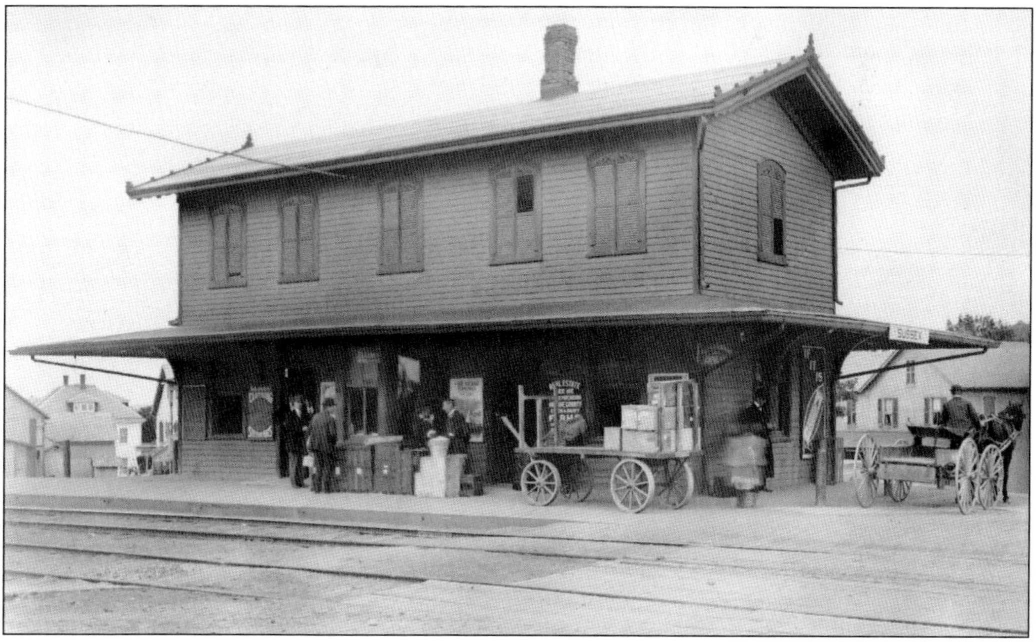

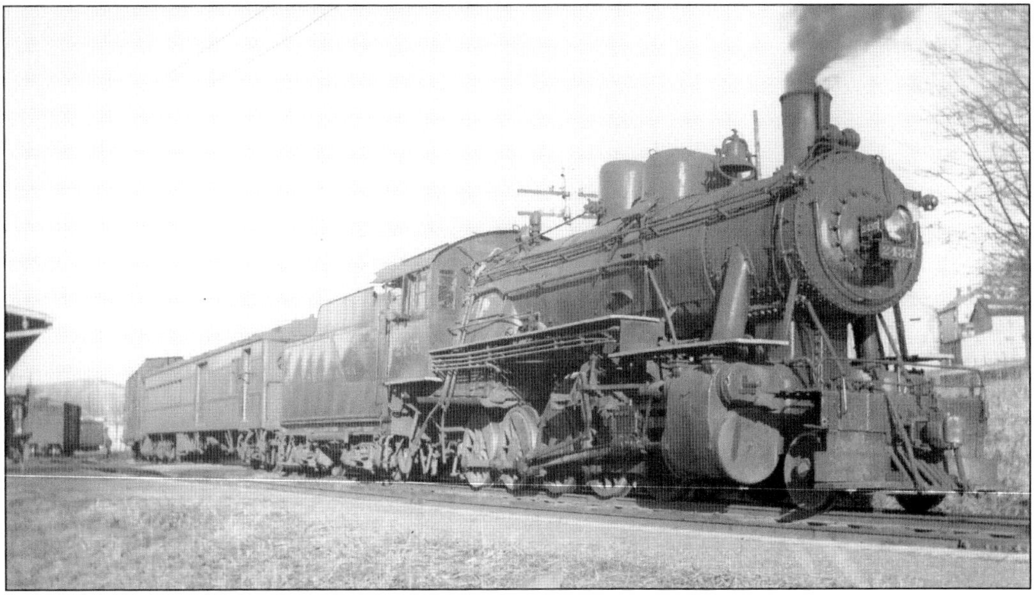

It is January 1, 1941, as NYS&W 2-10-0 2435 leads the eastbound mixed train past the Sussex depot. Earlier the 2435 leading the westbound mixed train had dropped the combination car at Sussex and continued to Hanford Junction to interchange with the M&U. Upon returning to Sussex, it would pick up the combine and return to Beaver Lake and continue on to Butler, New Jersey. (Railroad Avenue Enterprises Collection.)

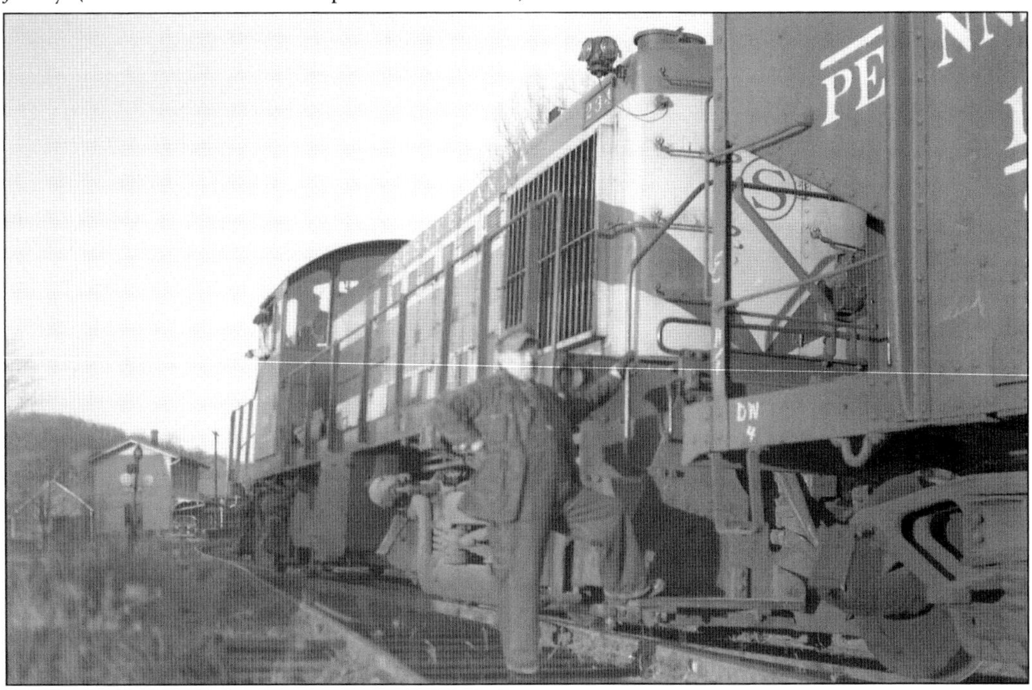

RS1 234 is westbound at Sussex leading the M&U job on November 11, 1948. The Sussex depot is in the background. John Rosner is the engineer in the cab of the 234 with Clark Day, brakeman in the foreground. Brakeman Day is standing on the siding that served the coal facility south of the depot. (John Treen Photograph, Robert Mohowski Collection.)

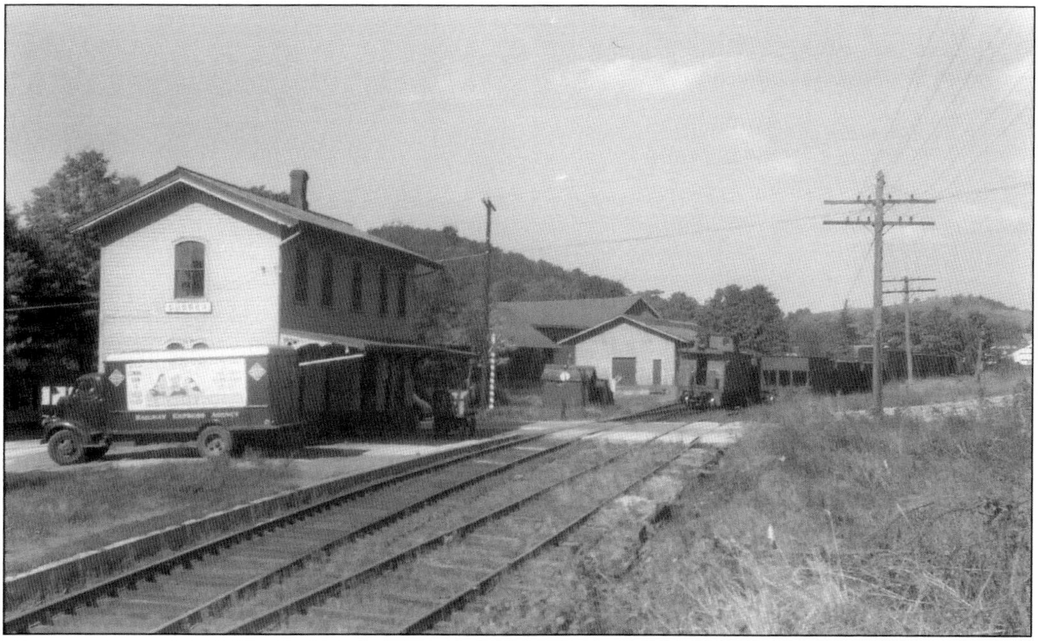

The westbound M&U job RS1 diesel is switching west of the freight station on October 11, 1945, as evidenced by the caboose and cars on the main line and siding. Upon completion of the switching, the train will resume its journey to M&U Junction. The Railway Express Agency truck will handle the less-than-carload traffic still being delivered to Sussex by the Hanford branch trains. (John Treen Photograph, Robert Mohowski Collection.)

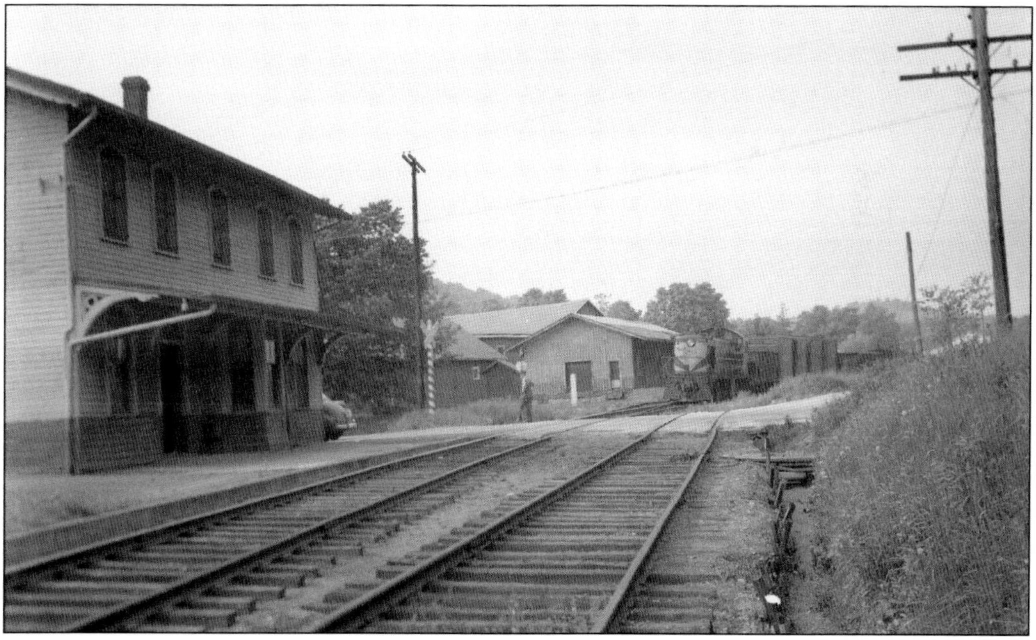

NYS&W RS1 250 is leading the eastbound M&U Job at Sussex on May 16, 1949, with a five-car train. The depot is to the left in the foreground while the freight house is to the left of the 250. A trainman is at the switchstand for the freight house track, most likely to flag traffic while the Hanford branch train crosses the highway. (John Treen Photograph, Robert Mohowski Collection.)

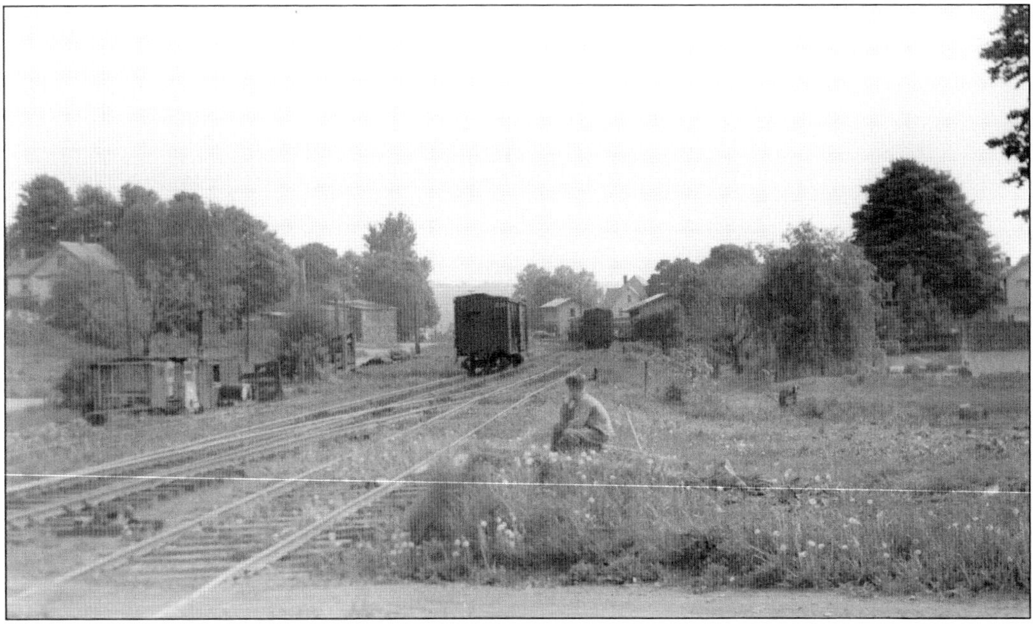

It is May 16, 1949, looking eastward as NYS&W RS1 250 switches cars between the Sussex passenger and freight stations. The view is eastward from the west end of the Sussex yard and includes a young boy who appears to be fascinated by the train in his hometown. Many train enthusiasts commenced their passion for railroads as an adolescent observing the activity of the local railroads in their hometown. (John Treen Photograph, Robert Mohowski Collection.)

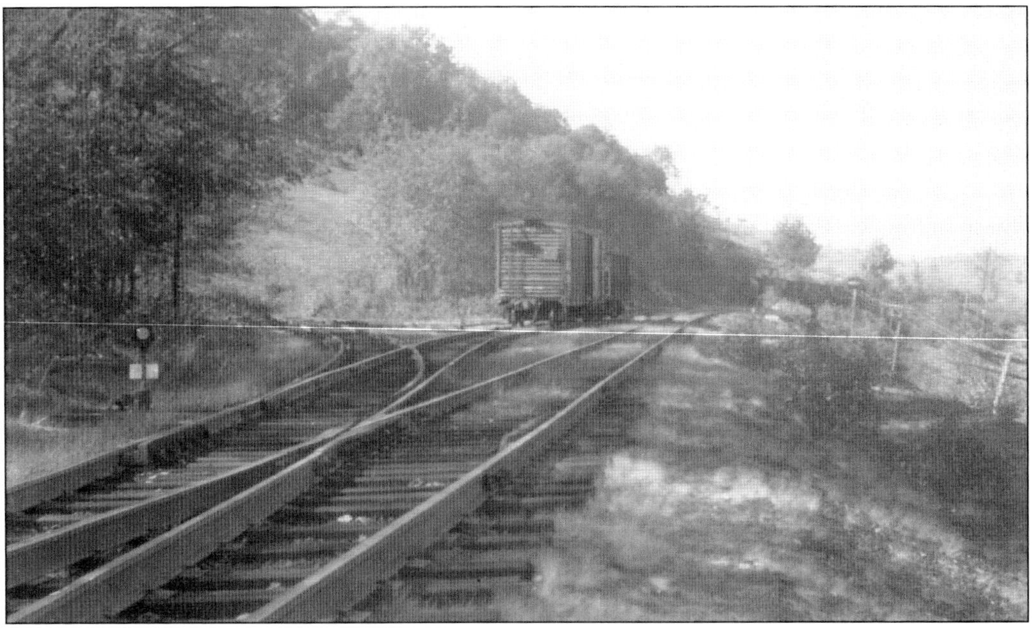

The east end of Hanford Junction consisted of a switch for the interchange runaround track that ran the length of the junction. Additionally there was a switch and track curving to the left to access the NYS&W turntable. On May 16, 1949, looking west to Unionville, the Hanford branch train is in the distance with five coal cars to be left for the M&NJ. (John Treen Photograph, Robert Mohowski Collection.)

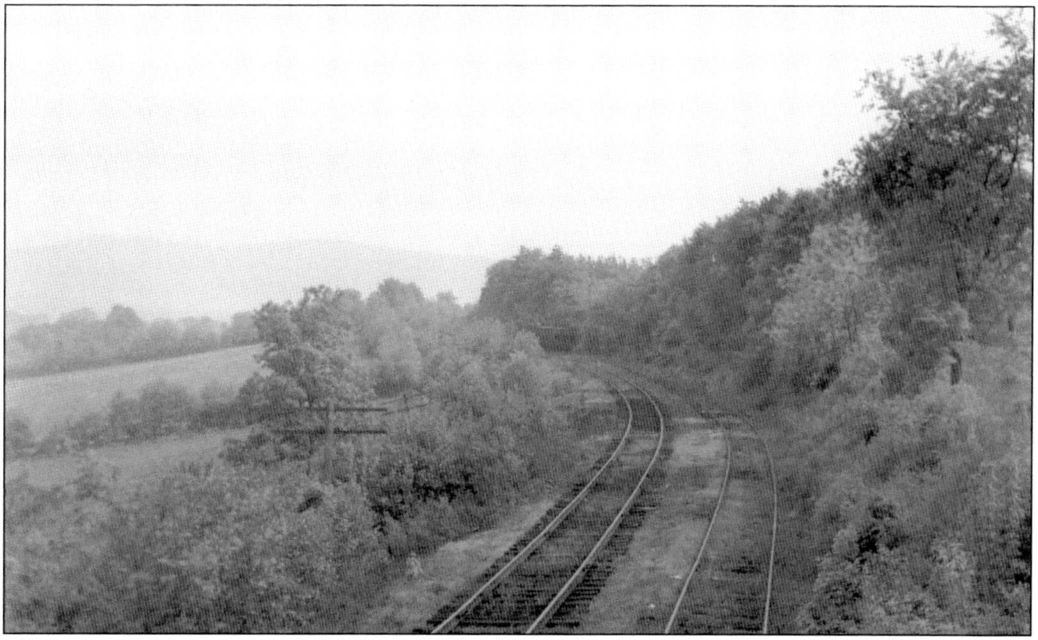

The NYS&W, M&U job is westbound on the interchange track on May 16, 1949, after dropping off the five coal cars for the M&NJ. The crew on the diesel locomotive has an easterly view of Hanford Junction, which consisted of just the main track and a runaround siding to the right. (John Treen Photograph, Robert Mohowski Collection.)

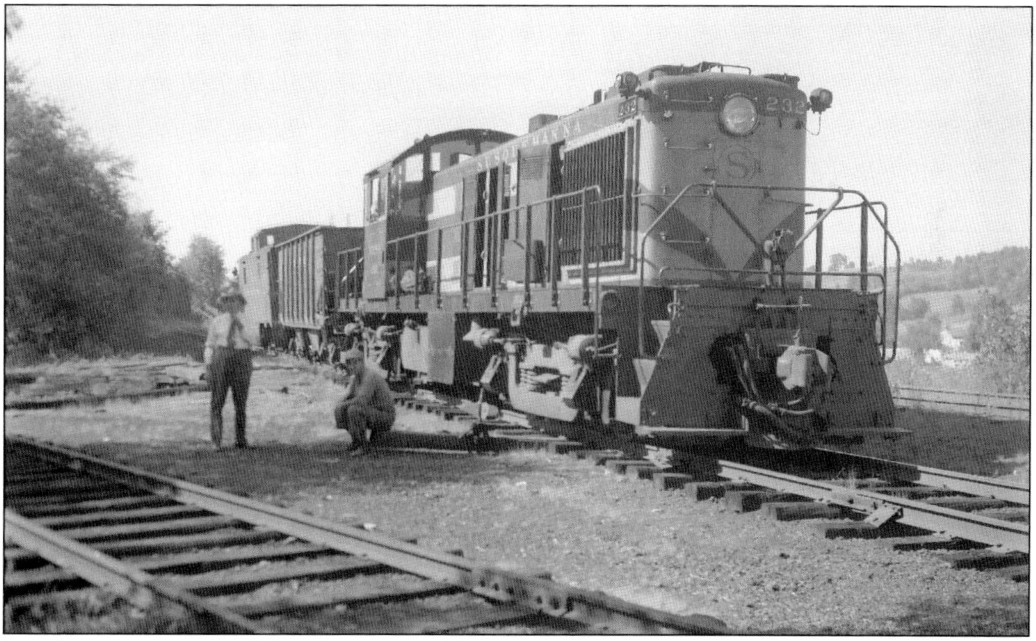

It is August 4, 1949, as RS1 232 is at M&U Junction waiting for the M&NJ to arrive with a few 'hot" cars for the NYS&W Hanford branch train to take east. Note the turntable lead track in the lower foreground with the turntable partially visible in the left background. Conductor C. S. Thompson is to the right and his father, a retired NYS&W conductor, is standing to the left. (John Treen Photograph, Robert Mohowski Collection.)

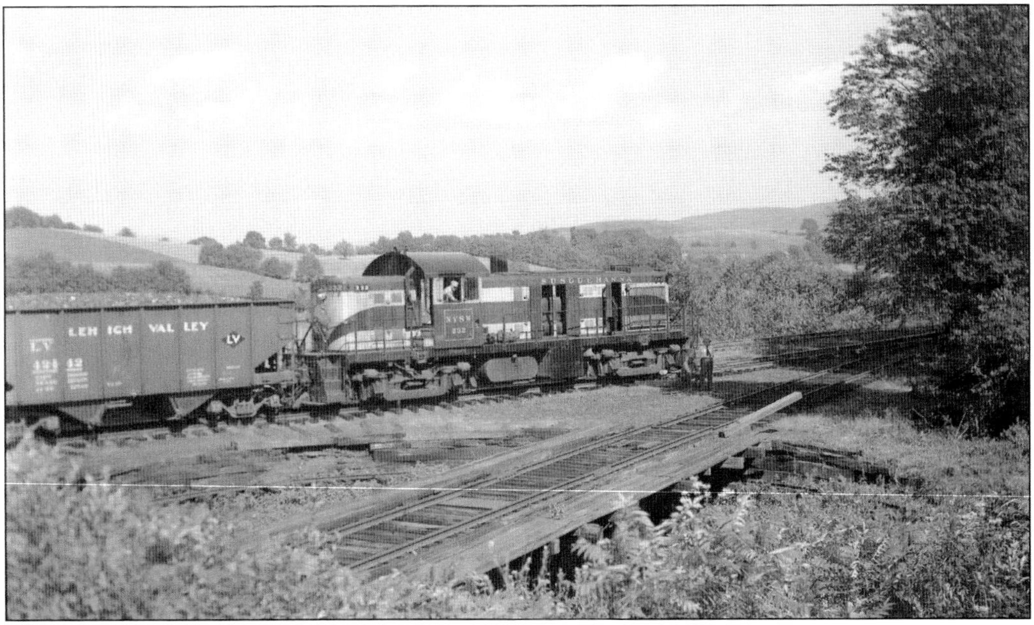

This scenic view of the M&U job at Hanford Junction on August 4, 1949, reveals 232 and a loaded Lehigh Valley coal car along with the NYS&W "Armstrong" turntable. The NYS&W needed this turntable during the steam era after the M&U became independent, because it did not want to pay to turn its engines in Unionville on the M&U or have to back their locomotives to Franklin Junction for turning. (John Treen Photograph, Robert Mohowski Collection.)

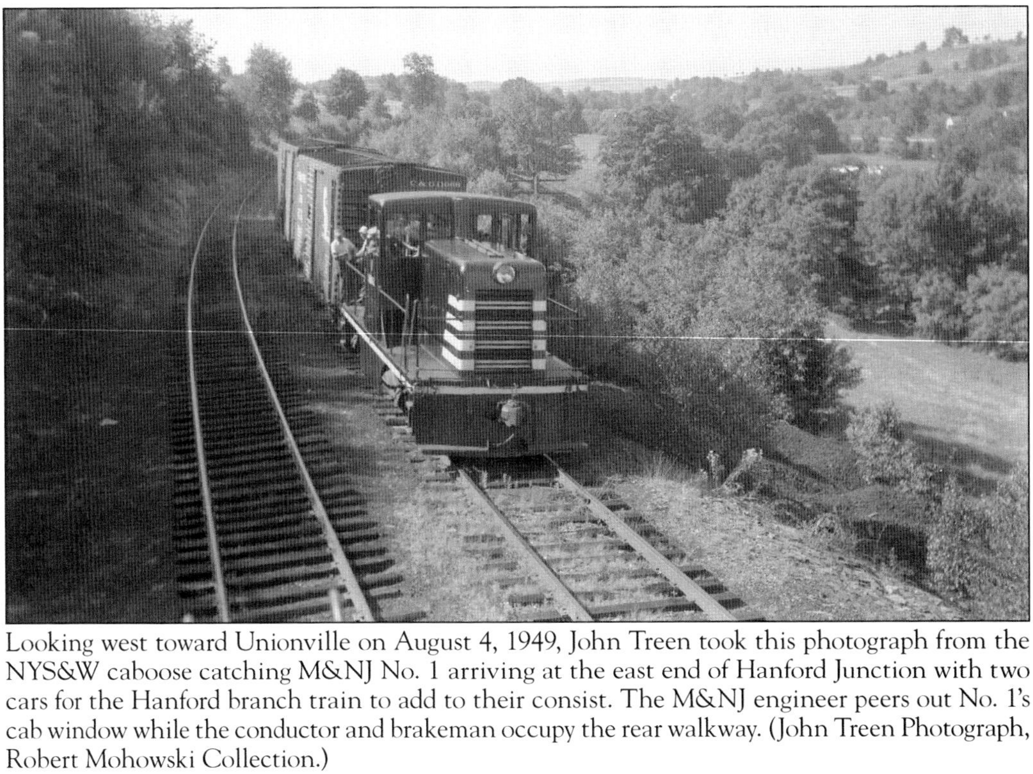

Looking west toward Unionville on August 4, 1949, John Treen took this photograph from the NYS&W caboose catching M&NJ No. 1 arriving at the east end of Hanford Junction with two cars for the Hanford branch train to add to their consist. The M&NJ engineer peers out No. 1's cab window while the conductor and brakeman occupy the rear walkway. (John Treen Photograph, Robert Mohowski Collection.)

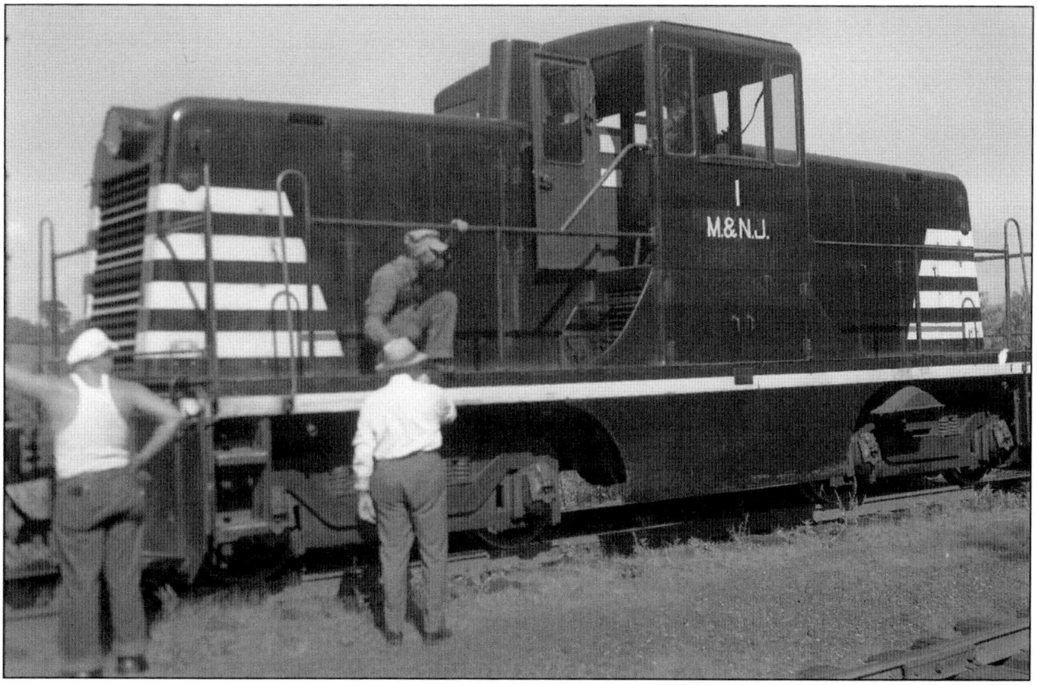

M&NJ No. 1 has reached the eastern end of Hanford Junction with the two cars in tow. The MN&J engineer is speaking to retired NYS&W conductor Thompson. A close inspection of the side of the engine cab reveals that the name Middletown and Unionville Railroad is still visible under the black paint and new lettering for the newly formed M&NJ Railway. (John Treen Photograph, Robert Mohowski Collection.)

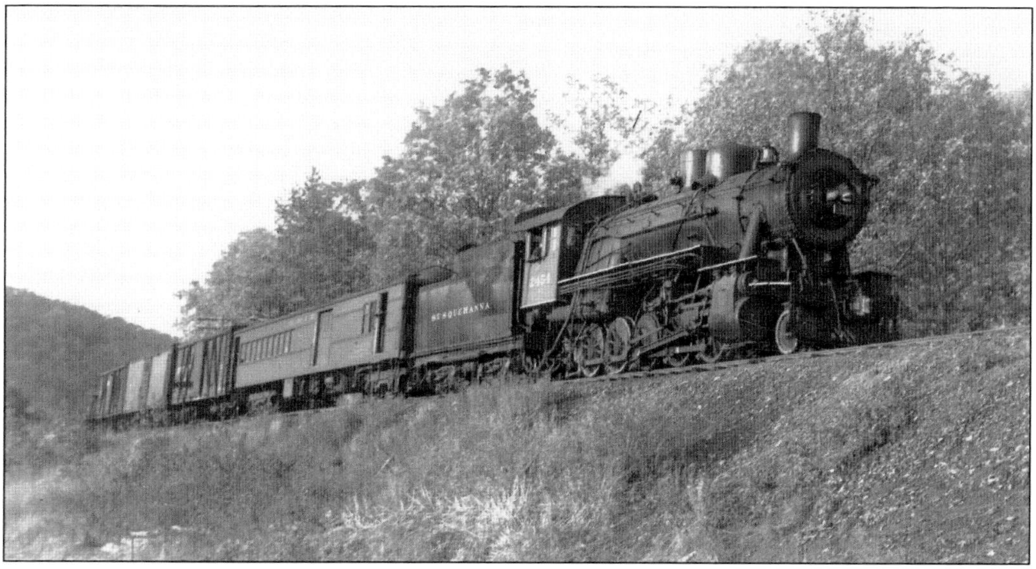

During 1940, NYS&W 2454 leads the eastbound Sussex mixed train at Stockholm, east of Beaver Lake, on the run to Butler, New Jersey. The combine car is behind the coal tender followed by freight cars from the M&U at Hanford Junction and customers along the Hanford branch. When the mixed train was annulled after March 22, 1941, the M&U job began running during the day. (Railroad Avenue Enterprises Collection.)

Bibliography

Barberio, Douglas. *The NYO&W Railway's Middletown Branch Part 1 Cornwall to Burnside*, O&WRHS *Observer*, 2005.

———. "Touring the M&U." M&NJRHS *Unionville Flyer* Vol. 11 Nos. 1–3, Vol. 12 Nos. 2 and 4.

Brill, Peter. "O&W Steam on the M&U." M&NJRHS *Unionville Flyer* Vol. 1 No. 3.

———. "The New York, Susquehanna and Ontario Company: Coal Trains on the M&U." M&NJRHS *Unionville Flyer* Vol. 3 Nos. 1 and 2.

———. "M&U No. 7, Mr. Knox was Proven Right." M&NJRHS *Unionville Flyer* Vol. 5 No. 2.

———. "End of the Steam Era on the M&U." M&NJRHS *Unionville Flyer* Vol. 7 No. 1.

———. "The Middletown & Sussex Transit Corporation." M&NJRHS *Unionville Flyer* Vol. 14 No. 1.

Cohen, Marvin. *Middletown*. Charleston, SC: Arcadia Publishing, 2001.

———. *Middletown Revisited*. Charleston, SC: Arcadia Publishing, 2008.

Deserto, John. "Middletown & Unionville Freight House." M&NJRHS *Unionville Flyer* Vol. 1 No. 4.

———. "The Middletown, Unionville and Water Gap Railroad." M&NJRHS *Unionville Flyer* Vol. 2 Nos. 2–4.

———. "History of DG Yard." M&NJRHS *Unionville Flyer* Vol. 6 Nos. 3 and 4, Vol. 7 Nos. 2 and 3.

———. "Susquehanna Operations and Facilities at Hanford, NJ." M&NJRHS *Unionville Flyer* Vol. 4 No. 4, Vol. 5 No. 1.

Detwyler, Carl. "That Unionville Train." O&WRHS *Observer*, 2002.

Flynn, Elaine. *Wawayanda Our Town Royal*. Fireworks Press, 1999.

Mohowski, Robert. *The New York, Susquehanna, and Western Railroad*. Johns Hopkins University Press, 2003.

The Town of Minisink Bicentennial Commission. *Minisink a Bicentennial History*, 1988.

Treen, John. "A Typical Day on the M&U Job." M&NJRHS *Unionville Flyer* Vol. 8 No. 1.

About the Historical Society

The Middletown and New Jersey Railway Historical Society was formed in 1994 with the encouragement of the M&NJ Railway president Pierre Rasmussen, his son, Harold the engineer, and conductor Peter Brill. The M&NJRHS has published a quarterly newsletter the *Unionville Flyer* for each membership year. Our newsletter contains articles concerning not only the M&U and M&NJ but also the Erie, NYO&W, NYS&W, Erie Lackawanna, Conrail, and other local area railroads. Current railroad topics and local railroad history in Orange County are included when articles have been submitted. We maintain a Web site at http://www.mnjrhs.org and have meetings on the second Friday of the month in September, November, February, April, and June at the First United Presbyterian Church at Roberts Street in Middletown, New York, at 7:30 p.m. We maintain an archive of M&U and M&NJ original documents, along with slides and photographs of the M&U/M&NJ railroad and its connections. For more information contact our society at M&NJRHS, P.O. Box 848, New Hampton, New York 10958-0848.

Consistent with our mission to preserve history on a local level, this book was printed in South Carolina on American-made paper and manufactured entirely in the United States. Products carrying the accredited Forest Stewardship Council (FSC) label are printed on 100 percent FSC-certified paper.

MADE IN THE USA